Homo Criminalis

Also by Mark Galeotti

We Need to Talk About Putin
A Short History of Russia
Downfall (with Anna Arutunyan)

Homo Criminalis

How Crime Organises the World

Mark Galeotti

EBURY
PRESS

EBURY PRESS

UK | USA | Canada | Ireland | Australia
India | New Zealand | South Africa

Ebury Press is part of the Penguin Random House group of companies
whose addresses can be found at global.penguinrandomhouse.com

Penguin Random House UK
One Embassy Gardens, 8 Viaduct Gardens, London SW11 7BW

penguin.co.uk
global.penguinrandomhouse.com

Penguin
Random House
UK

First published by Ebury Press in 2025
1

Typeset in 11.5/17pt Baskerville MT Pro by Six Red Marbles UK, Thetford, Norfolk

Printed and bound in Great Britain by Clays Ltd, Elcograf S.p.A.

The authorised representative in the EEA is Penguin Random House Ireland,
Morrison Chambers, 32 Nassau Street, Dublin D02 YH68

A CIP catalogue record for this book is available from the British Library

Hardback ISBN 9781529148220
Trade Paperback ISBN 9781529148237

MIX
Paper | Supporting
responsible forestry
FSC
www.fsc.org   FSC® C018179

Penguin Random House is committed to a
sustainable future for our business, our readers
and our planet. This book is made from Forest
Stewardship Council® certified paper.

*I dedicate this to Anna, for her own fascination with bad guys,
and to Masha, for not being a bad girl.*

'When a man is denied the right to live the life he believes in, he has no choice but to become an outlaw.'

– Nelson Mandela

Note: Although it may seem odd to standardise on both the US dollar and the British pound, I have kept both to avoid some especially jarring anachronisms. Obviously, currencies fluctuate all the time, but as of writing, a pound is worth around $1.35.

Contents

PART FOUR: BRAVE NEW WORLD

Introduction

The gang was disciplined, ruthless, well ordered. Its thugs swaggered around the city as if they owned it. Maybe they did: everyone knew who they were, and the corrupted police never dared take them on. They each knew their trade and their place within the gang's hierarchy, their operations orchestrated by a cunning godfather who understood the value of loyalty. Each sworn member had no trouble reconciling his violent trade with his devout Roman Catholicism. Not that they had much option: the godfather was also a great fan of the monopoly. Criminals on his turf had a simple choice: accept his leadership or die. Even so, most joined not out of fear but because membership in the gang offered security, the prospect of wealth, and even respectability. After all, not only does money have a cachet all its own, but the godfather was as much a mediator and powerbroker as gang boss. People came to him willingly to have their disputes settled and their grievances avenged, knowing that his 'justice' was rather quicker and more insistent than that of the courts.

This could so easily be the Mafia in its heyday, whether in its Sicilian bastions or the Little Italies of New York or Chicago; the gang boss who is at once arbitrator and avenger steps straight from the pages of *The Godfather* (1969). Yet it is actually the description of a fictional but factually based brotherhood of thieves from *Rinconete y Cortadillo* by the Spanish writer Miguel de Cervantes.[1] Best known for his *Don Quixote*, Cervantes also wrote a series of 'Moral Tales', one of which concerned the two rogues Rincón and Cortado, who travel to Seville in search of ill-gotten gains, but come to realise the extent to which the shadowy Señor Monipodio's criminal organisation dominates the town's underworld. When Rincón incautiously asks, 'Can it be that thieves in this country have to pay a duty?' the porter who first tells them of the real power in Seville warns them that 'If they do not pay ... they at least have to register with Señor Monipodio, who is their father, their teacher and their protector; and I accordingly advise you to come with me and render him obedience, for if you do not do so and dare to commit a theft without his approval, it will cost you dearly.' Through charisma, charm, threats and detailed records, Monipodio and his 'priors', his lieutenants, preside over a complex array of burglars and bravos, conmen and bag-snatchers. Even retired criminals retain a role as so-called 'hornets', scouting out likely targets for future thefts. Monipodio also has friends – or clients – in high places: when an *alguazil*, a magistrate, comes to solicit his assistance in retrieving a stolen purse, Monipodio is happy to help, for the official is 'a friend and does us countless good turns every year'.[2]

In many ways this seems an astonishingly modern account, yet it was published in 1613, and was derived from other, even earlier tales of brotherhoods of thieves in Spain. Many seem to think that organised crime began with the migrations of the Irish and Italians to the United States in the nineteenth century – especially daring works may present the pirates of the Spanish Main as primordial Mafiosi. However, despite common assumptions about it being an essentially modern phenomenon, ancient and pre-modern societies offer plentiful examples of organised crime or at least its recognisable ancestors. From the olive growers of ancient Greece, whose groves, cultivated over generations, were prey to protection racketeers with threat of axe or fire, through the rise of banditry in early modern Europe, to the contemporary organised crime that now operates across the world and dominates an underworld turnover estimated (very crudely) at up to more than two trillion dollars annually, organised crime has taken many guises.[3] The brotherhood of thieves Cervantes describes was clearly meant to be an extreme example, but there is nothing in *Rinconete y Cortadillo* which suggests that he thought he was describing some outré phenomenon that no one would consider credible or at all unfamiliar. We cannot necessarily take literary accounts at face value. Yet Luís Zapata's *Miscelanea*, written well before *Rinconete y Cortadillo*, refers to 'a brotherhood' of thieves that 'has lasted longer than the principality of Venice; for although the law has caught a few unfortunate ones, it has never been able to run down the leader of the gang.'[4] Even if often embroidered, reflecting the assumptions and prejudices of their chroniclers, these tales also tended to have a core of truth to them. For example, while it is highly unlikely that the fifteenth-century French gang known as the Coquillards really had their own elected 'king', as was claimed at the time, they certainly did have a secret dialect, subsequently popularised by the poet François Villon.[5] In itself, this says something about their cohesion and sense of common identity. Besides, there are many more such contemporary tales of historical villainy, as well as official documents, personal accounts, and even archaeological evidence. From them, we can see that organised crime has been around as long as organised society. Indeed, as thieves have their own codes, structures and sense of common identity, their 'underworlds' often mirror the 'upperworlds' of ordinary society.

You and me, we are thieves. Crooks. Criminals. Odds are, all of us will have done something to break the law, from exceeding the speed limit to drinking under-age, from smoking an untaxed cigarette to sneaking some questionable 'expenses' into our tax return. It is human nature to look for the loophole, to balance risk and reward, to test that tension between the desire for a safe and orderly society and our own self-interest. And we always have been thieves: it is hardly coincidental that one of the most pervasively common figures in pre-modern mythology was the trickster, often little more than a polite way of describing the lawbreaker. Coyote among the Native Americans of the southwest, Raven in the north-west; Anansi the spider in West Africa; Loki for the Norse; and the Monkey King for the Chinese. Later, the trickster would survive in new forms, whether the roguish vagabond hero of picaresque literature, Mr Punch, Q or even Jerry the mouse (of *Punch and Judy*, *Star Trek* and *Tom and Jerry* fame, respectively).

We crave security, yet chafe against the demands it makes of us. We admire the rogue and the reprobate, even as we fear and confine them. There is a reason why crime, both true and fictional, has colonised our bookshelves, cinemas, televisions and podcasts. It is nice to keep the criminal safely at arm's length, to bolt the door and bar the window, before settling down to a cosy night in front of the TV, watching other people have a miserable time. However, our relationship with crime is an intimate one. We – the supposed good guys, legitimate society, the 'upperworld' in contrast to the gangsters' underworld – are the ones who really *define* crime. We decide what is legal and what is not. Sell the horse tranquilliser ketamine to a veterinarian, and you're a dealer in medical supplies; sell it to a pusher who will market it as a 'club drug' under such street names as 'Special K', and you're a narco-baron. As societies become more organised, as borders become more controlled, as states become more expansive, then the tally of goods and activities we ban, control, tax and regulate tends to increase to match. The ancient Babylonian Code of Hammurabi embodied just 282 laws, rules and standards. By contrast, Title 18 of the United States Code has 2,005 sections and five appendices – and that is just the main criminal code of the federal government. There is also a vast body of regulation, to say nothing of the distinct criminal codes of each of the 50 states.

So crime doesn't just pay, it tells. It is the dark shadow of the upperworld, its shape defined by the contours of the society which cast it. First of all, what we choose to ban and what we do about it, says something about us. Today, slavery is rightly decried as not just a crime, but a sin. To the Romans, though, to free another's slave was more than a crime but a challenge to the very fabric of the social order. Today, we pass laws rightly condemning animal cruelty, but in the Middle Ages, animals were considered to act from conscious volition and could be tried for their 'crimes'. In 1379, in the French village of Saint-Marcel-le-Jeussey, two herds of pigs were believed to have 'rioted' in support of three sows who trampled and killed the son of a swineherd. The three sows were sentenced to death for murder, but while the other pigs were tried as accomplices, one of the herds belonged to the local priory, which petitioned Philip the Bold, Duke of Burgundy, for clemency. They were duly pardoned.[6] From setting the age of consent or of criminal responsibility, to defining what is illegal and what is not, law and crime are expressions of the values of state and society.

Crime also maps the gulfs between the moral economies of the state and its people. Criminals flourish in the gap between the law, and what communities think is justice. As states organise, they pass laws and levy taxes, central to their role and existence. This often criminalises previously accepted activities and creates a competitive pricing advantage for criminals able and willing to evade customs and other duties. Prohibition in the United States handed organised crime a market worth perhaps $3 billion per year (equivalent to half the federal budget in 1920, when it was applied), and one that many Americans thought was entirely moral. Likewise, Russian society has traditionally drawn a definite distinction between *prestupleniye*, crime as defined by the laws, and *zlodeyaniye*, what is regarded as immoral.[7] Centuries of autocratic and selfish misrule by narrow elites – whether tsarist aristocrats, Party bureaucrats or today's politician-businesspeople – have kept those two concepts far apart, as the state tried to criminalise activities ordinary Russians regarded as their right (like picking firewood in the tsar's forests because, after all, he had more than enough), while society frowned on activities that the state either sanctioned or regarded in a much less serious light (such as corruption and horse theft).

The presence of crime in general and organised crime in particular is also often a good indicator of stresses in society. As Nick Fisher concluded from his study of ancient Athens, 'The relative stability of the society, the absence of serious rural or urban social discontents and unrest, powerful feelings of family solidarity and strong localised community spirit all worked to keep levels of this sort of crime relatively low.'[8] That stability and balance are hardest to maintain in times of rapid economic, social and political changes, though. Any era and society is prone to the destabilisation they bring, and resulting evolutions in crime. New Dynasty Egypt under the Ramessid pharaohs, between the twelfth and eleventh centuries BCE, was a period of expansion and economic change that exposed the elites to foreign influences and new sources of wealth, and in the process laid the basis for a period of unrest, instability and a crisis of values across the empire, as new beliefs and interests began to challenge the old.[9] The fall of empire can be even more disruptive. Across the Middle East's Fertile Crescent, the decline of second millennium BCE empires such as the Sumerian, Hittite and Egyptian was accompanied by the tales of the depredations of miscellaneous bandits, raiders, mercenaries and outlaws collectively known as Habiru (or ʿapiru, which effectively can be translated as 'filth'). When Korea's Goryeo Empire fell under the pressure of bloody internal intrigue and repeated Mongol invasions, it heralded such an explosion of banditry and insurgency that it effectively opted to become a Mongol vassal state in 1270.

As human history has unrolled, though, the pace of those changes has tended – with all kinds of variations – to accelerate. They elevate social groups who have not yet a commensurate stake in the status quo, such as the educated middle classes who would be at the heart of the revolutionary movements of nineteenth-century Europe.

They open up new opportunities that the state is not able or willing to regulate, whether forced marriage and baby-selling in pretty much any century until the twentieth, or virtual cryptocurrencies today. They throw into question old certainties and weaken or break once-strong structures of social control. Industrial revolution, for example, forced or attracted peasants to the cities, where suddenly they were cut off from all the old constraints, from the disappointment of their families to the authority of the village elders. No wonder they were unruly enough to be considered the 'troublesome classes', and the disdain in which they were held only encouraged their drift into hooliganism and street gangs: crime as a proto-revolutionary act of class and cultural defiance. As well as winners, dramatic changes also create losers, faced with the option of accepting a diminution of their status or wealth or finding new, illegal ways to retain it. In Italy and Japan, for example, gangsters profited from the comprehensive transition to modern economies and democracies after defeat in the Second World War; similarly in Russia after exhaustion from the Cold War.

Finally, the changing character of crime also delineates the reach, power and legitimacy of the state. As it manages to shrink the 'grey zones' where criminals can evade their authority – from the deep woods frequented by bandits, to the lawless slums of the cities – then criminals have to be more organised to survive. In a Darwinian process, the smartest, the most efficient, the most ruthless and the best connected enjoy the fruits of their labours and pick up the turfs and businesses of their less fortunate or effective rivals. However, crime can also be an excuse for states to constrict and control. For the French philosopher Michel Foucault, 'with the generalized policing that it authorizes, [crime] constitutes a means of perpetual surveillance of the population: an apparatus that makes it possible to supervise, through the delinquents themselves, the whole social field.'[10] In other words, more crime – or at least more public fear of crime – can also mean more repression. So many can, in their own narrow and dog-eat-dog ways, benefit from the crime industry.

Most crime is not organised, but nonetheless this book will focus on the activities of the gangs, mobs, mafias and dark networks, because exploring the underlying relationship between underworld and upperworld, the way as the one becomes more complex, so too does the other, and the manner in which they buttress as often as challenge each other, tells us most about ourselves, and how we end up organising ourselves.

But what is it? Definitions may often be dull, but here they are necessary. After all, organised crime is more than just crime which is organised. Almost any crimes committed by more than one person and with premeditation will involve some degree of coordination. Stealing grain from maize storage bins was sufficiently common in Aztec society, for example, that the law specifically laid out different penalties for the two key roles: the man who actually got into the bin and the man who helped him climb into it. The former was regarded as the ringleader and would be enslaved for this crime.[11] Nonetheless, this is hardly organised crime in any meaningful sense. Instead, organised crime is a business, non-ideological in that while its members may seek political influence or even power in order to protect themselves and further their activities, they are first and foremost out for profit. They do not want to change the world, just own it. Terrorists may turn to the tactics of organised crime to raise funds for their activities, whether Northern Irish paramilitaries dealing drugs in pub car parks or Islamic State at peak making over a million dollars a day smuggling oil out of the regions of Syria and Iraq they controlled in 2014–15, but that does not make them the same as the gangs.

Organised crime is social, with multiple members, who enjoy close interaction. They may be kin, or come from the same street or village, or they may meet at a bar, a workshop, a rarefied club or the lowest dive. One way or the other, they share a sense of community, a set of common values, at least a minimal level of trust. This shared identity may well also be communicated and perpetuated by a variety of means: oaths of brotherhood, tattoos, distinctive slang, even a secret language. Japanese Yakuza affect elaborate and artistic body tattoos, for example, but not around the neck, hands or forearms: these are for private show, and the gangster must be able to pass in licit society. The more visible tattoos of traditional Russian *Vory* ('Thieves'), by contrast, are not just marks of belonging to an underworld fraternity, they are also a means of communication, encoding everything from the criminal's beliefs to his résumé.

It has a hierarchy, with those who give orders and those who obey. Some gangs are very pyramidal, with a leader at the top, captains and lieutenants in the middle, and numerous foot soldiers at the bottom. A Chinese Triad gang, for instance, is led by a Mountain Master, who relies on his Incense Master and Vanguard to manage rituals and discipline, and organisation, respectively. Beneath them are the Red Pole, White Paper Fan and Straw Sandal – responsible for enforcement, administration and liaison with other gangs – and a mass of initiated 49ers and apprentice Blue Lanterns. Sadly, most gangs lack such poetic appellations. While others may seem almost egalitarian, especially smaller or simpler street organisations, even where there is no formal hierarchy, there will be members of the group able to get their way through strength, seniority or sheer charisma.

Finally, and even more obviously, the group carries out crimes – in other words, acts which are illegal by the standards of the times. When no laws apply, or they sanction violent, predatory and arbitrary behaviour, you may have warlordism, thuggishness, immorality and exploitation, but you cannot truly call it crime. Thus, and with all due credit to Howard Abadinsky, who came up with perhaps the most widely-used definition,[12] for the purposes of this study, which will seek to set Roman bandits alongside Sicilian Mafiosi, and twenty-first-century Chinese Triads by their seventeenth-century ancestors, a working definition would be:

> Organised crime is a continuing enterprise, apart from traditional and legal social structures, within which a number of persons work together under their own hierarchy to gain power and profit for their private gain, through illegal activities.

Of course, any such expansive a canvas as the whole of human history needs to be painted with a very broad brush. There are all kinds of details and nuance that will be overlooked, and national particularities omitted. My own experiences and biases drive me more towards European examples, I acknowledge. Furthermore, definitions such as 'ancient', 'pre-modern' and 'modern' are inevitably impressionistic. Take a look at the streets of contemporary Russia and it is undoubtedly 'modern', but the personalistic court which Vladimir Putin has built around himself is deeply reminiscent of pre-modern tsarist practice. Likewise, one could debate whether Golden Age Amsterdam in the late sixteenth and early seventeenth centuries, at the heart of the Northern Renaissance, prosperous, literate and tolerant, was really any less 'modern' than contemporary Caracas (still holding its crown as the most violent capital city in the world) or Damascus (coming bottom of *The Economist*'s 'Most Liveable Cities' index year after year), for all that the latter have the internet, airports and fast food.[13]

Armed with our definitions, then, let us embark on exploring the story of the world's changing values, of the rise of the state and the emergence of modern society, as told through the evolution of its underworlds and through crimes from pre-modern banditry and eighteenth-century English tea smuggling to today's industrial-scale traffickers in drugs and people and the high-tech crimes of tomorrow.

PART ONE
THE AGE OF STATE-BUILDING

CHAPTER 1

'ROBBERS OF THE BETTER SORT' AND MAKERS OF STATES

By 1655, Chinese emperor Shunzhi had had enough of his eunuchs. He issued a decree, which was then carved onto an iron tablet, thundering that:

> The employment of eunuchs has been a tradition since ancient times. However, their abuses have often led to disastrous disturbances. They misappropriated power, intervened in government affairs, organised secret agents, murdered the innocent, commanded troops and brought their evil practices to the border regions. They even engaged in conspiratorial activities, framed those who were loyal and good, instigated factional struggles and encouraged fawning and flattery, until the affairs of state deteriorated day by day, and corruption occurred everywhere.[1]

In Imperial China, eunuchs had come to play a powerful role at court from the second century onwards. Many parents had their sons castrated, hoping it would give them a chance to escape poverty – a large number, though, would never get a position. What happened to the unsuccessful ones, those who had been mutilated for nothing? Scorned, despised, no wonder that while some turned to begging or fortune-telling, others – frustrated, angry, outcast – became bandits.[2] When they did, they joined a hardy tradition of marginal-ised, impoverished communities, from demobilised Mongol soldiers to ordinary farmers in times of bad harvest, turning to crime as a means not just of survival, but also to create alternative communi-ties and power structures in which they could feel they had a place. As Shunzhi found, trying to reduce the numbers of eunuchs at his court, from the high of 70,000 in 1644, only added to the numbers of these eunuch bandits.

Banditry was, of course, a time-honoured and even respectable trade in many pre-modern societies. Brent Shaw notes that while by the fifth or sixth centuries BCE, the Greeks were using the terms *lesteia* and *lestes* in a negative context, for pirates and brigands respec-tively, before then, the words had had no pejorative connotations. 'They merely signified another way of making a living, of acquiring economic goods by plundering and raiding': banditry thus became one of the five basic livelihoods Aristotle described, alongside hunt-ing, farming, fishing and herding.[3] Yet this is not simply an ancient practice. In the early sixteenth century, Ming Dynasty China's cap-ital region was plagued by the Xiangmazei, the 'Whistling Arrow Bandits', known for their use of arrows with grooved heads to make a fearsome sound as they cut through the air. These became so infa-mous that merchants would abandon their goods and flee just on first hearing the distinctive keening of these weapons. Meanwhile, right through to the twentieth century, the Bedouins of northern Arabia enthusiastically and unapologetically practised the *ghazw* (*razzia*), in which a small band would raid another tribe – hopefully without bloodshed on either side – for plunder, especially camels. As the seventh-century poet al-Qutami put it, 'Our business is to make raids on the enemy, on our neighbour, and on our brother, if we find none to raid but a brother.'[4]

However, banditry often reflected a crisis in society, whether an over-production of eunuchs, an under-producing harvest, the dislocations of war or the perverse result of peace. The Jewish Roman writer Josephus noted how crop failures led to 'a harvest of banditry', as people were forced to steal and raid to survive, for example.[5] War likewise often forced people into banditry – or even peace. The end of the War of Spanish Succession in 1714 meant hordes of muleskinners – mule-drivers – lost their livelihoods. They were considered morally polluted, not least because, as well as handling dead animals, they also buried the bodies of hanged criminals on behalf of the court. As a result, lacking legitimate alternative employment, they formed the core of the *Bokkerijders* ('Billy-Goat Riders'), who robbed and raided their way across the Meuse Valley and into other regions of the Low Countries beyond.[6]

Often, the bandits were mastered by local communities or power structures. The life of the samurai-turned-bandit Ishikawa Goemon and his exploits in sixteenth-century Japan have been thoroughly mythologised, making him everything from a revolutionary to a ninja assassin, but nonetheless it is clear that he was able to marshal a disciplined and efficient bandit army that robbed lords and merchants alike with impunity until he over-reached. Goemon was only caught in 1594 when he boldly, if incautiously, stole into the castle of Toyotomi Hideyoshi, the warlord who had become effective dictator of the country, with assassination on his mind. Goemon was seized and publicly boiled alive, the kind of death guaranteed to turn him into a folk hero, yet also which induced his gang to disband.

At other times, they were essentially co-opted. There is often a fine line to be drawn between warfare and banditry. Following the Norman invasion of England in 1066, for example, the Anglo-Danish lord of the Isle of Ely, Hereward the Wake, resisted them as much through bandit raids as military operations – his men looted Peterborough Abbey in 1070, 'to protect its treasures from the Normans' – before being crushed by William the Conqueror the following year. Hereward perhaps gained posthumous satisfaction by being immortalised as a dashing warrior and canny rebel in a series of romantic adventures and ballads, but it is impossible to tell how far in reality this could be considered guerrilla war and how far it was just banditry.[7]

Sometimes the bandits actually became instruments of statecraft. The way pirates could become legitimised as privateers will be discussed later, but just as bandits might find themselves openly recruited as soldiers (indeed, in the war that followed Russia's invasion of Ukraine in 2022, both sides have turned to enlisting convicts), so too were they at times employed more covertly. The Aztecs of the thirteenth to the sixteenth century established an increasingly effective centralised government, with military patrols along its roads, but highwaymen and similar bandits were still a common threat to the merchant caravans which travelled from city to city. Most of the raiders were no doubt simply out for profit, but, especially before the empire (or Triple Alliance) united the original three city-states of Mexico-Tenochtitlan, Texcoco and Tlacopan in 1428, there also seem to have been cases in which they were carrying out a kind of covert warfare on behalf of one or another of them.[8] They were still bandits, to be sure, but they were deniable agents, too.

Bandit kingdoms

However, the final prize was sometimes to become the founder of a state. To sociologist Charles Tilly, for whom 'banditry, piracy, gangland rivalry, policing and war making all belong on the same continuum', this 'continuum ran from bandits and pirates to kings via tax collectors, regional power holders and professional soldiers'.[9] The smartest predators, after all, understand the need to maintain their prey, leading to a process of state-building. The economist Mancur Olson theorised that there were two types of bandit, the roving and the stationary.[10] The roving bandit strikes, grabs whatever he can – even if that is everything the victim has – and moves on, while the stationary kind actually steals the whole community, and in the process acquires new incentives. The roving bandit will grab the goose that lays the golden eggs, steal however many have been laid, cook the goose for dinner, then look for another one tomorrow. The stationary bandit will try to keep the goose fed and healthy, in the expectation of taking his cut from a lifetime of golden eggs. In the process, the *smart* stationary bandit will only take what his prey can afford, protect them from other bandits who would kill or dispossess them, and perhaps even provide other public goods, so that as they become richer, he can take more from them in due course. In other words, the bandit becomes a monarch.

How far was a stationary bandit different from other sources of power? The ambitious Marcus Licinius Crassus became regarded as the richest man in late Republican Rome for his involvement in a wide range of schemes, but one of the most ingenious exploited the fact that the city had no fire brigade, even though blazes were commonplace. He established his own, but when it turned up at the scene of a fire, Crassus would offer to buy the property at, well, a fire-sale price. If the owner refused, Crassus and his men would stand back and watch it burn. Even later, some would still put their trust not in the state, but what the writer Apuleius called, tongue-in-cheek, 'the brave, steadfast, faithful robber of the better sort'.[11] He was operating within a state, but others created their own. Visigoth raiders settled and formed their own kingdom in the ruins of Roman Gaul in the fifth century.[12] In ninth- through eleventh-century France and England, the Danegeld ('Danish tribute') was paid to buy off Viking raiders, who themselves were the foundations of their own states.[13] This was part of an evolution, as small-scale hit-and-run raiders (before around 850) began to cohere into larger raiding armies that eventually set up in their own realms in Dublin, Northumbria, Normandy, Russia and so on, extorting tribute from neighbouring communities on pain of war.[14]

The bandits need not be outsiders, though. Frances Stonor Saunders wrote that 'knights were an instrument of force: they could use violence to build communities, or to destroy them'.[15] Setting aside the mythology of chivalry, in practice they largely acted as they willed. Hobsbawm called this the age of 'feudal anarchy',[16] while Barbara Hanawalt's study of what she wittily described as 'fur-collar crime' concluded that, except when it impinged on their own interests directly, 'both king and barons assumed that a certain amount of criminal activity was involved in being a noble and would be tolerated'.[17] Boys will be boys and knights, apparently, will be knights. The extent to which the law was not a constraint on the rich and powerful is a recurring theme of medieval commentaries. The fifteenth-century French poet Eustache Deschamps, for example, likened justice to a spider's web, which catches the small flies, but which is torn asunder by a larger insect. This analogy crops up time and again in other works of the period, from those of the English writer Thomas Hoccleve to the fiery Italian radical monk and reformer Girolamo Savonarola.[18]

It was often only when wilful and arrogant local tyrants fell foul of those above them in the food chain that they risked facing justice. In the fourteenth century, for example, Sir John Molyns was the terror of Buckinghamshire. A protégé of King Edward III, he stole land and had his enemies murdered or attacked – including the sheriff of the county – all with impunity, thanks to royal patronage and the protection of one of the king's judges. He juggled his role as a 'fur-collar criminal' with similar activities on the king's behalf, not least in 1337 when he was ordered to round up all the foreign merchants in London. The only exceptions were the king's own Italian bankers, whom one might speculate had paid well for their immunity and the ejection of their competition. It was only when he alienated Edward that he was brought to account for his crimes. Even so, as soon as he was needed, he was back in the king's favour, being pardoned in 1345 during the run-up to another war with France.[19] Likewise, members of the Russian gentry accused of banditry could often secure the suspension of any legal proceedings by taking on active service for the tsar, a practice which continued at least into the seventeenth century.[20]

Violent entrepreneurs

Those 'violent entrepreneurs' who were successful at wielding both force and political authority were creatures of their times. Although they would continue to emerge whenever states were weak and there was a demand for their services, they were especially prevalent in the chaotic interregnums between times of state collapse and the emergence of new ones. Indeed, Vadim Volkov originated the term violent entrepreneurs while looking at the anarchic emergence of Russia from the collapsing Soviet Union in the 1990s.[21] They were, however, even more common in earlier times, when armies were 'elaborate business ventures',[22] when the boundaries of nations and concepts of legality were equally fluid in practice, and when the whole concept of the state was still in gestation. From these violent entrepreneurs' expeditions of conquests and plunder emerged states and dynasties: banditry as a tool for state-making and social mobility. Those who successfully assembled and used armed power, while perhaps technically acting unlawfully, could parlay this muscle into political legitimacy by proving that they were good at it. As St Augustine put it in the fifth century,

If this villainy wins so many recruits from the ranks of the demoralised that it acquires territory, establishes a base, captures cities and subdues people, it then openly arrogates to itself the title of kingdom, which is conferred on it in the eyes of the world, not by the renouncing of aggression, but by the attainment of impunity.[23]

Thus, the feudal order emerged in Europe. Sometimes land was seized and its inhabitants subjugated through direct force, at other times they submitted of their own will in return for necessary protection in a violent and dangerous time. Effective violent entrepreneurs could find themselves elevated within the political order, if they survived long enough. The opportunist merchant Giovanni Agnello made himself lord of Pisa in 1364 thanks to the backing of the infamous English mercenary John Hawkwood (no one says that a violent entrepreneur needs to carry out the violence himself, merely be able effectively to control or unleash it). He had more strategy than luck, though: while immobilised in neighbouring Lucca in 1368 when a balcony he was standing on collapsed, he was overthrown in a counter-coup.[24]

Nor is this a uniquely European concept but one found in pre-modern societies across the world. In Imperial China, the stewards of Imperial lands typically gathered 'an assortment of deserting soldiers, local toughs and men who had managed to escape from the household registration system' as their protectors and tax collectors. Their leaders acquired such coercive power that 'many officials tacitly acknowledged the power of these de facto satraps'.[25] Muscle buys authority. A more unruly example emerges from Donald Crummey's study of banditry in nineteenth-century Ethiopia, undoubtedly a pre-modern society. He explores *sheftenat*, a combination of rebellion and robbery, largely led by members of the elite. One of the founding fathers of modern Ethiopia, Emperor Tewodros, rose precisely through *sheftenat*. Born Kassa Hailu, of noble birth, he practised wise governance over his own lands in Qwara while ruthlessly plundering the lowlands of western Ethiopia. Even after being made governor of Qwara, he continued to combine the roles of nobleman and bandit, using *sheftenat* to punish his enemies, enrich himself, and attract more warriors into his service with the promise of plunder and glory on the long road from bandit to emperor.[26] Such violent entrepreneurship, conducted in accordance with recognised conventions and through established and socially (if not legally) legitimised institutions and leaders, is the stuff of state-building.

A real state, though, makes its own demands. It has to be defended; its elite need to be bought off; it needs churches and temples, granaries and foundries, heralds to praise the monarch, and scribes to tally his wealth. All that requires money, taxation, and that means more than just plunder. But what can criminality tell us about the difference between taxation and extortion? In other words, what is the difference between a state and a protection racket? Let's turn next to that thorny question.

CHAPTER 2

BETWEEN EXTORTION AND PROTECTION

States must establish their authority to provide protection and adjudicate disputes, while excluding alternative providers of both services. When the state cannot or will not provide, others will fill the vacuum. The late medieval Scottish Marches, for example, were a no-man's land between the English and Scottish crowns, fair game for the Border Reivers, roving bands of brigands who would steal, plunder, burn and kill with virtual impunity. Their raids, often launched in the early winter months, when nights were longest and the livestock well fed from summer grazing, might be as small as a few dozen riders, to the kind of massed expedition involving hundreds, maybe even thousands, which scoured Cumbria in the early seventeenth century. Just one excursion apparently netted some 1,280 cattle and 3,840 sheep and goats.

Unable to fight, when they could the farmers paid raiders to stay away. These dues were known as *black mal* – 'mal' being Old Norse for agreement – whence comes the word blackmail. By the beginning of the seventeenth century, London was even contemplating rebuilding Hadrian's Wall, the old Roman fortified line dividing England from Scotland. Instead, though, James VI of Scotland acceded to the English throne in 1603 (as James I), and with the union of crowns and kingdoms, the particular conditions that had kept the Marches virtually lawless were gone.[1] However, over the years, some reiver families had become rich and secure enough to find themselves incorporated into the regional elites, especially on the Scottish side, as Marcher Lords. In other cases, 'black mal' deals had moved from simple extortion to something more positive, reiver families assuming responsibility for the security of the villages in their turfs. Protection can become authority, after all.

This protection has long been a basic commodity of life, a fundamental building block of the state, and also a core business of many criminals, especially organised gangs. Outside raiders may practise this as a kind of extortion. However, the smartest and most secure gangs inside communities, Olson's 'Stationary Bandits', come to realise that extortion – protection just from their own predation – can be turned into a much wider business of the provision of protection.

Mafias

This conjunction of gangsterism and protection has led to a scholarly debate over the term 'mafia'. The terms 'organised crime' and 'mafia' are often used interchangeably, even though the capital-M Mafia itself is a particular Italian organised crime culture, originating in Sicily and then migrating to North America. Indeed, the very origins of the word are still disputed, with theories ranging from the distinctly dubious claim that it is an acronym based on the supposed battle cry of the 1282 Sicilian Vespers rising against French rule, *Morte Alla Francia Italia Anela!* ('Death to France Italy Cries!'), to the more plausible derivation from the Sicilian adjective *mafiusu*, meaning 'swagger', or perhaps 'bravado'.[2] Other possibilities include carry-overs from Arabic denoting either arrogance or strong protector. It had become a popular term by 1863 when the Sicilian-language comedy *I Mafiusi della Vicaria* appeared. Set in the Palermo prison known as the Vicaria, it features the gangster godfather Gioacchino

Funciazza, a power in the prison, who demands his tribute from others (known as *u pizzu*) yet, for all that, protects those under his patronage and respects the old traditions.

The play was fiction, but rooted in the experiences of the time. Indeed, one of the playwrights, Gaspare Mosca, had consulted Gioacchino D'Angelo, a notorious member of the Camorra, Naples's equivalent of the Mafia, who had served time in Vicaria. Although, at the authorities' request – demand – the authors added a moralising final act in which Funciazza repents and urges his former acolytes to follow him to redemption, this was as unconvincing as it was unentertaining. The Sicilian Mafia, whatever its etymology, had already established itself as a distinctive form of local gangsterism, predatory and protective. After all, the Mafia was rooted in the specific circumstances of Sicily. The island's story is of foreign control, from the Greek and Phoenician colonies of the eight century BCE, to being a Roman province, a property of the Vandals and the Ostrogoths, a Byzantine holding, and then in the ninth century, briefly, a Muslim emirate until conquest by the Normans in 1071. The subsequent Kingdom of Sicily was controlled first by the French and then the Spanish, until eventual incorporation into the new Italian state by conquest in 1860. For Sicily, government was something imposed from abroad, of questionable local legitimacy, usually exploitative, and often incompetent.

The Mafiosi themselves were locals, men willing and able to use violence, yet also to establish themselves as intermediaries of a distant and weak state and of absentee landlords, as key figures in the centre of the process as 'the central government, the landlords, and the peasants arranged and rearranged themselves in conflict and accommodation'.[3] They could be the agents of those with the power, yet also defenders of those without – all for a price. Mafiosi resolved disputes and developed relationships between different interests and social groups. There is a reason why the original 'men of honour' were called godfathers, as in Sicily's fragmented peasant society they were also matchmakers, brokering marriages between villages and in the process gaining new allies and clients. The criminals could then leverage this provision of tangible and intangible services to their community to give them some of the authority and legitimacy due the state – and to justify their demands for tribute.

Since then, though, the word 'mafia' has also become a term of art for a specific form of organised crime exemplified by the Sicilians. In his *Mafia Business* (1986), Pino Arlacchi suggested that, as well as directly criminal businesses, a mafia engages in three particular activities that replicate or supplant functions of the state: providing protection, repressing those disliked by the social mainstream, and mediation between a variety of legitimate and illegitimate actors. Diego Gambetta then took this further, focusing purely on the provision of non-state protection. In his *The Sicilian Mafia* (1993), Gambetta argues that the key characteristic defining a mafia is that it does not just run predatory protection rackets through which victims pay them off, but it also sells protection from other gangs, even the state or commercial rivals. This form of organised crime is thus a symptom of a state which is unable to meet the needs of its citizens, or which they do not trust, creating a market opportunity in security for the criminals to exploit. Others have applied Gambetta's model to a range of other societies where such a market opportunity has emerged, from 1990s Russia (Federico Varese) to post-war Japan (Peter Hill).[4]

Antisocial bandits

In a way, this is a modern, post-Marxist take on the 'social bandit' thesis put forward by the leftist historian Eric Hobsbawm. In his wide-ranging, wonderfully readable yet also undoubtedly idealised *Bandits* (1969), he lays out the notion of social bandits, 'peasant outlaws whom the lord and state regard as criminals, but who remain within peasant society, and are considered by their people as heroes, as champions, avengers, fighters for justice, perhaps even as leaders of liberation'.[5] To some degree this can be – and has been[6] – dismissed as Marxist romanticism, Robin Hood with dialectic. It is much easier to admire this supposed breed from the comfort of a foreign country and a different age.

While examples of Robin Hoods and bandit-heroes can be found across history and across the world, on examination, their progressive credentials usually end up looking a little tenuous. The fifteenth-century Korean outlaw Hong Gil-dong, for example, whose tawdry real life was later elevated by perhaps being confused with the tale of the sixteenth-century rebel Im Kkeok-jeong, who supplied grain to the hungry, such that there is now a Hong Gil-dong theme park in his home region of Jangseong.[7] Or Diego Corrientes Mateos, the eighteenth-century Spanish highwayman who acquired the nickname 'El Bandido Generoso', the Generous Bandit, for his reputed willingness to help out needy Andalucian peasants, although this seems to be a tale based on ballads more than records.[8] Or Tadas Blinda, the nineteenth-century Lithuanian smallholder who was driven to the wrong side of the law by his dispute with Duke Myko-las Oginskis, and who died with his head smashed by an angry mob for his horse-thievery, yet who was later reinvented by fabulists and nationalists as a hero who struggled against Russian imperialists and their local quislings.[9]

Yet ultimately, they all sought to maximise their profits and min-imise their risks. Those who robbed from the wealthy would have understood American gangster Willie Sutton's apocryphal answer to the question as to why he held up banks: 'Because that's where the money is.'[10] In practice, though, bandits generally prey at least as often upon the peasants as the rich and powerful, because the latter can usually afford their own defenders. Indeed, such predation is often one of the drivers of the rise of states and militarised elites: Hobsbawm might have been advised to watch a few more Westerns (or, indeed, *The Seven Samurai*), exploring as they do just how a peasant community can defend itself from bandits by finding specialist warriors, whether knights, gunslingers or samurai, to do their fighting for them. If someone is going to oppress you, at least find someone who will do it in an orderly and predictable manner, and not to your extinction: mercenaries, not bandits.

In fairness to Hobsbawm, he does not wholly ignore the sound practical reasons why criminals seek positive relations with their host societies, at the same time as they steal from them. Even gangsters have to sleep, and they will generally be outnumbered by their prey. They also rely on the locals not turning them in to the authorities or appealing to their rivals. Thus, it is always useful to create myths that either suggest the criminals are somehow on the people's side, or at least that they are the least objectionable or dangerous exploiters around. This is a pattern that outgrew peasant society: when the Australian bushwhacker Ned Kelly and his gang raided the bank in Jerilderie in 1879, they did not just loot it for their own gain, they also burnt the townspeople's mortgage deeds, winning them considerable public sympathy. In post-war Britain, the notorious Kray twins from London's East End created for themselves a useful image as 'bad boys' who nonetheless looked after their communities, paying for old ladies' teas at a local cafe on Bethnal Green Road and donating to Repton Boys Club, where they had started out as juvenile boxers. This was an image far from the reality of these violent and petty sociopaths' reign of terror but, combined with the fear generated by their murderous reputations, ensured that for years the police were unable to get anyone to testify against them. Only their ill-judged decision to kill one of their own, Jack 'the Hat' McVitie, began to turn opinion against them. Consider even the name of the Cosa Nostra – 'our thing' – with its implication that the Mafiosi preying first and foremost on the Italian immigrants into the United States were nonetheless 'theirs'. In their own ways, the Mafia in both Sicily and America's 'Little Italy' were stationary bandits, as might the Krays have been, with a little more forethought and better impulse control.

State-builders

Of course, states and their elites have long used the *tactics* of organised crime. In the fifth century BCE, ancient Athens used its naval power to force lesser Greek city-states within the Delian League to pay to be protected from pirates. Even after the threat of piracy was gone, Athens still expected to be paid, though: the implicit threat was that were the tribute to stop, pirates would suddenly reappear. Likewise, in the seventeenth and eighteenth century, the Maratha Empire of central India demanded a tribute known as the *Chauth* ('the fourth') from neighbouring states that wanted to avoid conquest. And even after it had outlawed the trade within its own borders, the British Empire fought two wars with China in the mid-nineteenth century precisely to punish it for trying to stop opium from British India from being imported through its ports. These were, of course, all technically legal acts of statecraft, even if under other circumstances we might consider them protection racketeering and extortion.

So, as St Augustine wondered, what distinguishes the state from the gang? The rather uncomfortable answer would seem to be that very little distinguishes a state in essence from a *well-run* criminal organisation in form and operation. Where, after all, do we draw the line between extortion and protection? There are, of course, the most crass and exploitative of criminals who demand money for nothing more than leaving the victim alone today (even if he might be back again tomorrow). However, successful organised crime groups understand the importance of a kind of legitimacy, a kind of social contract. If the deal is that your victims pay today and you leave them alone the rest of the month, then if you decide to take from them again tomorrow, they know they cannot trust you. Some will still pay up, some will fight, some will simply flee.

More sophisticated criminals come to appreciate the value of being, for want of a better way of putting it, reliable and honest in their extortion. What starts as a pragmatic business decision becomes a habit, and a habit becomes tradition, and yesterday's predator becomes tomorrow's legitimate protector. As sociologist and historian Charles Tilly famously put it,

> If protection rackets represent organised crime at its smoothest, then war making and state making – quintessential protection rackets with the advantage of legitimacy – qualify as our largest examples of organised crime.[11]

Admittedly, he himself accepted that this was just an analogy, to illustrate his depiction of Europe's historical 'war makers and state makers as coercive and self-seeking entrepreneurs'.[12] One of the main thrusts of his ground-breaking analysis was that 'the distinctions between "legitimate" and "illegitimate" users of violence came clear only very slowly' and if anything it was precisely the process of state formation, and thus the consolidation of the state's monopoly on the use of violence, that draws these distinctions.[13] In earlier times, while there were laws which defined the legitimate use of violence *within* communities – and even these were often loose and regularly ignored – there were few or no legal constraints on violence, theft and extortion *outside* and between those communities. One person's piracy, banditry or crime was likely another's audacious triumph. In this respect, if history is written by the victors, then 'crime' is the complaint of the loser, but defined by the winner.

Less bandit, more state?

There certainly was something of a correlation between the decline of banditry and the rise of the state in early modern Europe. The wild days of 'fur-collar criminals' within the élite were ending, and states were explicitly acknowledging not only that they had to subordinate themselves to law or custom but also that widespread illegality represented a weakness. Where banditry continued, it would usually be connected to temporary crises which undermined the capacity of the state, or else be relatively small-scale, focused on marginalised communities, whether defined by faith, location, ethnicity or employment. Rural crime remained fragmentary, opportunistic and transient. It was often no less dangerous, but early signs of the rise of rural organised crime would disappear. Or, rather, they would migrate to the growing towns and cities, finally to achieve their potential in their marketplaces, factories, workshops and rookeries.

Furthermore, the process of excluding and marginalising whole communities would begin, albeit only slowly, to come under question. Stigmatised ethnic groups such as the Jews or Romany or the Spanish Moriscos appear to have been drawn to crime not just for profit but also revenge against the prejudiced mainstream of society.[14] The emerging state could not wipe out banditry, but it was generally able to limit its sphere of operation. For example, the navvies – short for navigators – who built the railways which crisscrossed Victorian Britain represented a 'caste of specialised nomad labourers with their own habits and traditions',[15] certainly inclined to violent lawlessness. Their camps often became refuges for wanted criminals. However, their crimes – which could include virtually terrorising villages near their camps until their work took them on to their next prey – were essentially opportunistic and about extorting some money, blowing off steam drinking, brawling and gambling, and thumbing their noses at authority. They were happy to turn a blind eye to professional criminals in their midst, but not eager to build alliances with them. In the main, while states – and their police and judicial machines – were changing dramatically, even if the European bandit at the start of the nineteenth century had a flint-lock pistol rather than a sword, he otherwise was much the same in methods, mindset and motivations as his Renaissance ancestor.

This is a developmental rather than strictly chronological process, though. In Spanish-controlled Philippines, for example, a combination of poor governance and increasingly commercialised agriculture (which increased the population but also made it more vulnerable to floods, droughts, diseases and other blights) meant that up to and beyond the end of the nineteenth century, rural banditry remained a serious challenge. Rich and poor alike were subject to the attacks of often-flamboyant bandits, whether the vicious *dugong-aso* ('blood of a dog', in Tagalog), or the less dangerous *tulisan pulpul* ('fake bandits'), under such leaders as one Laóng, famous throughout the region for his silver ornamented hat.[16] Mobilised by local leaders and buoyed by society's belief that raiding was a perfectly respect-able means of supplementing their other incomes, these bandits very much reflected older traditions. However, even in the Philippines and other colonial territories, state-making would in due course make the rural bandit increasingly anachronistic.

Modern bandits

Is that it, though? In crisis-wracked yet fashion-conscious Venezuela, such are the prices of hair extensions that gangs of 'Piranhas' loiter around shopping centres, ready to pounce on long-haired shoppers and cut off their tresses for black-market resale. In 1980s Glasgow, rival ice cream vendors clashed violently over turf, with vans being burnt out or blasted by shotguns. (Although this was more because they were also selling drugs and stolen goods along with choc ices.) In the 2000s and early 2010s, British shops in neighbourhoods with substantial Romanian communities experienced a spate of thefts of chewing gum, with some supermarkets even being raided exclusively for cartons of it, because at the time, a shortage in small change back in Romania meant that sticks and packs were being used as a kind of currency.[17]

There will always be gangs, but outside war zones and failed states, modern societies tend not to allow bandits to rise and form their own territories and polities. Or do they? If bandit kingdoms are symptoms of pre-modernism, is the modern world not always at risk of sinking back into this state? Such phenomena need not be confined to the history books. Is the street gang, with its turf, its hierarchies, its colours and its customs, not a new incarnation of the bandit? But is it not also the case that just as states may fail locally or completely, so too the process of state-building never stops? In modern Africa, amid the detritus of failed and failing states such as Somalia and Sudan, one can see new authorities rising. Here banditry is rife as individuals and groups realise that where the state is absent and a Kalashnikov rifle can be bought for ten one-kilo bags of maize flour or a medium-size goat (once the going rate in the Horn of Africa[18]) there is space for new state-builders. In Somalia, for example, after the state all but collapsed in a long-running civil war, locals in the coastal Puntland region first turned to piracy and then tried briefly to reinvent themselves as a pirate-fighting force, with the help of money from the United Arab Emirates and training from South African mercenaries, in the hope that this would establish their claims to autonomy, if not independence.[19] Finding itself lacking international support and facing jihadist mercenaries, Puntland has begun to slump back into its old ways, but the bandits' desire to find stability and recognition (and money) by offering security demonstrates that this was not only a medieval phenomenon.

Whenever the upperworld state seems weak, distant and exploitative, and the opportunities in accepting its rule seem insufficient, new, primordial state-building bandits will emerge. In the 'wild 90s', for example, when post-Soviet Russia seemed in freefall, and violence and political pull trumped law and decency, how could anyone protect themselves, let along enforce contracts? The answer turned out to be organised crime. Gangs started as predators, extorting money from the new generation of capitalists, but the smarter criminals came to realise that not only did it make sense not to kill the goose laying the golden eggs, but the fatter the goose, the bigger the eggs. They had more cash than they knew what to do with – why not invest it in businesses under their wing? They had muscle and friends in high places – why not use that to collect debts and enforce contracts? As one young entrepreneur on the make told me at the time, 'The most important business decision you make starting out is whose "roof" [protection] you'll shelter under.' Pick the right roof, and no one would threaten your business, no one would welch on your debts. And some of the younger, more flexible mob leaders, the *avtoritety* – 'authorities' – started to become semi-legitimate businessmen, almost without even knowing it.[20]

Many successful gangsters cultivate some rough-and-ready legitimacy, from Mafiosi distributing money to the local poor on saints' days to infamous Colombian narco trafficker Pablo Escobar building schools, homes and football fields in and around his home city of Medellín. In Japan, the process was less personalistic. On 11 March 2011, for example, a magnitude 9.0 earthquake under the Pacific Ocean, 72km east of Japan, caused a tsunami. Forty-metre-high tidal waves smashed into the city of Miyako and flooded the coastal region of Sendai; almost 20,000 people would die. The tsunami was accompanied by deep snowfall, and the government's relief efforts were inevitably overmatched by the crisis. Into the gap came hundreds of trucks laden with food, water, warm-weather clothing and blankets, courtesy of the Yakuza organised crime groups.[21] Just as during the 1995 Great Hanshin Earthquake, they had realised that this was an opportunity for them to burnish their distinctly tarnished reputations at relatively moderate cost. Nor could the government really turn away the much-needed aid; it was, one could say, an offer they could not refuse. As one justice ministry official ruefully admitted to me, 'Whatever good the government does is never enough, but the little good the criminals do, is always more than enough.'

Instead of thinking of mafias as illegitimate stand-ins and substitutes for states, maybe we ought to be thinking of states as well-organised mafias which have been around long enough to accrue legitimacy? And how is the legitimacy of the state exercised and demonstrated? Through laws, armed force and the like, of course, but at the heart of much of this is its capacity to accumulate, distribute and define what it depends upon to operate: money.

CHAPTER 3

COCOA BEANS AND CURRENCY COUNTERFEITERS

To the Aztecs, the cocoa bean was a gift from the god Quetzalco-atl, the Precious Feathered Serpent. It was the key ingredient of the bitter, spicy, cold chocolate drink *cacáhuatl* or *xocolatl*, a privilege of warriors and princes, and a part of their holy rituals. King Montezuma II allegedly drank gallons of it each day, not least for its purported aphrodisiac properties. However, it was also a currency: one bean would get you twenty small tomatoes, and a hundred would buy you a slave or a turkey hen. Billions circulated within the Aztec Empire and associated cultures. When Nezahualcoyotl, lord of Texcoco, died in 1472, he was buried with millions of beans to show off his wealth and to provide for him in the afterlife.

Given the centrality of the cocoa bean, and the fact that most were hoarded or traded rather than used as an ingredient, no wonder that a thriving counterfeit economy emerged. Fake beans were made out of clay or wax, avocado pits or amaranth paste or, in the most extreme cases, dried dung. Genuine beans were emptied of their cacao and filled with ash, mud or sand before being resealed. Much of this was individual enterprise, but serious counterfeiters relied on economies of scale, and also what we could call 'cocoa laundering'. There was always the chance of a bean being inspected or, more damning yet, used to make *cacáhuatl*, and Aztec laws were far from liberal in their treatment of fraud. The penalty was death, the only real question being which of their creatively gruesome array of means was chosen, from strangulation to being burnt alive in a pyre. So the more effective and organised counterfeiting rings not only mixed fake with real beans, they made sure that travelling merchants would carry them to distant cities and markets, in the hope that as they changed hands again and again, it would become impossible to track their provenance.[1]

As mobile bandits became stationary ones and then state-builders, they no longer necessarily depended on others' currencies and definitions of value and began to create their own. There is a reason beyond vainglory why monarchs tend to put their heads on coins: one of the fundamental marks of legitimate authority is power over money. The capacity to control currency – to mint and define it – is crucial. Those who debase it and, worse yet, copy it, not only generate wealth outside the channels the monarch can tax, they devalue the state's economy and authority and thus pose a danger to that monarch's future. As a result, states tend to be brutal in their treatment of counterfeiters. The seventh-century Laws of the Visigoths mandated that anyone involved in counterfeiting should lose their right hand, but this was positively delicate compared with how Britain's 1741 Counterfeiting Coin Act simply declared that this was high treason, punishable by hanging, drawing and quartering – in other words, noosed until near death, disembowelled, beheaded, and chopped into four pieces.

How to catch the miscreants? The banknotes of the Chinese Empire during the fourteenth- to seventeenth-century Ming Dynasty warned that 'to Counterfeit is Death'. In a bid to encourage dishonour among thieves, they added that an 'informant will receive 250 taels in silver and in addition the entire property of the criminal'. Considering that this weight in silver had a value equivalent to £20,000 in today's money, that was no mean inducement. Those who would challenge the state's control of money thus need to be smart and organised, and be willing to take the greatest of risks.

Shaving and plugging

Cowrie shells, from small sea snails found in seas from the Pacific to the Indian Ocean, had been used as a currency of sorts in China and India since the Bronze Age, and the classical Chinese character for money actually originated as a stylised Maldivian shell.[2] As a result, bone, clam shell and ivory duplicates were also in circulation, although it is unclear if these were legal substitutes or counterfeit. The ancient Egyptians used scraps of silver, simply assessing their value by weight, so when, 1,200 years ago, the conquered Canaanites could not get enough silver, they took to adulterating it with copper, coating it with arsenic to make it shine like the real thing. The first actual minting of money, though, was in around 600 BCE, according to the ancient Greek historian Herodotus. The Lydians of western Asia Minor made coins of electrum, a natural alloy of gold and silver. They did not have a standard weight and value and instead were stamped with the royal seal of King Alyattes, and their specific value. Invent the coin, and you invent a range of coin-related crimes, though. Archaeological digs have thrown up evidence of what are now known as *fourrés*. These are made by 'shaving' or 'clipping' small amounts of metal from the edges of coins (one reason why so many later coins have serrated edges, to make this more difficult) and using this scrap to plate a fake made of some cheaper, base metal. Given that electrum is already an alloy, another approach was to melt down these coins and then adulterate the material further with copper and forge more of them. However, when Alyattes's son Croesus – hence the phrase 'rich as Croesus' – replaced these coins with a standardised one, the gold Croeseid, the greater value of the raw material tempted people into simply shaving them for the gold.

The value of non-paper currency depends on the component metal, the imprimatur of the monarch or nation backing it, and the preferences of the potential users. In times of myriad local currencies, frequent adulteration of the specie, and a lack of reliable scales and measures, different societies and even professions sought particular coin. In Renaissance Italy, for instance, Genoese cattle traders expected to be paid in gold doubloons, while grain merchants and Calabrian silk traders favoured the local Milanese silver scudi. English and Provençal merchants used the Spanish real, but their Italian counterparts preferred Venetian ducats (later called zecchini).[3] In such conditions, it was sometimes worthwhile making what could be called 'honest counterfeits' – melting down one coin to make another, but keeping to the right weights and purity – but also rather easier to create dishonest ones, that skimped on both.

Indeed, larger coins could also be 'plugged'. A hole could be bored through the middle and filled with base metal, with the face of the coin then hammered to cover it, although this was difficult with any but the simplest designs. Or it could be sawed in half, and the middle shaved away and replaced with cheap metal in a sandwich. (This practice persisted long enough to explain such phrases as something being 'not worth a plugged nickel'.) This was all a difficult, specialist art. Some goldsmiths practised it as individuals, but the real money was to be made – in every sense of the word – by scaling up the operation. This required space, connections and a degree of impunity, and a number of Renaissance Italian aristocrats maintained their own workshops of artisans manufacturing a range of fake coins. Like the Aztec cocoa bean counterfeiters, they sought to reduce the chance of detection (and of crashing the local economy) by using their agents to dispose of them in other jurisdictions, especially by using itinerant priests, who could easily cross from one city-state to the next.

This was an especially complex monetary ecology that created particular opportunities for the counterfeiters, but the question of local preference is not unique. Ethiopia had relied on a range of primitive trade tokens, such as bars of crystallised salt and iron rods, until the eighteenth century, when Austria's silver Maria Theresa dollar, also known as the thaler, began to be circulated there by traders and quickly became the coin of choice. Even other silver coins might be rejected or accepted only at a discount. This persisted for the next two centuries: in 1935, after its conquest of Ethiopia, Italy secured from Austria the right to strike thalers precisely because this was necessary for trade in the country and also to pay local levies.[4] One result was a small business in counterfeiting thalers with precision – again, using the right amounts of silver – so that traders could avoid the unfavourable rates for rival coins.

Knockoff notes

Banknotes may have appeared later, but offer their own distinctive opportunities for criminality. They evolved from promissory notes underwritten not by a monarch or a government but individuals. In early China, they were written on pieces of leather, while in Carthage in the second century BCE they might be parchment. The first proper paper currency originated in, as with so many such inventions, China in the seventh to the eleventh centuries. By the thirteenth century the Song government was issuing its own standardised, woodblock-printed banknotes. Over the centuries, the idea then spread to the Middle East and Europe along trade routes, with pieces of cloth with specific values in silver being used in Prague by the tenth century, although actual banknotes as we would recognise them only emerged in Sweden in the seventeenth.

A coin is at least something that can be weighed and tested, even cut open to see if it has been plugged, but verifying banknotes is rather more difficult. The designs of early Chinese notes became increasingly more complex in the hope of challenging the counterfeiters, with additional seals, stamps and signatures, and printed in up to six coloured inks. They were printed on paper made from the bark of the mulberry tree, and by the fourteenth century, guards were being posted around mulberry forests to stop people stealing offcuts from which they could make their own. Later, notes were printed from engraved copper plates, which allowed for even greater detail, and by the seventeenth century, European ones also were acquiring watermarks in the paper.[5]

Little by little, as notes came to predominate and as the technology behind them improved, counterfeiting moved from the artisan to the organisation. By the twentieth century, the need for highly detailed, engraved plates, offset printing presses and special paper meant that the crime demanded not just skill and space but also considerable up-front investment. The individual forger moved to other documents, from passports to bills of sale, and counterfeiting became the preserve of relatively few, mass producers: the scale economy had even reached this criminal business. Between 1994 and 1998, for example, two-thirds of all counterfeit money in the UK was produced by a single gang, run by one Stephen Jory, out of a garage in Essex. After some teething problems, not least with the watermark of Queen Elizabeth II's head, which initially and unflatteringly seemed to give her a beard, he and his partner, a retired printer by trade, managed to produce extremely creditable £20 notes – some 50 million pounds' worth of them by the time the police eventually caught up with them.[6]

Money wars

The adoption of the banknote reflected two interconnected trends: the growing competence of government and the expansion of trade, which made lugging around metal coins increasingly onerous and impractical. It is hardly coincidental that China, with its extraordinary (if periodically interrupted) record of state-building, features so prominently in this story. All currency is, to a degree, a consensual fantasy, depending on everyone agreeing that this metal button or that paper slip is worth something real. Specie, at least, has some intrinsic value, even if no one can eat gold. Banknotes, though, are dependent upon the increasingly fictional promise that someone will, if required, exchange that piece of paper for gold, silver or some other concrete value. In short, banknotes depend on the emergence of a state that is solvent enough to back its paper (the institution that issued those first notes in Sweden, Stockholms Banco, went bankrupt within three years after it printed more notes than it had funds to guarantee), stable enough that people expect it to last and legitimate enough for its imprimatur to have credibility.[7] As upperworld society became more organised and effective, the criminals had to evolve to keep pace.

However, just as the legitimacy and value of a currency, especially paper money, depend heavily on the credibility of the state which is backing it, the inverse is just as true. States jealously guard their control over their currency for a reason – and anything that undermines this can be a serious threat. This has also meant that counterfeiting has been weaponised as a means of striking at the effective operation of an enemy's economy and thus the very legitimacy of its state. Since the Renaissance, this has been recognised by a succession of ruthless leaders willing to engage criminals as instruments of statecraft. According to some accounts, in the 1470s, Milan's Duke Galeazzo Sforza organised the counterfeiting of Venetian zecchini, with deliberately lower gold content, in an imaginative but unsuccessful bid to undermine the maritime trading state's economy.

However, the first to put this kind of economic warfare onto an almost industrial scale were the British. During the American War of Independence (1775–83), they set out to devalue the rebel currency by establishing their own counterfeiting operation, most notably on a boat anchored in New York harbour. A network of 'shovers' moved the fake dollars into the colonies, with two of the most notorious, David Farnsworth and John Blair, being hanged in 1778, caught in possession of $10,000 in counterfeit. Later, Napoleon adopted this tactic, ordering the forging of Austrian and Russian banknotes, while revolutionaries also saw in it a way simultaneously to undermine their enemies while raising operational funds. These tended to be amateurish and small-scale operations, though few were as tragicomic as Habsburg Prince Ludwig Windisch-Grätz's quixotic effort to fund a coup against the Hungarian government and at the same time punish France for its role in drafting the 1920 Treaty of Trianon that stripped Hungary of almost all of its former territory. By his own account, his goal 'was to avenge my country upon France' by 'sending the franc crashing to nothingness on a tide of counterfeit inflation'.[8] He had 100 million francs in 1,000-franc notes printed, and had procured enough paper to print 200 million more, which he hoped to distribute through a network of émigré Hungarians (and fascist fellow-travellers). However, the quality of the fakes was sufficiently poor that the plot was uncovered almost at once, with only a few notes put into circulation.

All these efforts paled before Germany's Operations Andreas and Bernhard, which produced impressively accurate British banknotes during the Second World War.[9] The aim of the original operation, Andreas, was to flood Britain with counterfeit notes to generate hyperinflation, but this was succeeded by Operation Bernhard, which was instead intended to generate revenue, by exchanging the fake notes for genuine Swiss francs and US dollars. This effort drew on the full resources of the Nazi state, from chemists testing the composition of the water used in the manufacture of the paper, to code-breakers cracking the algorithm that determined the number sequencing. The workers of Operation Bernhard were

Jewish inmates of Sachsenhausen concentration camp, who had to replicate the natural wear and tear of notes by standing in lines and passing the notes between them. Some would even be pinned in the corner, the way bank clerks would bundle genuine banknotes, or had numbers or even names and addresses in English scribbled on them. Anything up to £300 million were manufactured, but relatively few were ever used, especially as the British were alerted and introduced controls on notes in circulation. Nonetheless, it represented the most ambitious attempt to use counterfeit for warfighting, dwarfing Operation Sugi, the analogous effort by Japan's secretive Ninth Army Technical Research Laboratory to undermine the Chinese economy.[10]

Plastic and virtual, but always political

Since then, there has been a variety of similar campaigns, even though there is a constant struggle to create new forms of currency beyond the counterfeiters' art, with bimetallic coins, polymer notes and microprinted notations. Nonetheless, someone always manages eventually to find a way. These days, this often turns out first to be the North Koreans. They produce the most perfect replicas of the US $100 'superbill',[11] largely because they are printed in the government's own mint and used at once to bypass sanctions and levy a minor revenge on Washington, all managed by Bureau 39, in effect the hermit kingdom's Ministry of Crime, of which more later. In this way, technology continues to take counterfeiting away from the craftsman and gives it to big operations and big operators.

Of course, the emerging challenge is coming from the cryptocurrencies such as bitcoin, wholly virtual, and so far largely out of the grip of governments, already being used by criminals to move, cache and launder their funds. These truly fictional currencies – which some dismiss as little more than giant pyramid schemes which eventually collapse on duped investors – for now look as if they may be completing the circle, taking money back out of the hands of states. This also helps explain why they are regarded as so dangerous. In 2022, for example, Rostin Behnam, chair of the US Commodity Futures Trading Commission, called them 'potentially a threat to national security'.[12]

After all, what are the core attributes of states? Put very crudely, the capacity to assemble and control resources and then to use them to deploy force, whether in the offence, the defence or simply the preservation of the status quo. If bandits and other violent entrepreneurs were at the heart of the rise of the organised and settled community which, in time, became the state, then their capacity to control their own currencies was central to their capacity to maintain them. For all the David Farnsworths and Prince Ludwig Windisch-Grätzes of this world, counterfeiters were generally motivated by profit, not politics. Nonetheless, what they were doing was, whether they liked it or not, intensely political. Counterfeiters may not think of themselves as revolutionaries, but nonetheless, as states consolidated their grip on the financial infrastructure of the world, this was another place where crime and politics collided, unintentionally but inevitably. As a result, as in so many other ways, it was the growing organisation of the state that forced the growing organisation of crime. As cash replaced barter, as it became harder to get away with counterfeiting it but also potentially more lucrative, then the criminals had to organise, both to be able to commit these more technically demanding crimes and to be able to get away with them. This was, however, just one aspect of the consolidation and professionalisation of crime that would emerge as the state became more complex.

CHAPTER 4

GAMBLERS, CRAFTY CRIMINALS AND THE EARLY ORGANISED UNDERWORLD

The old adage has it that 'war is long periods of boredom punctuated by moments of sheer terror'. No wonder, then, that it was often fighting men, whether Roman legionaries, Aztec jaguar warriors or crusading knights, who indulged in games of chance to pass the time between those moments of terror, or to recreate the adrenaline highs thereof. Roman soldiers stuffed into their packs lightweight cloth boards to play board games such as Tabula (a little like backgammon) or Ludus Latrunculorum (a kind of chess), typically for money or traded duties. Although played throughout society, Aztec warriors were known to be obsessed with the board game Patolli, which dated back to the second century BCE, invoking Macuilxochitl (or Xōchipilli), god of games and flowers, instead of their usual, more martial deities. The dice game Hazard, a perennial of the Middle Ages, was traditionally said to have been invented by bored crusaders during the five-and-a-half-month siege of Tyre in 1124.

However, it is important to remember that this was a time when the fighting man was either the social elite (as with the Aztecs and the medieval Europeans) or the elite's essential instrument (as in Rome). They needed to be kept disciplined, united and, in the former case, solvent. As states began to become more secure and expansive, as they drew boundaries around the uncontrolled neighbourhoods and controlled their finances, they also began to look to policing morality, not so much because they cared about the souls of their subjects and citizens, but because of practical politics. Gambling, in particular, widely came to be seen as a threat to the very social order, associated with brawling, destitution and blasphemy. As Chaucer's Pardoner put it, gambling is 'the very mother of lies and deceit and cursed foreswearing, blasphemy of Christ, manslaughter'.[1] Not only did governments become increasing alarmed at the extent to which gambling created the danger of violence and penury, it also distracted workers from more profitable activities, whether working on the fields or military training.

Gambling against the status quo

Above all, it undermined the social order: the nobility could become – and were becoming – impoverished, in debt, and unable to meet their obligations to the crown. This has long been a concern, the spectre of the elite gambling away the resources they needed to maintain not just their status but also their value to the state. Even in the Indian mythic epic the *Mahabharata*, the god Yudhisthira wagers a hundred thousand gold pieces, a thousand elephants, his army, his slaves, and the freedom of his family, all in one game! England's King Richard I, during the Third Crusade, is meant to have tried to ban anyone who wasn't a knight from gambling, and confining even them to playing only until they had lost up to 20 shillings in a single day, a sum equivalent to the cost of a simple draught horse. That said, one doubts that made any difference given how pervasive games and gambling remained in medieval literature.[2] Almost as alarming a thought as that the nobility could become poor, was that commoners might become rich or, worse yet, gain power over their indebted social betters. Once

again, then, the authorities criminalised activities essentially to preserve their own interests and their status quo.

Hence the common pattern of attempts to control or ban gambling. In 1276, the authorities in the Norwegian city of Bergen gave
officials the power to fine gamblers half a silver mark – a considerable sum – and also confiscate all the money on the gambling table.
In 1388, dicing and other games (including football) were banned in
England, with archery practice being the only acceptable pastime.
Through China's Song, Yuan and Ming dynasties – from the tenth
to seventeenth centuries – successive efforts were made to stamp out
gambling, although as officials were among the worst offenders, this
never amounted to much.

Of course, occasionally it was less about moral control and the
preservation of the social order, but economic opportunities. Some
of these draconian measures were really aimed at extracting lucrative fines or licence fees from the activity. It's not a crime when the
government does it. In 1463, the British parliament forbade the
importation of playing cards and dice, but not their use: the idea was
to encourage locally sourced gambling and help domestic craftsmen.
In 1694, it authorised the first official national lottery, and then, in
1721, outlawed the numerous private lotteries to give it a monopoly.
The state clearly appreciated that what could not be banned could
at least be taxed.

Gambling increasingly became an opportunity for more organised predators, not just running rigged games, but also offering the
pawnbroking and loan-sharking services inveterate gamers needed,
and protecting venues for higher-stakes games than the laws might
permit. In Japan, the professional gamblers known as *Bakuto* were
among the various criminal castes that cohered into what became
the Yakuza crime syndicates. Indeed, their very name is from *ya-
ku-sa*, a losing card hand. While there were still many individual
dice-riggers, card sharps, and other miscellaneous rogues, even they

often would need to pay off the local gang to continue to fleece their marks without risking a knife in the dark. In many parts of Europe, laws were introduced banning gambling in private houses, inns' cellars or, in the town of Kotor in what is now Montenegro, even caves, precisely to try and limit the scope for the kind of gambling the gangs would run. In the medieval Islamic states, because gambling was *haram* – forbidden – gangs with suitable premises, or suitable protection, would organise everything from competitive chess and backgammon tournaments to wagering on sporting contests. They would also provide a suitable *muhallil* ('legaliser') who, by participating in the game but without contributing to the stakes or taking any winnings, created a technical loophole in the law that an organisation with the money to secure a capable jurist could use in case of an official raid, to be able to deny that this was gambling for money.

Yet why did illegal gambling become an economy dominated by gangs and career criminals? The rise of gambling reflects a wider economic change in the nature of professional (or semi-professional) criminality, in the early modern era. As subsistence and barter economies increasingly became cash ones, as the cities grew, and with them the kind of urban anonymity that meant that the person you cheated today was not necessarily the person who would be working the field alongside you tomorrow carrying a large, sharp scythe, the criminals were quick to adapt, as crime began to professionalise.

Crafty criminals

Even before the true onset of industrialisation, urbanisation was reshaping the criminal world. Mary McIntosh characterised this as the rise of 'craft' thieving because it essentially became an occupation through which ordinary citizens could sustain themselves without living obviously beyond the bounds of the law, the way rural bandits did. Instead, professional criminals from gamblers to pickpockets, confidence tricksters to burglars, could make a decent or at least bearable living through routine small-scale thefts perpetrated against a large number of victims. This was the secret: the crimes could be numerous, but individually small enough in scale not to trigger substantial security measures or social control (in this respect, they were much like many of the crimes of the computer age). McIntosh uses the example of Victorian boy pickpockets who 'could earn their keep from other people's pocket handkerchiefs and no one would consider keeping his handkerchief on a chain or under lock and key'.[3] Nonetheless, craft thieves typically work in groups and over extended periods of time, with 'elaborately worked out techniques, a detailed division of labour among the participants and a great deal of lore about the best time and places to work, the best victims and so forth'.[4]

This was not unique to Europe, nor even necessarily a purely urban phenomenon. From the thirteenth century, India was troubled by the *thuggee*, gangs of murderers who would waylay travellers and steal their possessions. However, their real heyday was in the seventeenth and eighteenth centuries. They have been mythologised originally as blood-crazed religious fanatics strangling hundreds of thousands in the name of the Hindu death-goddess Kali, and subsequently as misunderstood, dispossessed and demonised victims of colonial misrule or prejudice.[5] The truth of the matter appears to be that they were examples of primordial but also cross-generational and professional early organised 'craft' crime.[6] Gangs – which could be as small as 5 men but typically numbered 15 to 25 – followed a well-practised standard routine on India's long and under-patrolled roads, winning the trust of travellers only to turn on them at a prearranged signal (often the phrase 'bring the tobacco'). Stripped of their valuables, their victims' strangled bodies would be disposed of in wells or shallow graves, while the gang quickly moved on to its next prey or else a safe haven to divide the spoils. They were hierarchical, under a leader called a *jemadar*, and demonstrated a degree of specialisation, with scouts, inveiglers (who made friends with prospective targets), stranglers, grave-diggers and 'hand-holders' (who immobilised victims by wrapping their arms around them).[7] Older thugs might be employed to distract the prey or identify new targets, while there was a constant quest for suitable new recruits to train up as the next generation, whether the sons of thugs, or promising outsiders. The *thuggee* had no wider organisation, but did share a common culture, folklore (which included good-luck devotions to Kali, but not the fervour some British colonial observers believed), recognition codes and signals, and even *Ramasee*, their own argot. To establish for themselves safe havens, they would also typically cultivate local petty rulers or landlords, paying them off in return for protection. As it was, the *thuggee* were largely suppressed in the 1830s in a campaign marshalled by the East India Company, through a mix of effective intelligence and ruthless policing, perhaps one of the first examples of the kind of campaign able successfully to root out organised crime.

The *thuggee* were, arguably, ahead of their time. The rise of urbanisation would begin to revolutionise European crime in the eighteenth and above all nineteenth centuries, creating pressures encouraging the organisation of crime both in the countryside and, especially, the cities. The result was to further the development of rookeries, the lawless slums discussed in the next chapter, creating a critical mass of urban criminals who at last were numerous enough and could spend enough of their lives within this social environment to create a genuine criminal subculture. This subculture not only defined its members through its habits, rituals, slang and values, it also embodied an increasingly sophisticated internal economy and labour market.

Within this underworld, criminals could learn a trade and find apprenticeship into a life-long career, and these subcultures germinated more complex economic models. In most cases, early modern European crime worked as an artisanal 'craft' activity, with a mix of 'sole traders' and gangs, relatively small and still quite transient. This remained true in the nineteenth century, but the criminalised socio-economic environment in which they lived and worked became increasingly large and complex. As well as larger criminal groupings, it could also support a growing number of specialists able to respond to the new needs of the market, from professional forgers such as the itinerant 'jarkmen' of Elizabethan London (who started faking begging licences and then diversified to documents of all kinds)[8] or the *raky* ('crayfishes') of the late nineteenth-century Russian slums known as *yamy* ('pits'), tailors who could overnight transform stolen clothes, adding brocade to a coat, turning a fur collar into a stole or changing the buttons on a shirt, all so they could safely be sold.[9]

Criminal cultures

What emerged was a culture, a criminal underworld. On the whole, people did not fit into hierarchical criminal organisations, they were simply part of the criminal milieu. In the German criminal cant, *Rotwelsch*, they were simply *Kocheme*: cunning and smart folk willing to break the law.[10] Likewise, consider the underground argot of Russia's nineteenth-century *vorovskoi mir* or 'Thieves' World'. As well as 'world', the word *mir* also means 'peace' and, more appropriately, a peasant commune, underscoring the extent to which this was a world, a community unto itself. The criminals called themselves *lyudi*, 'people' – by extension, the law-abiding were something less than people.

As Mary Perry put it, based on her study of early modern Seville,

The underworld was a fluid subculture. Although these people could be distinguished from the dominant culture of the city by vocabulary, social attitude, economic activities, social organisation, ideology, and amusements, their world was not an isolated enclave . . . The underworld was a parallel culture running through all classes, actively participating in the life of the city.[11]

This was, after all, a pattern become increasingly evident even in rural banditry. The days were gone in which substantial, organised bandit gangs could live for months or years in the woods or wilds, covertly interacting with locals, and sallying out of their home district to raid and plunder. Growing populations were encroaching onto the wilds and the forests were shrinking. More to the point, local communities were increasingly effectively integrated into national structures of control, policing and surveillance, and the state could martial more effective forces to eliminate such gangs. The Japanese were rather ahead of the curve, by the eleventh century appointing officers known as *kebiishi* to fight rural banditry, later effectively replaced by military officers, the *tsuibushi* and *ōryōshi*.[12] However, from the fourteenth century northern Italy saw the rise of the *Campari* field wardens, and from the sixteenth century, Muscovy's Banditry Office was chartering local officials to police the countryside.[13] Little by little, the cities would begin to assert their writ more comprehensively on the countryside.

The underworld could no longer be a thing apart, it had to submerge itself in licit society or migrate to the new counterparts of Robin Hood's mythic 'greenwoods', the urban slums. Local informal underworld communities emerged, drawn from a variety of sources (vagrants, members of shunned professions, and those with a 'licit' place in society but also a willingness to engage in extracurricular crime for the excitement or loot); people who came to know each other through common acquaintances, drinking at the same taverns, attending the same rough entertainments, hiding from the same hue and cry.

Modes of production

The underworld became a labour market, too. Before the factory came to shape society, urban economic life was often built around the artisan's workshop, typically comprising a master and a number of apprentices and journeymen.[14] Gangs such as the *thuggee* essentially followed this model, recruiting likely new members and handing down their craft skills to the next generation. This was, though, an essentially limiting stricture. For more complex work, different specialists would cooperate in production in what Braudel called 'a sort of constellation of "disseminated manufactories" or a milky way of individual workshops', each taking responsibility for their own stage of the process.[15] This model was also manifest in the underworld connected with certain criminal professions. Counterfeiting, for example, required those who gathered the 'raw material', those who actually shaved or forged the coins, and those who then sifted them into the legitimate economy. It also reflected the way many urban criminals of this time lived on the border between underworld and upperworld, perhaps doing some honest labouring today, yet being recruited to commit a crime tomorrow. Looking at bandits in seventeenth- and eighteenth-century Germany, for example, Uwe Danker found that simple thefts tended to involve between one and three criminals, organised burglaries four to six, and raids in which violence was expected might be carried out by up to nine.[16] The criminals belonged to a wider 'gang', which in many ways was just a collection of likely lads who knew and could trust each other. When someone spotted some opportunity or simply needed the money, he would recruit a 'crew' – to use a modern Mafia term – from his peers. The actual composition would vary each time, depending on the size of the crime, its needs, and who was available. Finally, major projects in the pre-modern economy such as shipbuilding required a model closer to the factory we know, with workers hired and managed by a single public or private employer. While least often encountered, one could also argue that some criminal enterprises even began to mirror the factory model, not bandit gangs of armed freelancers, but specialists engaged along a supply chain, such as the more serious counterfeiting operations run by magnates and aristocrats, who also retained scouts to ensure no intrusion into their workshops and distributors who would sift the fake coins into the legitimate economy.

Where would all these criminals go, though? How could they socialise and recruit, plan their crimes and enjoy their fruits safely, away from the constant threat of authorities which were beginning to take policing rather more seriously? The common signals of subculture helped distinguish insiders from potential informants – the tattoos flaunted by those who had committed to Russia's *vorovskoi mir*, or the five tattooed dots signifying a 'circle of friends' used by Vietnamese gangsters – just as an argot helped keep the criminals' secrets to themselves. However, all of these had their limitations. Gang signs might attract unwelcome attention, and even if a police spy could not understand their slang (and many were themselves recruited from the underworld), it marked out its users. In earlier times, the answer was to escape outwards, going beyond the reach of the law, into the seas, hills and forests. With the rise of the cities, the answer was instead to build such havens in the very belly of the state.

CHAPTER 5
BEGGAR KINGS AND ROOKERIES

In seventeenth-century Paris, it was said that the city's beggars were ruled by their own king, known as the Grand Coesre.[1] He presided over a hierarchy of Cagoux, his 'captains', and below them the Archisuppôts and their apprentices, operating within a series of characteristic schools of begging. Each of the Grand Coesre's subjects had to pay him a different tax or fee depending on their mendicant speciality, from the lowly street children who begged as 'orphans', through the *marcandiers* (who presented themselves as impoverished merchants and paid twice as much in membership a year) up to the *sabouleux*, who smeared themselves with blood and chewed on soap to foam at the mouth (a distasteful but lucrative trick, so they paid the most). This had developed especially since the terrible Hundred Years' War of 1337–1453, which had precipitated a massive influx of its real and spurious invalided victims. At night, these 'crippled' and 'blind' mendicants would return to the fetid, winding alleys where they made their homes, lay down their crutches, unwind the bandages from perfectly healthy eyes and otherwise put aside their working guises. Thanks to these wondrous transformations, these beggars' quarters became known ironically as *cours des miracles*, 'miracle alleys'.

Victor Hugo, in his *The Hunchback of Notre Dame* (1831), later brought one of the *cours* to life as a place . . .

which no honest man had ever penetrated at such an hour; a magic circle where the officers of the Châtelet and the sergeants of the provostry, who ventured there, disappeared like crumbs; the city of thieves, a hideous wart on the face of Paris; a sewer, from which there escaped every morning, and to which there returned every night to stagnate, that stream of vices, poverty and vagrancy . . . in short, an immense dressing-room, where dressed and undressed at that time all the actors of that eternal comedy, which robbery, prostitution, and murder enact on the pavements of Paris.[2]

This was the most notorious of Paris's dozen or so *cours*, Rue Neuve-Saint-Sauveur. Around this street arose a dangerous and defiant rookery, rich with brothels, drinking hells and gambling dens. Of course, much of what people believed about them was largely fanciful. Stories of beggar kings, secret societies and their private languages long predated the Grand Coesre, and reflected the fears of the time, as well as the genuine emergence of coherent subcultures outside the cultural mainstream, whose organisation and unity grew in the telling. Certainly, these *cours* became havens for criminality which afflicted the rest of the city. Those looking for whores would flock to Rue Neuve-Saint-Sauveur, organised burglary rings would plan their next raid on the homes of the rich and fence their loot in the dives along Rue Montorgueil, and the gambling dens around the Convent of Filles-Dieu saw many a crafter or tradesman impoverished. The city was the cradle of modern states and economies; so too, it nurtured a new form of criminality in its rookeries and 'thieves' kitchens'.

Crime and the city

The cities were at the heart of the European Renaissance. They recovered disproportionately quickly from the ravages of the Black

Death, culturally, politically and economically, especially in Italy, Flanders and the Low Countries.[3] They were not just political centres but the hubs of ever more intricate trading and financial networks that spanned the continent and beyond, connecting it to markets and possessions from China to the New World. To them flocked merchants and migrants, opportunists and dreamers, and with them came influences of every kind. In custom, language, even cuisine: the cities became, if not melting pots, at least casseroles. In *Coryate's Crudities* (1611), for example, the English traveller Thomas Coryate observed in famously multicultural Venice, 'many Polonians, Turkes, Jewes, Christians of all the famous regions of Christendome, and each nation distinguished from another by their proper and peculiar habits', while others noted the number of visitors and residents from even farther afield.[4] Some intermarried, some stayed resolutely within their ethnic neighbourhoods, and most conducted themselves somewhere in between, interacting, allowing the edges of their othernesses to be rubbed off in the hustle of day-to-day life.

There had, of course, been travel and trade before, and even great cities with strong multi-ethnic and multicultural nature: Jerusalem with its Christian, Jewish and Islamic influences, Russo-Mongol Moscow, Istanbul at the crossroads of Europe and the Middle East, Timbuktu astride the Saharan trade routes moving gold, salt, ivory and slaves. But this became increasingly normal, and in the teeming streets and markets of these cities, people found themselves facing new challenges without the comforting habits of long-established tradition, and outside the social controls of the village. At the same time, urban life, for all its hubbub and confusion, was more closely monitored and regulated by the state than the countryside. When a serious crime was uncovered in Florence, for example, three cannon shots would signal that the city gates should be closed to anyone without a special permit to leave, river traffic along the Arno halted, and barges inspected before they could pass on. At the same time, officials in neighbouring villages would ring the church bells to warn local farmers to assemble to help search for fugitives and tip the authorities off if they came across any suspicious strangers trying to get away from the city.[5]

Boys in the 'hood

Edward Muir noted that during the European Renaissance, 'the idea of community was crystallised in three ways: community as a social interaction in an institutional guise, community as a certain kind of space, and community as a process of social exclusion.'[6] Applying this to crime, gangs and underworld subcultures were not just defined by their membership and their social relationships with each other and outsiders. They were – and are – also defined by *space*, by the environment in which they operate. Whether the overcrowded, cheek-by-jowl tenement slums of Manhattan's Little Italy of the late nineteenth and early twentieth centuries, in which the Cosa Nostra could thrive, or the inaccessible marshes around Liangshan Mountain from which twelfth-century bandits could strike into China's heartland, to understand criminals one also needs to understand where they were raised, the streets and hillsides they call home.

Ancient Rome, for example, was a sprawling, bustling, entrepreneurial capital, where business, politics and crime intertwined themselves effortlessly amid the hubbub of the forum, in the shadows of unlit side streets and lurking in the markets and wineshops. At its peak, its population was over a million sinners, saints, senators and suckers. At night, the main thoroughfares were clogged with commercial goods traffic, the carts and oxen barred from the busy streets by day, but the alleys became places of lurking danger. Juvenal warned that to leave one's home at night without having made a will was downright careless[7] and there were established gangs of robbers, killers, burglars, fraudsters and housebreakers (sometimes literally:

poorer buildings in the early times were made of sun-dried brick, all too easily dug through or prised apart). Their crimes, their routines, their opportunities (and, often, their ends) were largely defined by this social and architectural space. However, there was little evidence of hard-and-fast divisions of the city into rich and poor neighbourhoods, controlled and uncontrolled. The institution of patronage, whereby the rich and powerful extended personal guarantees to clients who owed them honour and obedience, helped knit society together. Neighbourhoods, even the poorest, had patrons, whose status and power depended on their being able to control and police them. As a result, the habitual solo criminal and the gang alike had to keep a low profile. They had their drinking dens and other places to meet and connect, but if they became too brazen, too obvious, too much of a challenge to the status quo, then if not the Imperial authorities, some local strongman and a posse of heavies would mete out rough justice of a more peremptory kind. Lest this sound a distant historical artefact, until their formal illegalisation in 1992, the Japanese Yakuza operated a very similar form of local stewardship: businesses within their turfs paying protection could also count on the organised criminals to keep the disorganised ones in check. Petty thieves and shoplifters risked being dealt with ferociously, as the Yakuza defended their 'honour' – and asserted their territorial concern and the reason to keep paying protection money – which helped explain the paradox of a relatively safe and peaceful country with a large and powerful mafia.

Conversely, if Roman crime was constrained by its environment, Brazilian urban gangsterism was liberated by it. In the late nineteenth century, for example, elegant and cosmopolitan Rio de Janeiro was known as *Cidade Maravilhosa*, the marvellous city. However, a growing influx of migrants from southern Europe, farmers looking for work and recently freed but impoverished slaves led to the accelerating rise of shanty towns known as favelas. Everyone deplored the insanitary conditions, the overcrowding, the criminality, but no one seemed to have the will or money to address the problem, so by the 1970s, they were sprawling out beyond city limits. Largely abandoned by the authorities, shunned by the well-to-do, these favelas quickly became no-go zones, within which gangs metastasised. Electricity was stolen by ramshackle illegal taps off existing power lines, businesses paid tribute to the criminals, as well as – or instead of – taxes to the state, and even before the gangs rose to their current heights of power, the police rarely bothered chasing criminals through the favelas' winding and narrow streets, let alone seeking to protect their denizens. These are modern rookeries with the admixture of cocaine money and automatic weapons and, in their own brutish and predatory ways, the gangs become states, at least in the sense of imposing their own kind of law and demanding obedience and tribute from those within their grasp. Place matters.

Thinking about urban crime

Much excellent scholarship has gone into locating crime within its social environment. Historians, anthropologists, criminologists and many others have understood and explored the way organised crime is about people, about communities of some kind, however violent, exploitative and parasitic they may be. However, studies concentrating on the human side of the problem miss part of the context which condition those organic interactions. 'Environmental criminology' certainly exists. The 'Chicago school' emerged from Chicago University's sociology department, which carried out ground-breaking studies mapping crime and social ecologies in and after the 1920s.[8] They found crime concentrated in the so-called 'zone in transition' – the hazy, growing and impoverished border region between the central business district with its shops and offices, and the concentric rings of stable working- and middle-class housing districts on the way out, towards suburbia. This zone was essentially confused and confusing, impoverished and yet dynamic. Cheap rents, absentee landlords and inadequately enforced regulations meant that here came the new immigrant communities, the dispossessed and the desperate. Those who made it, moved out, those who did not, or who preferred to live in an area where people moved quickly and asked few questions, stayed. Here the 'Chicago school' saw a process the sociologist Edwin Sutherland called 'differential association'. Taking the notion of the dangers in people 'hanging out with the wrong crowd' to its logical next step, it presupposes that different neighbourhoods and groups have their own norms and values. Those living in criminalised environments will learn criminal values and skills from existing criminals. Theft, fraud and gang membership become not a deviation from the cultural mainstream but – within their own terms – quite normal.[9]

The towns and cities of the European Renaissance did not harbour a substantial 'criminal class', but what they did offer was an environment in which a criminal culture could begin to form and flourish.[10] The cities were places in which the ambitious, the alienated and the acquisitive could meet and, separately or together, seek the kind of fortunes to which no peasant could ever aspire. Very few would ever make these fortunes, but that was hardly the point: crime is driven by dreams as much as by desperation. The cities had concentrations of riches which not only moved from hand to hand but were often in easily portable – stealable and sellable – form: goods and coin, not the rather less amenable land and herds which represented rural wealth. The cities were also cosmopolitan, offering greater options for social mobility for those with the cash and the connections, two resources into which native cunning, ruthlessness, wit and violence could be converted. The cities also offered a degree of anonymity for both criminal and victim, especially given the degree to which criminals either moved from town to town or else preyed on merchants, pilgrims and other travellers. Lauro Martines notes that 'life in the Italian walled-in city of about 1300 went on in a tight world of personal relations and public settings'.[11] In such an intimate setting, people tended to know their neighbours and the familiar faces they encountered in their daily lives. Strangers were noted, the subject of scrutiny and perhaps suspicion.

As the towns and cities grew, though, the influx of transient and heterogenous populations of peasants-turned-labourers, traders and travellers diluted old social bonds. The sometimes cosy, sometimes suffocating older models of community control became increasingly untenable. Thus, whole urban spaces were becoming 'zones in transition' as the Chicago school defined them, areas in which old social controls did not apply or else were weakened, in which values were negotiable, and within which people could lose themselves in the crowd.

The rookery

Looking at Renaissance Florence, John Brackett identifies five components to the city's small but growing underworld of professional criminals: assassins; prostitutes; illegal gamblers; corrupt police officers; and, largest of all, thieves and those who fenced their loot.[12] By themselves, none of these represented anything more than a marginal phenomenon. Even together, they were hardly that significant. Yet it is in the interactions between them that the real signs of organised crime can be discerned. The brothels, for example, also fenced loot for the thieves and provided premises for illegal gambling (prostitution and gambling being the two main criminal industries of the time). This was a risky business, as prostitutes were registered and thus confined to known locations such as Via Maffia (unconnected with the Mafia, alas, but entertainingly wedged between a monastery and the church of Santo Spirito). Having some amenable protectors among the police not only helped ensure no unwelcome raids, it also offered options if an unlucky punter refused to pay or cried 'cheat'. Of course, the final option was always the assassin's knife. Needless to say, this was not in any way an 'organisation' – even Señor Monipodio's Sevillian gang, mentioned earlier, is some time in the future – but it does show how an underworld economy of criminal services evolves and begins to form interconnections.

Many cities would begin to acquire their own 'miracle alleys', rookeries given over to vice, poverty and violence, largely beyond the reach of legitimate authority. Hong Kong's Kowloon Walled City was a virtual municipality of the Triad organised crime societies until the middle of the twentieth century. Manhattan's notorious Five Points slum was not only a haven for the most violent street gangs, including the infamous Roach Guards and Dead Rabbits, it even became something of an attraction precisely for its dangerous depravity. By the 1830s, tourists from Charles Dickens (something of a connoisseur of the slum) to Abraham Lincoln took a tour – during daylight. These were often virtual 'no-go areas' for the authorities. The police would only venture into such rookeries as Moscow's Khitrovka or St Petersburg's Haymarket when they had to, and in numbers. Likewise, it was said that for the Chief Justice to serve a warrant in London's notorious Alsatia rookery, south of Fleet Street, he needed a company of musketeers as an escort.[13] In medieval times, this had been the Liberty of Whitefriars, a neighbourhood outside the direct control of the crown's laws but instead under the jurisdiction of the church. This made it a sanctuary, and wanted felons could shelter here for 40 days (unless their crimes were especially heinous). As a result, its winding alleys and grimy tenements became home to criminals, debtors, prostitutes and runaways, even after the right of sanctuary was finally removed by the Escape of Debtors, etc. Act of 1696. Defying any attempts at slum clearance and gentrification, its denizens relied less on traditional rights to keep the upperworld at bay and more their own efforts. Any intrusion by ambitious law enforcers would be met by a cry of 'Rescue!' at which point dozens or hundreds of locals would rally against them, with whatever weapons they had to hand. In extremis, they could escape to other slums such as nearby Mint neighbourhood in Southwark (which retained a special status until the Mint in Southwark Act 1722) and just return home when the coast was clear.

It was dubbed Alsatia – after the no-man's land of Alsace on the French–German border, recently ravaged by the Thirty Years' War – by Thomas Shadwell. A year before he was appointed Poet Laureate, in his restoration comedy *The Squire of Alsatia* (1688), he wrote:

Was ever such impudence suffer'd in a Government? Ireland's Conquer'd: Wales Subdu'd: Scotland United: But there are some few spots of ground in London, just in the face of the Government, unconquer'd yet, that hold in Rebellion still. Methinks 'tis strange, that places so near the Kings Palace should be no parts of his Dominions: 'Tis a shame to the Societies of the law to Countenance such Practices: Should any place be shut against the Kings Writ . . . ?[14]

The infamous Mitre Tavern in Fleet Street, for example, was known for a back door leading into the even more notorious Ram Alley, which led in turn into the nearby Temple Gardens, which had its own right of sanctuary. Fugitives would dash through it when challenged by the law. The Temple neighbourhood, though, had been occupied by lawyers since the fourteenth century and, while jealous of their traditional privileges, they became increasingly aggrieved at being surrounded by ne'er-do-wells and riffraff. As far as they were concerned, the 'beggars, vagabonds, and sundry idle and lewd persons' passing through their grounds were turning it into a 'common and most noisome lestal' or dung heap.[15] So, in 1691, they brought in builders to brick up the Whitefriars Gate through which they would pass. In response, the 'Alsatians' mobbed the labourers and demolished their newly built wall. The sheriffs of the city arrived with their men, and the result was a riot in which one man was fatally wounded by a blunderbuss. Later, the alleged leader of the mob, the self-styled 'Captain' Francis Winter, was arrested and hanged, in a case that arguably pushed the authorities into clearing up the 'Liberties' of London.

Ironically, though, the presence of rookeries represented not a retreat by the state but an advance – for there to be rookeries, it means that there must be other, wider parts of the cities which *are* under some degree of lawful control. Of course, the legitimate authorities were not so keen to see their cups as being half full; when they chose to recognise the existence of these districts, they saw them as subversive not just to the law and public order but also wider morality. Just as chroniclers and magistrates alike had chosen to see the Coquillards and beggars as some mirror-image of the lawful state, with their own laws, taxes and hierarchies, so too the authorities often presumed that the rookeries needed to have some kind of underworld power structure to function.

In 1667, French King Louis XIV, the mighty Sun King and not a monarch to tolerate virtual no-go zones in his own capital, had instructed Gabriel Nicolas de la Reynie, the first lieutenant-general of police and father of French law enforcement, to end the 'miracle' of Paris's Grand Cours. It took major deployments of troops and police and some hard fighting, but the rookery was cleared, and many of its inhabitants were killed or sent to crew the galleys Louis XIV was building for his Mediterranean fleet. Needless to say, though, clearing one rookery hardly ended prostitution, crime and lawlessness in Paris. While a powerful symbol of the state's growing desire and ability to enforce its writ across the country, this largely dispersed the problem and displaced it to new rookeries.

This was in many ways a recurring pattern in the early modern era. States became more concerned about urban districts outside their effective control, as sources of crime, disorder and perhaps sedition, infecting the rest of the city and thus the wider body politic. Indeed, it is striking how often the image of 'infection' is used in contemporary accounts, as an understandable concern about the diseases incubated in squalor became a metaphor for wider moral and political corruption. While the authorities relatively quickly acquired the coercive resources to attack such rookeries, they were not always guaranteed an easy success. When New York's Dead Rabbits and Bowery Boys gangs clashed in 1857, a local tussle in Lower Manhattan soon escalated into a city-wide criminal struggle involving up to a thousand gang members and several hundred more opportunist looters. With the police outmatched, eventually two regiments of the New York State Militia had to be marched into the city. Even so, slum neighbourhoods such as Five Points would resist clearance and gentrification for decades to come.

The criminal service sector

More to the point, clearance only addressed symptoms. The rookeries emerged because there were impoverished and hopeless communities with nowhere else to go in a time of urbanisation and in due course industrialisation, and because there were widespread demands for illicit goods and services. The bayonet and the cudgel, improving sermons and the workhouse, can only go so far in addressing such problems which, after all, still bedevil modern societies. Reynie's men were able to break one *cours* but others emerged to take its place. The expulsion of the Moriscos from Seville in 1609 helped cleanse their San Marcos district of its reputation as a fences' and smugglers' haven, but did nothing to reduce fencing and smuggling in the city; indeed, by 1651, San Marcos was once again infamous for contraband.[16]

There is always the need for places where the law's hand rests light. There, the criminals could find the fences whose services were essential to convert stolen goods to spendable cash, and who also sometimes acted as underworld bankers, holding funds and even sometimes lending money. The rookeries offered congenial and safe locations to burn their ill-gotten gains on high living and the necessary tools and assistance for future criminal activities. Perhaps most importantly, they also provided security and community, a distinct social world in which the legal state had little purchase. Sometimes, indeed, the creation of no-go districts even represented an inchoate form of active political resistance, crime as a means of empowering or liberating the political and economic have-nots. The martial art known as *capoeira*, whose dancelike moves, often performed to music, fuse combat, ritual and performance, emerged within the slave culture of Brazil. In the slums of nineteenth-century Rio de Janeiro, though, *capoeira* – often practised also with knives and clubs – became a powerful tool in the hands of gangs drawn from the lower classes, free and slave alike. Known as *maltas* or *badernas*, they staked out their own territories under *capoeirista* leaders given such picturesque names as Quebra-Coco ('Skull Buster') or Boca-Negra ('Black Mouth'), which they defended against both police and rival gangs.[17] Time and again, across the world, as modernity saw the city expand and the differentials between rich and poor widen – and be seen to widen – criminals looked to create microstates within it – or at least havens within which the state's writ did not apply.

This was especially important because by the nineteenth century, even beyond Europe and North America, the criminal culture was often increasingly at odds with the cultural mainstream. Once, 'the law' may have seemed an often alien and exploitative concept existing to further the interests of a small, privileged minority: 'it was their rulers – landowners, entrepreneurs, magistrates and judges – who were deviant' in the eyes of the majority.[18] However, this would change, as states rooted their existence and legitimacy in the psyches of their peoples, and as courts and police forces became ever more inescapable. Once demonised as agents of control, in due course they were more likely – though by no means by everyone, everywhere – to be seen as sources of security, as the cultural gap between the common 'us' and the dominant 'them' narrowed. Less able to rely upon the tolerance or even support of ordinary society, professional criminals instead had to retreat into and rely more heavily on their own subcultures.

Modern rookeries

Today, you can still find rookeries all across the world, from the slums of Bogotá's Ciudad Bolívar, a haven for the FARC narco-terrorists, to Cape Town's Cape Flats neighbourhood where, in 2019, the army had to be deployed. After 11 months, the troops withdrew, with Cape Flats unreformed and unpacified. A self-proclaimed reformed gangster wryly commented: 'There comes the army. There goes the army.'[19] The problem was a lack of both carrot and stick. The state is often unwilling or unable to maintain sufficient force in these areas to establish its authority. Yet nor will it spend the money on social and economic uplift sufficient to make these communities believe that it is on their side – and there to stay. Instead, the authorities rely on raids and interventions that may take out a particular kingpin or roll up an individual gang, but then withdraw, leaving a vacuum instantly to be filled by an almost identical predator.

This is, after all, a serious challenge. In the 2000s, for example, the situation in the favela slums of Rio de Janeiro reached such a pitch that the Brazilian government adopted a strategy that was akin to the conquest of hostile territory. Well-armed criminal gangs, largely involved in the drug trade, had essentially taken control of them, even levying their own taxes on the local population. With Rio having been chosen to host both the 2014 FIFA World Cup and the 2016 Olympics, addressing this violent anarchy became a priority. The new strategy was pioneered in 2008, when the elite paramilitary BOPE Special Police Operations Battalion was deployed into the notorious Santa Marta favela. From their distinctive unit patch of a skull, knife and crossed pistols, to their use of slab-sided armoured personnel carriers, they gave the appearance more of an invading force than a friendly local bobby. When 1,300 police swept into Rio's Jacarezinho favela in January 2022, a bastion of the notorious Comando Vermelho or Red Commando drugs gang, state governor Claudio Castro made no bones that it was intended 'to reconquer the territory'.[20] These heavily armed police have been accused by Amnesty International of a range of human rights abuses up to and including extra-judicial murder. Indeed, in training they would sing:

The interrogation is very easy to do
Get the slum dweller and beat him till it hurts
Interrogations are very easy to finish
Get the criminal and beat him until he dies.

> A criminal from a slum
> You don't sweep up with a broom
> You sweep them up with grenades
> With a rifle and with a machine gun.[21]

In they duly went, with rifle and machine gun, hunting down known local criminal kingpins, searching for weapons and drugs stashes, and generally trying to make one fundamental point: we are the biggest gang in town. In due course, the BOPE were withdrawn, and in their place came a new unit with the Orwellian name of the Pacification Police Unit. The intention was that this unit would be permanently based in the favela to try and fill the authority vacuum left after BOPE had chased out the gangs. It certainly had considerable success, with 'treated' areas experiencing diminishing violent crime rates, rising property prices and new investment. These new police came straight from the academy, in the hope that they would also not yet have acquired the habits of corruption and abuse of their power which so undermined the authority of many forces.

To a large degree this simply pushed the gangsters into other neighbourhoods, though. Sometimes they had trouble establishing themselves, and at other times they had to fight ensconced groups for the turf – leading to even more violence – but overall, some progress had been made, albeit at a huge cost in both economic and political terms. No wonder, as a Colombian police officer told me, 'We don't have the resources, the support from our politicians, even from the public, to do anything like that. And I don't know when we will,' rue-fully adding, 'unless Bogotá gets to host the World Cup.'

Rookeries still exist cheek-by-jowl with prosperity. Back in 2006, I was invited along on a New Jersey State Police raid into a particu-larly rough part of Newark, itself a particularly rough city with a murder rate up to seven times the USA's national average.[22] The task force assembled well outside city limits and rolled into Newark in the early hours: the warrant went live at 6am, and the intention was to kick down the appropriate door at 6:01am. Newark is in many ways a mirror image of its neighbour and near-namesake New York, though. Here live many of the men and women who do the low-paid night work in Manhattan: the cleaners and bouncers, dishwash-ers and streetwalkers. Thus, at that time of the morning there is a reverse commute, and Newark is busy with people making their way home to bed. What was striking was how many of the street-corner newspaper sellers, as soon as they saw our convoy, started pulling out their phones. They were, of course, spotters working for vari-ous local gangs, and one such tipoff could earn them more than a month of their legal employment. When the troopers went in, what also struck me was just how many were forming a heavily armed perimeter – just the month before, a similar operation in Trenton, New Jersey's state capital, had been subjected to a drive-by machine-gunning, and they were taking no chances. The streets were blocked off by police cruisers and SUVs, their lights dappling the plastic sidings of the houses in blue and red. Dogs snuffled at the stoops, and men with shotguns keenly scanned the roofline. At that moment, it was the troopers who were unquestionably the biggest gang in town. But they, and all the people furtively peeking out through their blinds, knew that in an hour or a day, they would be off somewhere else, and the streets would again be the property of the gangs. This was bandit country, literally within sight of the gleaming towers and spires of Manhattan.

Post-modern rookeries

However, in many ways, the concept of the no-go zone has migrated to the virtual: the darkweb, the secretive recesses of private banking, secure messaging. One way or another, criminals will find their rookeries. The darkweb, for example, is the portion of the internet that cannot be accessed by regular programs and search engines but rather via an anonymising browser such as Tor. While technically legal (as are more than half the sites on it), because of that anonymity, the darkweb is also a haven for those seeking and offering criminal services, from trading stolen goods and information to offering contract killers for hire. It is not that the authorities cannot access the darkweb, and there have been successes in taking down sites and identifying users, but it is that much harder and more resource-intensive.[23] As a rueful FBI agent once admitted, 'The problem is time – when you have too many targets and not enough technically skilled personnel, you know you're only going to be able to go after the baddest of the bad. Or,' she added, 'the most stupid.'

Likewise, criminals have enthusiastically adopted the range of encrypted secure messaging options, from ProtonMail email to Signal chat. Indeed, some have even tried to create their own. Sometimes this comes back to bite them. In 2019, the FBI and the Australian Federal Police turned a source who had been working on a secure, encrypted messaging system for criminals and began developing a sting operation. The result was a company called ANOM that claimed to be able to provide totally secure phones that could be wiped remotely and even programmed with 'duress passwords' which would signal if a user was being coerced. Over time, some 300 organised crime gangs in over 100 countries ended up acquiring more than 12,000 of these devices. After 18 months of careful monitoring of 27 million messages, a multinational operation involving 20 different police agencies around the world was sprung. Operation Greenlight/Ironside/Trojan Shield led to more than 800 arrests and the seizure of 32 tonnes of narcotics, 250 guns and more than $48 million in various worldwide currencies.[24]

While such operations are noteworthy and demonstrate just how effective international law enforcement can be at its best, the struggle to compromise criminal communications is a constant back and forth. New apps, new tactics, are constantly emerging. For a while, the Sky ECC messaging app become the drug barons' method of choice, until that was cracked in 2021. By the time this book is out, there will no doubt be another – and the police will be desperately trying to decrypt that, too. Indeed, the challenge of mustering resources commensurate to the task is even more difficult when it comes to tracking money and coping with the jealous security of private banking, offshore trusts, freeports and other havens for the high net worth and highly criminal alike. Nothing is impossible with enough resources, but, as will be discussed later, few police agencies have enough powers, forensic accountants and financially literate prosecutors to tackle more than a fraction of the cases they would like to handle.

So, bandits create states, and states create cities, but cities create rookeries, state-free zones. Then, as the physical rookeries become more limited and controlled, new virtual ones emerge, drawing on the very resources and capacities that make cities so important, from technological innovation to imaginative financial engineering. As our worlds expand, collide and interpenetrate, the race to find the frontiers of legality – or to head off the creation of new bandit kingdoms – is, it seems, never-ending, especially as the growing ease of trade and travel and the rise of modern capitalism and bureaucracy all open up new vistas for the criminals.

PART TWO
THE AGE OF CAPITALISM

CHAPTER 6

HURRAH FOR THE PIRATE KINGS

The US Navy really owes its origins to North African pirates. The Barbary Coast had long been home to raiders who preyed on shipping across the Mediterranean, but by the sixteenth century they were hunting as far north as Iceland, and south along West Africa's Atlantic seaboard. The pirates seized ships, raided coastal settlements for slaves to be sold in the Ottoman, Middle Eastern and North African markets, and practised crude protection racketeering, extorting payments for promises to hold off their attacks, promises they almost invariably broke. The Danish church, for example, raised funds to supplement the state's *slavekasse*, its slave fund, used to ransom captured seamen; of course, the unintended consequence was that Danish prisoners were highly prized, as they had a guaranteed cash value. By the later seventeenth century, the pirates were on the decline, their crude galleys outsailed and outgunned by European warships. Nonetheless, those who did not have the protection of these navies were still at risk. When America declared independence from Britain in 1776, the Royal Navy stopped protecting US ships, and they became fair game. This led to the formation of the US Navy in 1794, but even so, it was not yet fit to deploy to the distant Mediterranean. By 1800, fully one-fifth of the US federal government's entire budget was going into paying off the Barbary pirates. This was neither sustainable nor acceptable, and so Thomas Jefferson instead sent a fleet to sink their ships and bombard their ports. The two Barbary Wars of 1801–5 and 1815 essentially ended the practice.

The high seas have always been both crucial trade arteries and uncontrolled territories. Piracy and war were almost indistinguishable in antiquity, and later the privateer – essentially, the state-sanctioned pirate – was a staple of European maritime conflicts. Indeed, London actually encouraged the Berbers to prey on US shipping during the Anglo–American War of 1812. Bottlenecks in global shipping routes such as the Malacca Straits between the Indian and Pacific Oceans, as well as crucial arteries of empire and trade, such as the trajectories of the 'gold ships' returning to Spain from its South American possessions, all were prey. Even today, it is impossible to eradicate it, with Somali fishermen-turned-pirates taking oil tankers heading for the Suez Canal and heavily armed criminal gangs operating in the Gulf of Guinea. However, for all their freewheeling reputation, the operations of pirates were and are shaped by the market and constrained by logistics. Pirates cannot continue to pirate without not only a steady and lucrative stream of targets, but also the opportunities to repair their boats, restock their supplies and, most important of all, monetise their plunder. The evolution of the pirate is thus also a story of the evolution of maritime trade and international capitalism.

Early pirates

Early pirates were simply maritime bandits with a side-hustle as mercenary raiders. According to the ancient Greek historian Herodotus, the captain Dionysius of Phocaea, who led the Ionians in their failed resistance to the Phoenicians in the fifth century BCE, then became an 'honourable' pirate who only attacked the ships of non-Greeks, although he appears to have had no formal connection with any Greek city-state. A cynic would wonder if these scruples had anything to do with the fact that this meant he could rely on a warm welcome in Greek ports. On the other hand, Philip V of Macedon secretly engaged the pirate chieftain Dikaiarkhos and gave him 20 ships to raid the Cyclades islands in 205–204 BCE in what today might be classed as a 'deniable' operation against an enemy power.[1] For a while, the fleets of Athens provided some check on their activities, but after their defeat in the Peloponnesian War (431–404 BCE), Mediterranean piracy entered a golden era. The lines between piracy and war remained unclear. With so many pirates, no wonder that there were also numerous cases when they were simply hired as mercenaries: the massive army which the Macedonian prince Demetrios raised to conquer Rhodes in 302 BCE reportedly included fully 8,000 of them.[2] As it was, after a two-year siege, Demetrios had to come to terms with Rhodes, gained the derisive nickname Poliorketes, 'the Besieger', and watched the scrap metal from his abandoned siege engines melted down to build the statue later known as the Colossus of Rhodes. Meanwhile, Greek islands such as Samos and Kythira became pirate havens, while other coastlines were regularly ravaged – in many cases, peoples moved inland precisely because of pirate attacks.

Similarly, essentially from the ninth to the eleventh centuries, the Vikings, raiders from Scandinavia, ranged as far afield as the lands of the Rus' (where they eventually established their own principalities around cities such as Kyiv and Novgorod), Byzantium, the Mediterranean and even North America. These were warbands formed by landowning chieftains from their own retainers and enthusiastic volunteers, launching hit-and-run raids for plunder. Although the practice was sometimes seen as somewhat grubby – the word *víkingr* did mean 'pirate' – it was a common way for young men to win a name for themselves (and some loot) and for chieftains to distract potentially troublesome rivals.

A common theme of these early pirates was that they would raid foreigners, and were either connected to or dependent on existing social elites. The Vitalienbrüder, the fourteenth-century German raiders who ravaged the shipping of the Hanseatic League in the North and Baltic Seas, were initially founded largely by noblemen from the Duchy of Mecklenburg, for example, and Denmark appears to have been happy to offer them havens in order to force the League to raise expensive and divisive levies to patrol their waters.[3] The much-feared Moro pirates of the southern Philippines from the sixteenth century were essentially maritime raiders gathered by charismatic local chieftains. In alliance, they could assemble whole fleets, such as the 36 large ships and 2,000 men from multiple tribes who besieged Lubungan in 1754. Thanks to the presence of Chinese engineers, the pirates even built medieval-style siege towers before a Spanish contingent was able to relieve the town.[4] In many ways, though, the continued strength of piracy in the Sulu Sea bounded by the Philippines and Borneo, occurred precisely because Spanish imperial power was never able adequately to conquer or co-opt local power structures, fixing a pre-modern pattern of raid and conquest. Elsewhere, as states began to become more jealous of their monopoly of violence, though, and as the room for manoeuvre for 'violent entrepreneurs' within the aristocracy shrank, piracy would also have to evolve.

And it is, it is, a glorious thing/To be a Pirate King!

Even when Gilbert and Sullivan immortalised those lines in *The Pirates of Penzance* (1879), the age of the pirate seemed long since over. In Heywood and Rowley's drama *Fortune by Land and Sea* (1607–9), the pirate Purser crows that they 'raign'd as Lord / Nay King at Sea, the Ocean was our realm'.[5] Yet by the end of the play, Purser has mounted the scaffold, and the rest of the pirates are in prison. This was a time of state-building, of the emergence of genuine standing armies (and navies), state bureaucracies, and meaningful, controlled national borders. European states still had to cope with the old scourges of banditry and lawless local elites, but the scope for these old-style criminals shrank. Even piracy was increasingly often defined by the state. This could be a negative process, the corsairs and buccaneers avoiding areas and routes patrolled by increasingly effective naval forces. Alternatively, it could be through being co-opted. Ancient Greek pirates had often been little more than rapacious agents of a city-state, but this was largely out of choice. Many later pirates had to become privateers out of necessity, whether during the struggle for the domination of the Baltic in the fourteenth century[6] or the mercantile-military squabbles between Venice, Naples and Genoa in the thirteenth to fifteenth,[7] even though privateering was only really formalised in the seventeenth century.[8] They were in effect state-sanctioned pirates, maritime mercenaries granted the legal right to raid the ships of an enemy power. Privateering used the methods of piracy and enriched both the crown and individuals – often including wealthy officials, who invested in these ventures – but was more an example of outsourced warfare than crime.

Of course, the boundaries between the two were often blurred, sometimes deliberately so. Queen Elizabeth I was prone retrospectively to sanction raids by her favoured captains, such as Sir Francis Drake and Sir Walter Raleigh, on Spanish ships and ports (and gladly took a cut of the profits in return).[9] Indeed, the English were especially infamous for this practice; a Venetian ambassador to Spain warned that nowhere in the Mediterranean was there safety from 'this accursed race' which had 'grown so bold that it goes everywhere without hesitation, using barbarous cruelty and sinking ships'.[10] In an age when naval officers also received bounties on the value of enemy vessels captured, though, it was perhaps inevitable that patriotism and greed would find common cause.

Greed was generally the greater of the two and the pirate king was really a pirate merchant. In earlier times, entrepreneurs might hope to gain from the plunder of pirate missions. In the mid-sixteenth century, for instance, Meadhole on the Isle of Wight became infamous for its markets which sprang up when raiders had plunder to sell, attracting traders from as far as London and Bristol. At other times pirates would simply set up shop in friendly harbours, as their 'ships became the equivalent of a floating bazaar, operating as an informal market for commodities which were subsequently redistributed ashore'.[11] While an individual might deal with the pirates, their main commercial contracts were men of business, victuallers who supplied them what they needed, and merchants who would buy this plunder wholesale. The latter seem in the main to have done very well out of the relationship, as the pirates were in a relatively weak position, needing to convert loot into food, coin and repairs, and typically impatient, at that. By the account of the notorious Welsh pirate-turned-privateer John Callice, for example, he often received no more than half the market value of his plunder, with Spanish wool fetching £3 a sack when it was worth £6 or more, and a captured cable and anchor worth £20 selling for just £7.[12] Murderous rogues though the pirates were, they rarely proved a match for hard-nosed merchants.

War by other means

The model of pirate as floating wholesaler worked well enough so long as raider and trader could interact relatively freely. By the end of the sixteenth century, a combination of pressure from the authorities and the new opportunities for privateering would change the relationship between the two. Soon enough, entrepreneurs were instead looking to bankroll raids rather than just seeing them as a handy source of cheap goods. In 1602, for example, the captain Richard Gifford set sail from London in his private warship the *Charles*. His consortium of backers included Sir Robert Cecil, Earl of Salisbury and the Lord Privy Seal. He bore letters of marque authorising him to raid Spanish shipping, but he ignored his ostensible mission and instead headed for the easier pickings of the Mediterranean. There he bought an additional ship, naming it the *Fortune*, and attacked two French ships with Dutch cargoes. One of these they took and sailed to Algiers, where it was sold and most of the profit used to buy olive oil. They then sailed to the Italian port of Livorno, where they sold their cargo to an English merchant.[13] These were hardly the pirates of popular myth; just as in earlier times adventurers might well juggle the roles of bandits, feudal lords, soldiers and wheeler-dealers, so Gifford and his like were essentially peripatetic armed entrepreneurs, raiding and trading as the opportunities arose.

Privateering would be a feature of the seas until the nineteenth century, although in practice its last major upsurge was during the American Revolutionary War (1775–83). There were times of greater tolerance, typically during wars between naval powers such as the First Anglo–Dutch War (1652–4) in which the British were able to make dramatic inroads into Dutch revenues from trade and their colonies, and the War of the Grand Alliance (1688–97) in which the British were instead on the receiving end of French privateering. On the other hand, even at an early stage there were those who regarded privateering as either morally wrong or practically unwise, fostering a mutually dangerous climate of lawlessness at sea. On hearing that his Lord High Admiral was encouraging raiding (he automatically received a tenth share in the profits of any privateering venture[14]), Elizabeth's successor King James famously exclaimed, 'By God, I'll hang the pirates with my own hands, and my Lord Admiral as well!'[15] However, while James and his son Charles may have been hostile to the notion, during the Cromwellian Commonwealth era and after the restoration of the monarchy, British privateers such as Henry Morgan ravaged Spanish ports and shipping in the New World. He was arrested for the sack of the Spanish colony of Panama in 1671 (after the official end of hostilities between London and Madrid), but ultimately exonerated, knighted and made lieutenant-governor of Jamaica.[16] The fact was that, in Fernand Braudel's words, privateering was already endemic: 'All, from the most wretched to the most powerful, rich and poor alike, cities, lords and states were caught up in a web of operations cast over the whole sea.'[17]

Nonetheless, over time this practice was to fall from favour. Although still a potentially lucrative business investment through the eighteenth century and a feature of the War of the Austrian Succession (1740–8), Seven Years' War (1756–63) and French Revolutionary Wars (1792–1802), the tide was turning, even though it would not be until the international Paris Declaration of 1856 that privateering would be generally proscribed.[18] This did not necessarily make the seas any safer. In some ways, quite the opposite. So long as they could earn letters of marque, pirates might feel under some slight moral and political constraints. Without this possibility, they preyed indiscriminately. After all, havens such as the ports of Madagascar and the North African coast still provided them with places to convert their prizes and loot into money, repairs, resupply and the more ephemeral alcoholic and libidinous needs of the crews. The European world was expanding, with mariners increasingly daring to cross seas once regarded as impassable (even as late as the seventeenth century, it was believed that ships venturing into northern polar waters would be 'dashed to pieces by the sea and torn apart by the magnetic force', while it had previously been thought that to travel south of the tropic of Cancer was to burn to death[19]). Colonies, evangelical missions and trading stations were spreading across Asia, Africa and the Americas, and economies becoming bound into international and intercontinental markets. Those powerful and maritime states which could wield privateering most effectively as a weapon were also most vulnerable to it, witness England's own problems at the end of the seventeenth century.

No country for old pirates

On a more philosophical level, the new age was one in which the freebooting warrior-adventurer was beginning to be replaced by the disciplined sailor and the merchant, so 'the privateer's heroics call[ed] into question the duller ethics of the merchant' just as 'the pirate's depredations threaten[ed] the very possibility of licit commerce'.[20] This was increasingly unacceptable to the dominant European maritime states, which had come to realise that privateering was indeed a two-edged cutlass. For example, while the English privateer campaign under Elizabeth undoubtedly had a profound impact on the Spanish economy and thus war effort, the 'reckless behaviour of the privateers' not only represented 'a continual source of embarrassment to legitimate [English] traders who relied upon the goodwill of foreign governments', but it also had a knock-on effect on other trade routes on which England relied.[21]

By the later seventeenth century, trade had become even more important to national economies and navies were increasingly sizeable and regularised institutions. Just as the mercenary bands of the Renaissance would be eclipsed by standing national armies, so too would privateering become increasingly rare, the gulf between freelance pirates and national navies becoming ever wider and more obvious. This slow repudiation of privateering represented a retreat from the 'fur-collar crime' model which scarcely recognised any meaningful distinction between legal and illegal theft, extortion and violence. States now appreciated that there was a difference, and while for pragmatic reasons they may sometimes have been willing to overlook this, they mistrusted illegal and independent violent entrepreneurs.

If piracy now had to operate without the sanction of the state, it had to find other ways of establishing a support infrastructure. Pirates needed intelligence on prizes worth seizing, and they needed safe havens at which to lay up, lick their wounds and recruit new crew. Above all, they needed the equivalent of the thief's fence, places where they could realise the value of their plunder. The kind of ad hoc approach that once had worked when the state was weak or cared little about their activities, the impromptu markets announced on the grapevine and low-key visits to home ports, these were no longer viable. Settlements which once had welcomed them for the money they brought to the local economy increasingly feared them. Either they disrupted trade or else they raised the risk of reprisals from the state. In the early eighteenth century, for example, the ports of South Carolina, once welcoming havens, were closed to the pirates. South Carolina's rice exports had begun to flourish, and a rising mercantile elite saw the pirates as a threat, and backed vigorous campaigns to drive them from their shores. At the same time, a rudimentary form of international law was emerging, with victims of piracy seeking redress through the courts of pirates' homelands or by petitioning their authorities.

Pirate havens

So while the bandits were moving from the wilderness into the rookeries, the pirates were pushed out of the upperworld: denied their old support structures, the pirate economy found new refuges in locations blessed by geography and cursed by economics, which found dealing with the pirates an offer they could not refuse. For example, the Spanish-claimed island of Hispaniola in the Antilles was settled by French Huguenot refugees and adventurers in the seventeenth century. They made what living they could by selling dried meats and other essentials to passing pirates in return for coin and ammunition. When the Spanish drove them out, not least because they traded with non-Spanish pirates as well, they settled on the smaller island of Tortuga, conveniently along the Windward Passage, the route Spain's treasure fleets took returning home from the New World. This became the haven of the multi-ethnic Brethren of the Coast buccaneers from the 1630s until the end of the century.

Jamaica's Port Royal – which earned itself the title 'Sodom of the New World' for its sailors' dives, brothels and drinking dens[22] – turned to the pirates of Tortuga for defence, and prospered thanks to plunder.[23] Bermuda and the Bahamas also became notorious havens, but this was not a purely Caribbean phenomenon. The island of Madagascar, its coastline corrugated with countless defensible inlets, sat squarely across the trade routes off eastern Africa and into the Indian Ocean. It provided a base for numerous raiders, including Thomas Tew, the so-called 'Rhode Island Pirate', who blazed the route later known as the 'Pirate Round'. Favoured by raiders from England or America, this began in Atlantic ports from New York to Bermuda, where the crew was assembled, then crossed the Atlantic to run down the western coast of Africa and round the Cape of Good Hope before docking at Madagascar to repair, re-crew and re-provision. From Madagascar the pirates would then raid Muslim shipping in the Red Sea or routes to and from India, making the return crossing of the Atlantic when they had made their fortunes or lost the appetite for more raiding. So secure did Madagascar appear to pirates that some even settled and made a living off the 'industry'. Most notable was Adam Baldridge, a pirate who raided from the Madagascar island of St Mary's. Establishing a base there, he made it into a favoured pirate destination, offering goods and services from naval stores to alcohol, much imported from New York.

These havens were typically islands close to valuable trading routes, under no or light metropolitan control, and with the least opportunities to prosper without the influx of pirate booty. Their relationship with the pirates lasted as long as it was convenient, until brought to an end by the application or threat of force (at the urging of the politically powerful East India Company, the Royal Navy broke the reign of the pirates of Madagascar in the early eighteenth century, for example) or a change in the economic context. Elsewhere, they emerged thanks to a combination of national, economic and religious interests. In the sixteenth and early seventeenth centuries in particular, the Barbary Coast of North Africa offered many berths for pirates in the Mediterranean, especially – but not solely – Muslim raiders preying on Christian ships and coastal settlements. Bejaya (Bougie) in Algeria became the most notorious such centre after the Ottoman Turks drove out its Spanish occupiers in 1555, and Tripoli, Tunis and Salé also played an active role, gaining slaves, loot and power as a result. Despite successive reprisal raids by the British, French, Dutch and even American navies, Barbary piracy continued into the nineteenth century and in part at least was driven (or at least legitimised) by the way 'Moslems and Christians were in a virtually permanent state of war in the Mediterranean'.[24] More generally, the spread of colonial empires destabilised old economies and created a moral and national rationale for piracy as a form of resistance, especially in Asia. The notorious Marathan raider, Kanhoji Angre, could raid British, Dutch and Portuguese shipping out of Mumbai in the late seventeenth and early eighteenth centuries thanks to his base at Vijaydurg Fort on the western coast of India, for example, and he later became Grand Admiral of the Marathan Navy thanks to his buccaneering activities.[25]

Pirate communities

After all, however crude and brutal the pirates themselves may have been, a great deal of organisation went into piracy. Pirate captains needed to hold together disparate crews of various skills and abilities, manage a ship, with all its needs for supplies and repair, and be able to fence what may sometimes have been substantial and unusual loads of booty. It was also rather harder for them to blend in with the population at large: even with the Jolly Roger hauled down from the mast, a pirate ship was a rather unsubtle beast, especially if it had seen battle. Thus, some pirates formed rough-and-ready communities of their own.

The best example would be the largely Anglo-American pirates who operated in the Caribbean and the Indian Ocean in the second and third decades of the eighteenth century. With a literally floating population of up to 2,000 members at any one time, these pirates shared both a common legacy (most had been privateers, merchant seamen or Royal Navy sailors) and a shared social order of their own, constructed 'in defiant contradistinction to the ways of the world they had left behind, in particular to its salient figures of power, the merchant captain and the royal official, and to the system of authority those figures represented and enforced.'[26] Broadly egalitarian, this culture made the ship's crew a social unit in its own right and exalted 'manly behaviour', a willingness to avenge attacks on their own (in 1720, for instance, Bartholomew Roberts – better known as 'Black Bart' – raided St Kitts following the execution of captured pirates) and also a common identity. This allowed ships to cooperate rather than compete, even between vessels whose crews were drawn from different nationalities. It was, however, also a brittle community. Their common cultural identity aside, the pirates had been brought together by a delicate balance of opportunities and risk. When states – and the Royal Navy in particular – focused their efforts upon them, offering pardons to some, suppression to the rest, it fragmented. Their culture survived, albeit as much in popular myth as reality, but their days were numbered.

Modern pirates

Piracy relies on a perverse relationship between anarchy and order. On the one hand, the pirates need havens outside the reach of the law. On the other, fully to enjoy the fruits of their trade, as well as to get the resources needed to continue to do so, they require a connection with the upperworld. Today's pirates find new uncontrolled spaces from which to operate, whether corrupted localities such as Venezuela's ports, insurgent territories including coastline held by MEND (the Movement for the Emancipation of the Niger Delta), or essentially failed states such as Somalia.

Even so, modern piracy is about more than exchanging looted gold, silks and cotton for rum and gunpowder, and relies on an invisible economy of facilitators. What can a dozen Somalis do with the 300,000-tonne tanker containing 2 million barrels of crude oil they have just seized? They can perhaps siphon off the oil to sell on the black market, but even then, that means ultimately finding buyers in the legitimate world. More likely, they will ransom the crew and the cargo. Even then, how do they know how to handle the negotiations, what they can plausibly ask, how they can get the money? Enter middlemen who will talk to the shipping company (or more likely their insurers) and – for a hefty cut – arrange everything. Indeed, it has been estimated that only about 30 per cent of the ransoms actually end up in the hands of the pirates themselves: another 30 per cent goes to paying off local officials, 20 per cent to organisers and middlemen, and 20 per cent on the operational costs of missions.[27]

In other words, pirates still depend on havens, even if those havens are often virtual, a laptop and a mobile phone in a coffee shop, rather than a fortified island port. Furthermore, as modern states became less easy to sidestep or ignore, as business becomes more regulated, then these havens – and the facilitators who allow the pirates to stay in business – must rely not on challenging them with gun and cutlass, but in developing and expanding the uncontrolled spaces within them. In short, on corruption.

CHAPTER 7

CORRUPTION, BUREAUCRACY, FORGERY AND FRAUD

How do you steal a country? The people who made the most money out of piracy, and with greatest safety, were and still are typically the backers, the middlemen, the patrons, the investors. They, in turn, will have others they have to pay off, those at the top of state or criminal hierarchies. The relationship between money and power is an intimate one, after all. When Renaissance political thinker (and doer) Niccolò Machiavelli wrote in his *Discourses on Livy* (1517) that 'gold is not sufficient to find good soldiers, but good soldiers are quite sufficient to find gold', he was making a point about the limitations of mercenaries and the value of adequate military power.[1] However, a central theme of his *Discourses* is the danger of corruption to the republic, and an awareness of the degree to which corruption is arguably the most serious threat to any state. After all, a highwayman may take your jewels, a robber empty your safe deposit box, and a fraudster empty your bank account, but corruption can steal the very state around you.

Once, it was obvious. After the assassination of Emperor Commodus in 192 (and of the unlucky individual the Senate tried to appoint in his place), the elite Praetorian Guards auctioned off the position of the emperor of Rome. One Didius Julianus eventually outbid his rivals, offering 25,000 sesterces for each soldier, which would have meant a total of some 200 million sesterces (perhaps equivalent to half a billion dollars in today's money), a massive sum he could not even begin to pay, and he was killed after just 66 days as emperor. Since then, it may be a little more subtle, but the sums involved and the potential payoffs equally eye-watering.

In 2011, for example, the US government launched a campaign to seize $70.8 million in property from Teodoro Nguema Obiang Mangue, son of the dictatorial President Teodoro Nguema Obiang Mbasogo of Equatorial Guinea. Teodoro Jr had been agriculture and forestry minister, and gladly presided over a campaign of ruthless deforestation, so long as the logging companies paid and paid. On the back of an official annual salary of less than $100,000, he accumulated more than $100 million in assets. What can one do with such a sum? Among other things, buy a $30 million Malibu mansion, a Ferrari, a Gulfstream personal jet – and, most surreally of all – more than 1.8 million dollars' worth of Michael Jackson memorabilia.[2] He may have lost tens of millions and been sanctioned by the UK on the basis of his alleged corruption, but this chip off the old block is as of writing still doing fine: dad made him First Vice President in 2016.

The corrupt society

Of course, corruption, the abuse of public office for personal gain, has a long and ignoble history, ever since there have been public offices and a line drawn between the legitimate and illegitimate use of power. In pre-cash ancient Egypt, when taxes were paid either in labour or in goods, tax collectors would frequently rig the scales they used to weigh out grain dues to cheat the farmers into overpaying, and then skim off the extra. Alternatively, the 'holder of the cord' and the 'stretcher of the cord', the two officials whose job it was to measure the size of fields, on the basis of which tax dues would be assessed (typically

10 per cent of the expected crop) could slightly overstate their size, especially when they were newly cultivated. Admittedly, they did face having their noses cut off – or worse – if they were found to have swindled the 'Treasurer of the Gods', the Pharoah.[3]

Nonetheless, there are always greedy officials, just as there are those looking to buy themselves access or assets, privileges or impunity. In thirteenth-century France, King Louis IX's efforts to wage crusade so consumed his government that, concerned potential taxpayers might buy their way out of fighting or paying, in 1254 he banned his councillors from accepting gifts of any kind.[4] This kind of prohibition would neither last nor, one suspects, be honoured all that assiduously. Although Louis IX was not unique, and there were similar campaigns in England and Spain, to a degree this was a sign of the times. The pressure of mounting the crusades to the Holy Lands demanded money (and thus more honest and efficient administration) and also a moral mandate (so the rulers had to demonstrate their virtue to the ruled). This would be a 'two steps forward one and a half back' process, at best, though.

In his *Inferno*, the fourteenth-century Italian poet Dante places the corrupt in the eighth or next-to-last Circle of Hell, with the 'barrators', those politicians who sold public office, immersed in a lake of boiling pitch. The very viciousness of this punishment reflects the pervasive sense of impotence at the time as to what to do with such criminals. It would usually take relatively complex and advanced societies to recognise the scale of the problem, let alone to police corruption at all effectively. Insofar as they do, of course. In earlier states, after all, closing a blind eye to a degree of corruption was a way of lightening the load on the public purse. With what the Russians called *kormleniye*, 'feeding', salaries could be kept artificially low, in the knowledge that it would be supplemented by a judicious degree of bribe-taking, embezzlement and sweetheart deals.[5] *Kormleniye* was officially banned in 1556, but even as late as the mid-nineteenth century, tsarist Russian officials were all but expected to complement their often-inadequate salaries with bribe-taking. The very first inquiry into corruption was only held in 1856 and it concluded that anything less than 500 rubles – equivalent to two years' average salary for a skilled craftsman in Moscow – should not even be considered a bribe as such, but nothing more than a polite expression of thanks. We should all get such thank-yous.

Corruption is, in its essence, a way of monetising privilege. One counter-argument that is sometimes made holds that it can make a system more efficient – as Samuel Huntington put it, 'In terms of economic growth, the only thing worse than a society with a rigid, overcentralised, dishonest bureaucracy is one with a rigid, overcentralised, honest bureaucracy.'[6] Maybe, but the notion that a certain amount of short-cutting and rules-bending provides 'a welcome lubricant easing the path to modernization' is a tempting fallacy. Corruption and rapid economic growth often go together, but arguably more because the latter creates greater scope for the former, not the other way round. Besides, if corruption offers a 'VIP lane' round irksome regulation – for a fee – then it also encourages bureaucrats to impose extra restrictions precisely to generate more income. In other words, the rule-makers win.

Likewise, it can seem to humanise inhuman systems that lock all sorts of privileges away from the masses. The king, the state, the Party may not want you to travel, to send your child to an elite school, or to let you jump the queue for medical treatment, but if it is important enough for you, you may be able to accumulate the money or favours to do it anyway. Often this is through the informal exchange of services and promises rather than cash – what is known as *wasta* in the Arab world, *blat* in Russia, and *guanxi* in China[7] – but even so, while this kind of corruption may have a superficially and momentarily humanising effect, it again creates a perverse incentive to keep a system dysfunctional and opaque, with scarce resources rationed and controlled. It ultimately funnels money and agency from the desperate have-littles to the powerful have-muches: again, the rule-makers win.

Simplifying vastly, corruption follows a bell-curve trajectory. The simplest of states do relatively little (so there is less scope for the abuse of public office) and tend to accept the exchange of gifts for access and advantage as both legal and moral. A Roman patron would be *expected* to pull strings for his clients. As the state becomes more expansive, then the opportunities to (ab)use it for private gain increase rapidly. The more that is taxed, banned, regulated and otherwise controlled, the better the business opportunities for the corrupt and the corrupter alike. Regulation tends to lag, not least because these simple states often lack the incentive or will to tackle the problem, until they reach a stage when they become developed enough that they can begin to dispense with practices such as *kormleniye*.

In the West, we are still a long way from being anywhere near having banished corruption, and our passion for taxation and regulation ensures that there are still good reasons to bribe or trade favours. We have made strides in changing the moral environment, as well as the legal one, though. Yet there are distinct limitations, especially to our willingness not to deal with the corrupt outside our borders – or at least their lovely, lovely money. Oliver Bullough has pilloried Britain as the *Butler to the World* (2022), unsparingly subtitled *How Britain Helps the World's Worst People Launder Money, Commit Crimes, and Get Away with Anything*, but in fairness this is hardly a British monopoly. (Even if the Brits are depressingly good at combining moral flexibility with a sanctimonious veneer of rectitude.) Fighting corruption is still either something done at home in the name of national and financial security, or weaponised abroad, to win contracts, to undermine hostile regimes, or otherwise further our own interests. I still remember the insouciance with which a Brussels eurocrat whom I tackled on quite why the first sanctions imposed under the new EU Global Human Rights Sanctions Regime, adopted in 2020, were all on people and organisations in Russia, China, North Korea, Libya, Eritrea and South Sudan. Did he not think that a more powerful message would have been given if it had included people from countries with which the Union had a closer relationship? In other words, did this not look cynical? He smiled at my naivety: 'But why would we want to criticise our friends?' Well, precisely.

Hijacking bureaucracy

More generally, as business and the state became more organised, the opportunities to enrich oneself through cunning and artifice rather than brute force became more evident. In early modern Seville, for example, it was quite common practice for criminals to act as false witnesses in court cases, but one then went further and began impersonating a member of the Spanish Inquisition (no one expected that), using his apparent office to arrest people and confiscate their goods, gathering a whole gang of fake officials to enforce his judgements. By the time his impersonation has been uncovered, they had fled with their loot to the Indies, effectively beyond the reach of the law.[8]

Of course, fraud itself was nothing new, and organised fraud, at that. In ancient Greece, it connected the social extremes: wealthy traders, lawyers, landowners and princes at one end, bandits and pirates at the other. Athenian court records contain suggestions of complex frauds carried out by traders and ship owners, whereby investors would be defrauded through such subterfuges as sinking ships that were so rickety they should never have put to sea, and claiming that their (non-existent) cargoes had been lost. Likewise, there seemed to be established criminal groups or networks – called *ergasteria*, 'workshops' – operating within the courts, whereby cases were won or lost thanks to collusion and the activities of gangs of sycophants, who were not above framing their rivals.[9]

Fraud was thus often also an explicitly political act, and forgeries could have massive social and geopolitical impacts. The (probably) eight-century Donation of Constantine purported to be a fourth-century decree whereby Emperor Constantine the Great transferred control of Rome and the western Roman Empire to the papacy. It was mobilised in support of all kinds of papal claims of authority over European secular powers during the Middle Ages. This was an especially expansive example of a long-running tradition of 'discovering' and disseminating convenient historical documents in the course of political negotiations or court cases. To give a smaller-scale example, in 1641, representatives of the Armenian community in what was then the Polish-owned city of Lemberg – now Lviv in Ukraine – submitted to the royal chancery what was claimed to be a charter, issued in 1062 by the Rus' Grand Prince Fyodor, in which he promised Armenian warriors the right to settle anywhere in his domains in return for military service. This was successfully used to win special rights for the Armenians, even though there was no such prince claiming those lands at that time, a deception only caught in the twentieth century, which was surely an impressive result for those enterprising Armenians.[10] Indeed, whole national histories were open to invention. In the name of giving his province a backstory to equal those of the rest of the Netherlands, Frisian scholar Suffridus Petri produced *Apologia pro antiquitate et origine Frisiorum* (1603), a detailed and entirely fictitious history of Friesland, claiming it had been founded in the fourth century by three Indian scholars with the rather improbable names Friso, Saxo and Bruno.[11] Another particular case is the widely distributed *Protocols of the Elders of Zion*, an anti-Semitic tract first published in Russia in 1903. Presented as the minutes of a conclave of Jewish leaders from around the world, its 24 bogus 'protocols' include plans to undermine the non-Jewish world and take over the global economy, and have inspired violence and discrimination in Russia, Germany and worldwide ever since.

Nonetheless, these were essentially forgeries motivated by politics rather than greed. Overall, the increased bureaucratisation of the state would create new opportunities to harness the power of law and paperwork to criminal ends, just as the spread of the movable-type printing press opened new vistas for forgers. Early modern Europe was deluged with all kinds of dodgy documents, from faked classical texts to bogus travel accounts. However, the real opportunities came from the state's increasing reliance upon official stamps and documents. It became useful for criminals to have access to forgeries (incidentally in Europe often carried out by members of the clergy),[12] with professional forgers rising as a criminal specialism, whether the aforementioned 'jarkmen' of Elizabethan London or the 'scratchers' of the inter-war American underworld. This was not just to bypass irksome laws, it was also to hijack their authority outright. In the still-anarchic territories of Spanish-conquered South America, for example, forged *titulos*, land grants, were hard to authenticate but relatively easy to produce. When the Ecuadorian forger Montoya was arrested and put to the question in 1803, he admitted that he bore fully seven fake royal charters, such that he could claim to be the *cacique*, or indigenous prince, of pretty much anywhere he wanted.[13]

This was why states came to treat forgery so seriously. According to some estimates, about a third of all capital crimes added in the eighteenth and early nineteenth centuries to Britain's 'Bloody Code' – so-called for the sheer number of offences for which the death penalty was prescribed – related to forgery in some form or another.[14] Likewise, according to the Jōei Shikimoku, the administrative code of thirteenth-century Japan, if a samurai committed forgery, his lands were forfeit, while anyone without holdings would be exiled or branded – along with the scribe who created the document. However, by the time of the later Tokugawa Shogunate in the seventeenth to nineteenth centuries, the punishments for forgery had been increased to crucifixion or burning to death. Forgery mattered, because the state was increasingly a beast built of paper.

The state unclothed

When the Renaissance brought new forms of banking, it also opened new avenues for financial fraud, especially as bankers and merchants often hesitated to expose forged letters of credit, lest they undermine the credibility of an entire economy increasingly dependent on such instruments. Today, things are different, aren't they? Not so much. One of the great challenges in dealing with cybercrime is precisely that many institutions extorted through 'ransomware' attacks – malicious software whose originators demand payment to neutralise – or plundered in data theft never report it. Their fear of looking incompetent or insecure is such that it has been estimated that only 28 per cent of cyberattacks on businesses in the UK are reported – and just 15 per cent in the USA.[15] Corruption likewise suffers from massive and endemic under-reporting, especially when it is not predatory (in which some official demands a bribe with a threat) so much as consensual (whereby bribe-giver and -taker are both happy with their deal, whether it is to arrange for a contract to be awarded to an uneconomic vendor or a traffic violation to disappear). In the latter cases, after all, it is often society that is the unknowing victim: the taxpayer foots the bill for an over-priced service, or a dangerous driver gets back on the road.

State power and commercial credibility alike depend on legitimacy, or at least the appearance of reliability, and this is often the fraudster's best weapon: the emperor must claim to be fully clothed at all times. Corruption and fraud can be used against the state, but are most easily, effectively and usually lucratively mobilised by those at the top of society. The frauds which emerged in the Renaissance, for example, often relied on corruption: it was officials who could provide the relevant stamps, approve the necessary permits or obstruct any inconvenient investigations. Just as the more far-sighted of the aristocracy would in due course convert their assets from land into investments, so too the 'fur-collar criminals' of medieval Europe became the corrupt officials of the early modern state. The men of power became arm's-length patrons, protectors, investors and initiators, usually while others actually committed the crimes and took the risks, from clipping and counterfeiting money to murder in the streets. Just as the beginnings of the capitalist system were evident in the banking houses and exchanges of Europe, so too did it manifest itself in a growing differentiation between a criminal 'proletariat' and 'aristocracy'. This was not just a European phenomenon: in asymmetrically comparable China, the 'gentry-officials and gentry-scholars who composed the local elite invested deeply' in a range of criminal enterprises, not least smuggling and piracy, while relying on their status and their distance from the dirty work to keep them safe.[16]

Corruption as such is not organised crime, or at least it need not be. However, it can be the most valuable force-multiplier for the criminals, the literal 'Get Out of Jail Free' card to divert investigations, derail prosecutions and deflect blame. For example, three officers from the Russian Federal Security Service's Directorate M, responsible specifically for rooting out corruption within the police, were arrested in 2024 for having taken bribes to the value of more than 5 billion rubles ($55.2 million), both to kill investigations and even to help expedite the criminal activities of those they were meant to be arresting.[17] Huntington's complacent thesis notwithstanding, it seriously affects national prosperity more broadly, distorting markets, diverting state spending, undermining investment (Malaysia's 1MDB development fund was plundered of some $3.5 billion[18]), and creating hidden monopolies. It can also be a direct threat to national security. In 2021, for example, corruption was estimated to cost Ukraine at least \$37 billion per year, equivalent to six times the total defence budget, even as Russia was preparing to invade.[19] Fortunately for the Ukrainians, corruption within the Russian procurement system also meant their soldiers' modern encrypted radios had been replaced with off-the-shelf Chinese walkie-talkies and their supply trucks were fitted with cheap and shoddy tyres that quickly shredded in tough conditions, rather than the robust military-grade ones that regulations required.[20] More generally, corruption can be used to influence foreign governments, shape media narratives and weaken public institutions, although that is a massive topic that has rightly been the focus of many whole books.[21]

In the process, it also exacerbates global divides between rich and poor, too. There is a cosy belief in the prosperous countries that while we may grumble about a case of political favouritism here or some corporate malfeasance there, serious corruption is a weakness of the impoverished. This complacency is reinforced by well-meant exercises such as Transparency International's Corruption Perceptions Index. This ranks countries on the basis of experts' and business leaders' sense of the levels of public-sector corruption, and countries such as Denmark and New Zealand routinely head the league table as the 'cleanest'. Yet in 2022, Denmark's largest financial institution, Danske Bank, paid \$2 billion to the US authorities for its role in facilitating the laundering of corrupt and criminal proceeds precisely from 'bad' countries.[22] Likewise, a serious concern has been raised that New Zealand's low level of financial cases may represent less utmost probity and more a failure to look into potentially embarrassing cases: only 1 per cent of all the complaints made to its Serious Fraud Office lead to prosecutions, and of the nearly 1,000 other cases, less than 1 per cent are passed to the police's Financial Crime Group.[23]

And who pays the bribes? Despite such measures as the US Foreign Corrupt Practices Act, the small-scale payments may come from local shopkeepers or restaurateurs, but the large-scale payments all too often come from corporations or even governments in the Global North. In 2022, for instance, Glencore Energy UK Ltd had to pay £281 million in fines after it emerged that it had paid £29 million in bribes for preferential access to African oil.[24] Even so, this was nothing to the $950 million US defence contractor RTX – formerly Raytheon – paid in 2024 following allegations that it had won arms contracts in the Middle East through bribery.[25] And these are just two examples of the stream of cases of Western corporations engaging in corruption on a massive scale.

More to the point, where does that money go? Teodoro Nguema Obiang Mangue bought himself a mansion in Malibu, not Managua, and typically the profits of industrial-scale corruption end up in Swiss banks or New York condos rather than kept, let alone spent, at home. In practice, bribes may be demanded or paid in poor countries, but one way or another tend to flow into the rich ones, even as the latter sermonise on the ills of the process and the moral failings of the former.

We may be exercised by the elevation of a prime ministerial friend to the British House of Lords, or the appointment of a generous campaign donor to some agreeable and elegant ambassadorial position, or when a minister appoints a mistress as an adviser, but it is easy to think that this doesn't really matter in the grand scheme of things. However, it all contributes to a sense of moral degeneration, that corrosive belief that 'if they break the rules, why shouldn't we?' in which other forms of criminality can flourish. Corruption demoralises or sidelines the honest, allows the ruthless to rise, and helps the entrepreneurial prosper by ignoring regulation, law and custom. All this again widens that crucial gap between the moral economies of the rulers and the ruled, and can put the public on the side of the criminals – or, rather, make them see little difference between them. Admittedly, though, this is really best visible in the case of smuggling.

CHAPTER 8

A NICE CUPPA AND SOME SMUGGLING

Never try and get between the English and their tea. Seriously, just don't. In the eighteenth century, so great was the crown's need for revenue, that customs dues on tea imports rose as high as 119 per cent. While it may have been understandable why the government sought to profit from the English demand for tea (just as Moscow later relied on vodka taxes[1]), unsurprisingly enough this created a huge market for smugglers. Britain's coastline is studded with towns such as Baytown in Yorkshire (now, appropriately, Robin Hood's Bay) or Deal in Kent, where cliffs were threaded with tunnels to bring in the haul of tea (or Dutch gin, or tobacco, or any of the other heavily taxed imports) and where half the town lived off the profits of smuggling. When the government decided to crack down on the smugglers of Deal in 1781, they had to send in 100 cavalry and 900 militia. But this was no one-sided contest. The infamous Hawkhurst gang was said to be able to muster 500 men within an hour and in 1747 even raided the customs house at Poole Harbour that had been presumed safely guarded by the guns of a naval warship (the gang waited until the lowering tide took the ship out of sight of the building).[2]

The scale of this phenomenon is hard to exaggerate, especially as it replaced banditry as an economic activity proscribed by the law, yet often accepted and encouraged by society. By the eighteenth century, smuggling may have accounted for more than half of all trade in and out of England.[3] The individual smugglers sometimes conformed to the popular image, from the 'tubman' who lugged a barrel of contraband up beach and cliff to a safe house, to the club-wielding 'batsman' who kept passers-by and Revenue officers at bay. As often, though, those behind these ventures were figures of substance within their local communities: merchants, aldermen, politicians and officials. Dissecting the accounts of Bristol merchants, Evan Jones found not only that corruption was routine and even registered in the books (such as payments to customs officers 'for their kindness') but that the roster of those involved included mayors and members of parliament.[4] Likewise noblemen were behind much of the lucrative salt smuggling into France, of which more in a moment,[5] as well as the strikingly similar operations bringing salt into China to avoid monopolies which accounted for between a third to a half of state revenue.[6]

Tax and spend

After all, states are essentially engines to raise and spend taxes. As they become more organised, as they do more, so too they need more revenue. This often means taxing goods and services, and this inevitably creates more markets and opportunities for the criminals. Ban something, and you create an illicit market, as buyers look to alternative suppliers. Tax something, and you likewise create an illicit market, as smugglers and black marketeers sell untaxed goods under the counter.

Medieval states' main outlays were on the court and war, and to a degree much the same was true of early modern ones. However, as the size and scale of warfare grew, so did its demand on the public purse, and the money had to be found somewhere. In the last decade of the seventeenth century alone, for example, the kingdom of France saw its overall government expenditure double, with three-quarters of that still going to the military. As a result, the state devalued its currency, introduced a new head tax known as the *capitation*, and increased the take from the *gabelle*, a tax on salt, which was so crucial for the preservation of food. However, the *gabelle* was set by each *pays*, or region of France, and so there were substantial variations between them. Mark Kurlansky cites the eighteenth-century statesman Jacques Necker, who reported that between disequilibria in tax and demand, a *minot* of salt (a unit of 49 kilos) that would cost just 31 sous in Brittany, would fetch 81 in Poitou and a whopping 591 in Anjou.[7] Needless to say, the result was a thriving domestic salt-smuggling industry, whose principals, the *faux-sauniers* (false-saltmen), were as well regarded by the wider populace as the English tea-smuggling rings. The state responded with the usual savagery: a *faux-saunier* could be sentenced to death if he also went armed, while those women who smuggled salt packed into ingenious pads that enhanced their curves, the *faux culs* or 'false bottoms', risked ten years' imprisonment. Any members of the nobility convicted of a repeat offence of even just buying contraband salt would be expelled from the aristocracy.

After all, these illicit smuggling operations were directly eating into the state's treasury for war-fighting and court. No wonder the authorities cracked down so hard (if rarely with great success), and that loyalists would frame this in political as well as moral terms. In his 'A word to the smuggler' (1783), the Reverend John Wesley asserted:

Open smugglers are worse than common highwaymen, and private smugglers are worse than common pickpockets. For it is undoubtedly worse to rob our father than one we have no obligation to. And it is worse still, far worse, to rob a good father . . . King George is the father of all his subjects and . . . he is a good father.[8]

Every crime has its price tag. There are cases where the state's and society's notions of criminality seem in stark contrast, such as whether or not soft drugs ought to be legalised, informed by a general sense of what is fair and what is not. When a necessity such as salt is made so expensive to enrich the state and monopolists, or when tea is taxed to such a degree, this crosses that invisible line, and smuggling becomes somehow justified as a blow struck against injustice. The Revenue man and the *gabelous* enforcing the salt tax are transformed from the representative of society to exploitative oppressors.

The immoral economy

This is something of a universal process, as people balance not just risk and reward, but their sense of the moral dimension. This is essentially what the Marxist historian E.P. Thompson described as society's (or in his case 'the crowd's') moral economy:

> a consistent traditional view of social norms and obligations, of
> the proper economic functions of several parties within the com-
> munity, which, taken together, can be said to constitute the moral
> economy of the poor. An outrage to these moral assumptions,
> quite as much as actual deprivation, was the usual occasion for
> direct action.[9]

He was thinking and writing about riots, but smuggling and other criminal acts are every bit as much expressions of that outrage. Pirating music or video today often reflects a belief that the price charged for an intangible download is iniquitous, and simply goes to overpaid performers and greedy executives, but the gap between official and public moral economies are most evident when it comes to basic staples, not just salt and tea, but also cloth and, indeed, any good

essential to the local economy. A period of especially onerous taxation of the wool trade in mid-fourteenth-century England did not
restore the royal treasury so much as lead to an upsurge in smuggling
and, just as importantly, an apparent decline in local authorities'
enthusiasm to police the trade, and jurors' willingness to find smugglers guilty.[10] They knew that these high taxes were making their own
clothes that much more expensive. too.

So often, the temptation to levy ever-higher taxes or impose
monopolies proved to be the trigger either for covert resistance
through smuggling or else direct protest, such as the 1781 revolt in
the Spanish Viceroyalty of New Granada (because of an increase
in the *alcabala* sales tax and new alcohol monopolies) or the 1864–5
revolt in Tunisia against the doubling of the *mejba*, the poll tax.

However, it can just as easily be manifest in luxuries. After the
American Civil War, the need to protect the domestic textiles industry was such that import duties skyrocketed. Silk, for example, was
taxed half as much again as before, and the 1890 McKinley Tariff
Act further restricted dress goods such as the finer cottons used for
lace and embroidery, which were mainly imported from France,
Germany and Britain. Yet the new rich of Gilded Age America were
keen to demonstrate their cosmopolitanism with the latest European
fashions, and from this emerged a specialised kind of smuggling. Mil-
liners might travel abroad to pick up clothes, cloth or designs, or
affluent consumers might head to Europe to buy a new trousseau
and hope to sneak it back into the country. So concerned was the
Treasury Department that it set up an office in Paris and stationed
agents across Europe to identify high-spending Americans whom
customs inspectors would investigate on their return home.[11]

In due course, the moral economies tend to converge, at least
enough to limit the scope of the organised crime gangs involved in
smuggling. In part, this usually entails the state recognising the unsus-
tainability of its levies and cutting back on taxes and tariffs. It also

reflects public concern that the smuggling gangs pose a wider threat out of proportion with their benefit. In eighteenth-century Britain, for example, there emerged a belief in the extent to which it undermined the wider peace. As one pamphlet of the time warned:

> Smuggling is not only highly injurious to trade, a violation of the laws, and the disturber of the peace and quiet of all the maritime counties in the kingdom; but it is a nursery for all sorts of vice and wickedness; a temptation to commit offences at first unthought of; an encouragement to perpetrate the blackest of crimes without provocation or remorse; and is in general productive of cruelty, robbery and murder.[12]

This was aggravated, though, by a concern that the smugglers were also becoming suborned into agents of the hostile French. As retired Admiral Edward Vernon warned, their criminal activities had 'converted those employed in it, first from honest industrious fishermen, to lazy, drunken, and profligate Smugglers, and now, to dangerous Spies on all our Proceedings, for the Enemy's daily Information'.[13]

Weaponised smuggling

After all, smuggling can be an outright political act against a national enemy or a system considered fundamentally wrong. For settlers in early America, smuggling was a blow struck against the 1651 and 1660 Navigation Acts that restricted trade and thus drove up prices for imports and limited export opportunities, especially for planters and traders in North Carolina.[14] As so many imperial possessions discovered to their cost, tariffs tend to be for the interest of the metropolis, not the provinces. In many ways, this was the first step on the way to the War of Independence, and passions ran high from the first. ('O Lucifer, I hope thou will soon fall into Hell like a star from the sky, there to lie unpitied and unrelented of any for ever and ever,' wrote a colonial smuggler to Captain Bursack of the British revenue cutter *Speedwell*, after he seized his ship.[15])

Commercial smuggling is usually only implicitly political. Smugglers are often deeply uninterested in their patriotic duty. English criminal entrepreneurs may have sold weapons to the Spanish Navy while they were building up their Armada for an attempted invasion of England in the 1580s,[16] just as Russian gangsters in the 1990s sold Chechen rebels guns with which they killed Russian soldiers.[17] The criminals tend to be happy to work with whomever pays. Chinese communities living in the Philippines took full advantage of Spain's efforts to conquer the Moro sultanates in the nineteenth century to create a large-scale smuggling enterprise that saw slaves seized by Moro raiders and rebels traded for guns that the Chinese would buy from Singapore and other trading stations – including, ironically enough, sometimes from Manila, capital of the Spanish East Indies.

Nonetheless, sometimes states themselves use, facilitate or support smuggling for their own goals. When Britain fought not one but two wars with China to prevent Beijing from keeping Indian opium out of its markets (1839–42 and then also alongside France in 1856–60), it was in part to maintain a lucrative trade but also to open up brand-new concessions. Was this smuggling, warfare, or economic coercion? A bit of all three, in that Britain was in effect acting as the protector of smugglers who sought to import a commodity into a country in defiance of local laws. Much more straightforward was France's assistance to the blockade runners who kept the rebels supplied and connected during the American War of Independence, or British smugglers' defiance of Napoleon's Continental System, that sought to strangle the 'nation of shopkeepers' by denying it access to European markets. Indeed, Napoleon also set up his own contingent of British-born smugglers to bring home from England escaped French prisoners of war, gold guineas and newspapers (for their intelligence value), financed by running French gin, brandy and textiles the other way. There was even a special compound for 300 of them in Gravelines near Dunkirk, the 'City of Smugglers' (or 'Ville de Smoglers', as it became known in mangled Franglais).[18]

Then there are those smuggling operations directly driven by the strategic interests of one state or another. During the American Civil War, blockade runners brought the South some 60 per cent of its modern rifles in an attempt to compensate for the industrial advantage of the North.[19] Today, sanctions-hit modern Iran facilitates networks secretly selling millions of barrels of its oil into global markets to raise funds to keep its economy afloat. Since its invasion of Ukraine triggered similar sanctions, so too now does Russia. 'Shadow fleets' of tankers owned through obscure front companies ship its oil around the world, 'grey market' facilitators buy sanctioned electronics to be delivered to some third country only then to re-export them to Russia, and organised crime gangs smuggle in everything from military-grade optics to Italian designer handbags for the Moscow elite.[20]

Even modern states must work with rather than against the market. As commodities rise and fall in fashion and demand, as taxes and regulations change in line with the thinking of the time, the disequilibria not just in supply and demand, but between legal prices and what people are willing to pay, continue to generate new opportunities. Sometimes, this means states looking to export their sanctioned oil or import Enfield rifles, but more often it is ordinary consumers looking for something that is banned or, as they see it, overtaxed. Tobacco has long been smuggled, but increasing taxes driven especially by health concerns have created burgeoning markets for counterfeit and smuggled, untaxed cigarettes and thus a lucrative 'buttlegging' industry. (An illegal factory raided in Bulgaria in 2019 was producing 2,000 such cigarettes every minute.[21]) Even environmental regulation can create new markets. As will be discussed later, when the European Union instituted tough new regulations on the safe and eco-friendly disposal of old fridges and other devices containing ozone-destroying CFC gases, necessarily ratcheting up the costs, Italian organised crime groups set up front companies apparently offering approved services at a reasonable price – and then dumped the fridges anywhere they could. States will tax, ban and regulate – that's what they are for. But every time they do, they risk creating new criminal opportunities in that crucial gap between state and society, a gap in which crimes can be ignored and criminals greeted as welcome suppliers. However, this is also a reminder that in the global age, it is not just legitimate goods that can illegitimately be moved – it is also a great time for anyone who has criminal assets that need to be fenced or otherwise disposed of.

CHAPTER 9

RUSTLING AND FENCING EVERYTHING FROM CATTLE TO CARS

In the tsarist Russian village, a horse literally could mean life or death or liberty for the whole settlement. Just the loss of one could mean not enough land could be ploughed. For peasants living a marginal existence at the best of times, that could force them to accept the land-slavery that was serfdom, simply to survive. For that reason, horse thieves were treated as the greatest threat – the greatest blights, the saying went, were 'drought, horse thieves and the Devil' – and the whole village would lynch any who were caught. Not for them the mercy of being handed over to the constables for a quick hanging. Rather, they would be killed in performatively gruesome ways, impaled on lovingly carved spiked poles, or their every bone broken before being nailed to a tree at the nearest crossroads, symbolically garrotted with horsehair just to make the point: horse thieves not welcome here.[1]

Not welcome if they came to steal, that is. The extraordinary value of the horse meant that there was a thriving market for horses, stolen or otherwise. After all, there could be no sentimentality in a hard life, and even if peasants knew a horse was stolen, if they could buy it, they would. No wonder horse thieves became increasingly organised, with larger and larger gangs using ever greater firepower and cunning, to defeat peasant resistance and exploit this lucrative market. The shadow economy became a sophisticated one, with stolen horses trafficked from region to region, so as to be sold far from their owners, their provenance concealed. From the cattle rustlers of the Wild West, to the modern-day car thief, the challenge is often less the theft than its safe monetisation: the fencing. This is what often distinguishes the individual thief from the organised gang – and it is the vastly greater opportunities for making money and avoiding punishment that make the former join the latter.

Those *raky*, the Russian slum tailors, could work overnight to convert stolen clothes into something that could safely be sold the next morning. It was harder for the horse thieves, even though wonders could be done with a branding iron, turning one mark into another. Nonetheless, it was pretty obvious if, say, a new line had been added to turn a triangle into an arrow, so instead, they would increasingly simply swap each other's stolen horses across provincial boundaries, confident that a horse stolen in one *guberniya* could safely be sold in the next. The trick, after all, was not necessarily to convince the buyer that the horse wasn't stolen, but to give them the comfort that the real owner wasn't going angrily to confront them, as well as plausible deniability: to be able to claim to be shocked, shocked to discover that it was dodgy. Of course, an alternative was to sell it to a horse dealer, who could hide the 'hot' mounts amid the rest of his herds and likely had the contacts to unload them without risk of alerting the authorities. Indeed, the authorities often were the buyer – the army was always in the market, and did not have to worry about any outcry from some peasant in the boonies.

Some stolen items are so mundane and comparatively low-value as to be relatively easily sellable, whether in the pub, at a car boot sale, or even on an online site. But what about more complex and identifiable items, such as cars with their Vehicle Identification Numbers? In the 1990s, organised gangs of European car thieves stole high-value vehicles to order, sending them to Albania, Russia and wherever else buyers had money to burn and didn't care about provenance; or, if they were more sophisticated, replacing the visible VIN plates. To be sure, this would not match other identifiers, but that would only come to light in a proper check. On the surface, this was a different car and again the buyer had deniability. Today, rustlers in northern Cameroon use middlemen to get stolen cattle to markets in northern Nigeria, in a manner nineteenth-century Russian horse thieves would recognise.[2] Meanwhile, organised burglary rings move back and forth across the open border between Northern Ireland and the Republic of Ireland, stealing on one side and fencing on the other.[3] In all these cases, the buyers likely have some idea that what they are getting – the cheap, used Mercedes with no log book, the cows with Cameroonian brands, the unusually large selection of 'granny's old jewellery' – was stolen, but the price is right and the risk seems manageable. For crime to pay – and that's the idea, after all – then you need to be able safely to sell what you steal, and that often demands organisation. It also frequently relies on that most human of characteristics, the willingness to turn a blind eye when it is in our own interests.

Rustling up a profit

So long as there is property, there will be theft, but in ancient times the constraints of transport and markets often limited the scale of physical robbery beyond the organised depredations of the pirate and bandit gangs which operated across the borders of tribe, clan or nation. (Of course, corruption and embezzlement still had free rein.) How could one sell or even use stolen goods within small social worlds where the victim could easily identify his or her property? Stealing a loaf of bread which could then be eaten was one thing, but identifiable goods – especially in an age before interchangeable, mass-produced wares – were quite another. (And a particular reason why vagrants, vagabonds and other itinerants were often treated with such suspicion, because they were in a better position to profit from petty theft.)

As economies shifted from barter to cash, as more and more people lived above the breadline, able to accumulate luxuries, then the scope for theft expanded beyond cloaks stolen from clotheslines or a cake from the griddle. So too did the means used to protect individual and commonly held property. Simple locks have been around for millennia, but it was the Romans who adopted locked safe deposit boxes of sorts in their home, the keys being worn as rings. There have, of course, always been complex crimes. In 1303, one Richard Podelicote stole more than 100,000 pounds' worth of jewels from the Royal Treasury, by spending four months burrowing into the vault from the adjacent Westminster Abbey.[4] However, this kind of long-term, high-risk and high-gain enterprise is more visible from the early modern era onwards. Typical was the theft of a treasure of gold and silver from a Coburg manufactory in 1733, which eventually proved to have been carried out by a skilled and daring gang of (mainly) Jewish robbers from Hesse who had carried out similar, if less lucrative, crimes across the German states. The 'ferret' – organiser – of the Coburg burglary had actually visited the manufactory as a customer over a year before and drawn up a detailed plan of the layout.[5]

As the most valuable prizes came under increasingly effective protection, and law-enforcement apparatuses became ever more sizeable and dangerous, some criminals adopted a 'fewer but bigger' approach. Instead of numerous low-yield crimes, whether holding up travellers, picking pockets, or fleecing gullible street-corner gamblers, they instead worked together to pull off the kind of 'big job' which has become a staple of the 'heist movie' genre, from *The*

Lavender Hill Mob (1951) to the since-remade *Ocean's 11* (1960 and 2001) and its sundry sequels. Mary McIntosh regards this as the final stage in the evolution of 'thieving': project crime, carrying out risky but potentially lucrative operations requiring skill, planning, violence and often the latest technology, whether Nobel's Blasting Powder, later renamed dynamite, in the late nineteenth century, the gangster's 'Tommy gun' in the 1920s, or drones today.[6]

There is much truth in this. Certainly when she wrote it in the late 1960s, North America and Europe were going through a spate of high-profile, sometimes complex and often violent operations such as the 1963 Great Train Robbery in Britain (in which 15 men stole £2.3 million, worth something like £30 million today) or the 1997 Loomis Fargo heist. Then, an armoured truck driver called Philip Noel Johnson pulled a gun on his fellow guards at a cash-handling facility in Jacksonville, Florida, stuffed his truck from floor to ceiling with $22 million, then removed the video surveillance tapes and even his own personnel file before disappearing. In what could be considered an ambiguous accolade, the *Washington Post* later ran his picture with this headline: 'Have you seen this man? He's 33, single, lonely, grouchy, rumpled and very possibly the richest thief who ever lived.'[7] Johnson was eventually arrested but perhaps this should have been considered a cautionary tale not to entrust millions to disgruntled employees being paid just $7 an hour.

In recent years, though, the tally of pay-roll robberies, lorry hijacks and bank hold-ups in more advanced countries has diminished as the pendulum swing of crime and countermeasures reversed itself. Armoured cash vans became more impregnable, connected by radio to the police, then tracked by satellite, and fitted with smoke generators to blind attackers and dye-packs to render stolen money unusable. Hard cash began to give way to plastic payment cards and even mobile phones. Cash-van robberies become more infrequent, and carried out by relatively skilled 'professionals'.[8] Even so, the real challenge has switched from the theft to – in an age when banknote numbers are scanned and tracked, diamonds micro-engraved and jewellery may even have embedded RFID identity chips – what to do with the loot.

On the fence

In ancient times, this was practical enough for relatively anonymous (and thus presumably relatively low-value) goods. A corner of the main agora or marketplace in Athens was the infamous 'villain's market' where stolen goods were bought and sold and nefarious characters could be found for shady tasks.[9] However, this was pretty small-time. The fences who traded in stolen tunics and cloaks (opportunistic clothes-snatching from washing lines or a victim's back was a widespread problem) and other trinkets did not make a living from such activities, they simply supplemented their existing stalls with this loot.

It was also dangerous. Under the Babylonian Code of Hammurabi, a thief and the fence who bought or tried to sell his stolen loot were equally condemned to death.[10] Likewise, Roman law explicitly addressed the need 'to abolish the protection of the powerful over armed criminal and bandits' and cautioned landlords from harbouring criminal gangs on their lands on pain of punishment.[11] Nonetheless, Roman officials and landowners were notorious for using their position to fence stolen livestock. The poet Ausonius even alluded to such practices in light-hearted vein when he wrote to ask a friend whether he was 'chasing thieves . . . who, finally fearing you, call you into partnership and share the booty? You, a gentle and idle chap, condone human bloodshed for money and call it all a mistake and impose a rate on rustled cattle and take the business from the courts.'[12]

Often then, just as since, fencing became the preserve of marginalised communities, who may lack the social capital safely to be involved in direct criminal operation, but have little enough to lose from being involved in such secondary activities. Jews, for example, often ended up with that role in Europe as they were excluded from so many legitimate economic opportunities. Anti-Semitism has a long and dismal pedigree. The Fourth Lateran Council of 1215 had denied them the right to own land or hold military or civil offices, while requiring them to wear distinctive yellow veils, hats or badges. Jewish populations were often subject to arbitrary expulsion, as from England in 1290, Spain in 1492 and Sicily in 1493, or forced to live in specific districts, locked up at night behind guarded gates in areas known as ghettos, named after the first such enclosure in Venice (in 1516). Within the ghetto, Jews were confined to a very limited range of occupations, notably pawnbroking, dealing in second-hand clothing and moneylending, thanks to a provision in Deuteronomy which permitted them to make a profit from providing credit, something otherwise banned as usury. Indeed, Pope Paul IV's openly anti-Semitic 1555 *Cum nimis absurdum* bull demanded that they confine themselves solely to trading in second-hand clothes, at least within the Papal States of central Italy. The Jewish communities of Europe had long learned the lessons of being a hated yet sometimes prospering minority in a time shaped equally by unreasoning prejudice and hard-headed pragmatism. Many communities had been spared thanks to 'taxes' or simple bribes paid to kings and other potential persecutors, just as others had been sacked or expelled when they could not pay. Whether out of fear of the consequences or genuine conviction, they had often been scrupulously law-abiding.[13] However, as the pressures increased and the legitimate opportunities narrowed, it is unsurprising that they accepted the role all but thrust upon them, of facilitating Gentile criminality.[14]

Pawnbroking lent itself to fencing stolen goods, as did dealing in second-hand clothing, especially given the common practice of their first mending such 'pre-owned' apparel.[15] (This was also a feature of the Japanese second-hand clothing business, notorious for handling stolen wares.[16]) Later, jewellers and goldsmiths of negotiable morals would also melt down or rework stolen gee-gaws for undetectable resale. Even allowing for the extent to which anti-Semitism colours the reports of their activity, from the early modern period onwards, Jewish traders, bankers and pawnbrokers appear disproportionately as fences in the European and later North American underworlds.[17]

It is important to stress that the Jews are given here as one example, not to be considered unique. All kinds of communities have been forced into fencing at different times because of discrimination or social stigma. Butchery was, for example, considered a spiritually polluting activity in both Korea and China. Butchers, as a result, often ended up dealing in stolen livestock – as they could quickly turn an identifiable animal into an anonymous and marketable collection of cuts – which in due course would extend to handling other illicit goods.[18] Camp followers in medieval European armies, often considered little more than 'ruined women', fenced booty from the battlefield (and opportunistic thefts on the march). The nomadic Yerukulas of India's Madras region were long held in suspicion by their settled neighbours, even before they were formally designated as 'addicted to the systematic commission of non-bailable offences' under the 1911 Criminal Tribes Act. It was hardly surprising if they combined their outsider status and itinerant ways to adopt a role as fences.[19] The 'Rascals' of Papua New Guinea, urban gangs of youths who felt alienated during the time of Australian rule (until 1975) and turned to petty and violent crime, spawned a generational evolution. Older figures no longer as keen to engage in the physical antics of 'Rascalism' on the streets instead set up businesses which fenced the loot gathered by their younger brethren.[20]

Of course, as with all such characterisations, it needs to be kept in context. Most fences are defined simply by their willingness to deal in questionable goods, and will be neither rebels nor outcasts.[21]

However, it is not simply greed which brings some into this business, but outright economic necessity and a sense that, having been excluded from mainstream society, they feel less reason to honour its values and laws. The Chinese would often regard Muslims, in the words of Chen Hongmou, an eighteenth-century governor of Shaanxi province, as 'nothing but unruly and rebellious people from the edges of civilization'. No wonder Sino-Muslims found themselves effectively nudged towards not just fencing stolen goods, but, according to Chen's broadside, a whole range of other crimes, including loosing flocks of sheep into others' fields, creating disturbances at public theatrical performances and, perhaps most outré, cat burglary.[22] (Which appears to have meant the theft of cats, rather than the second-storey antics of, well, a cat burglar.)

Theft, then, whether of a car or a horse, a diamond tiara or a DVD player, is a criminal act that, like so many others, largely only makes sense within a wider economic context. If crime is to pay, there needs to be an economy around it. As one prison inmate put it, with what *The Economist* described as 'impeccable logic', 'if there weren't these handlers, there wouldn't be no burglars'.[23] However, that wider economy, the world of the fence, is often shaped by society as well as law, by those who are cast out or cast down. For the thief, as much as the fence, this is likely to be an economic act, but it is also implicitly a political one, too. As the state tries to tax, ban and regulate, those who look to make a profit by defying it are not just engaging in crime but, however little they themselves may realise it, an act of rebellion. This is at its clearest when the crimes directly challenge the state's moral economy: its vision for how people should behave. Organised crime in particular thrives, after all, when the state takes something that people not only want but believe they are entitled to have, and tries to ban it, as we will see in the next chapter.

CHAPTER 10

WHAT'S THE PROBLEM WITH BOOTLEGGERS, PORNOGRAPHERS AND DRUG PUSHERS?

When the Volstead Act was passed in 1919 – more properly known as the National Prohibition Act – it turned the United States dry and handed a lucrative market over to the gangsters and bootleggers. Prohibition was never just about alcohol, but instead was a particular front line on a wider cultural and political war launched by traditional elites embracing 'nativism', as they felt their values and their power were being undercut by an ungrateful urban poor and, especially, waves of immigrants. The saloon became an easy symbol of moral depravity, political corruption, and social disorder, all at once. The 'drys' may never have won over the bulk of the population, but they did control Congress, and hence the introduction of measures to curb alcohol that were as sweeping as they were unenforceable. In the process it not only created a new wave of home-brewers and distillers, it massively empowered organised crime and wholesale smuggling of alcohol across the Canadian and Mexican borders. It was unwound in 1933, but had already created powerful mob syndicates that would simply diversify into new illicit markets afterwards.

This cautionary tale seems to have escaped the Soviet reformist Mikhail Gorbachev's team when, in 1985, they began a campaign against the endemic alcoholism that was a very real problem at the time.[1] After all, the typical family was spending up to half of its total household budget on booze by then, and drunkenness accounted for the majority of industrial accidents.[2] Gorbachev himself was not much of a drinker, and he was clearly out of step with his people. More to the point, the clumsiness of the late Soviet system was such that it was much happier banning than encouraging. What was originally envisaged as a multi-dimensional programme to wean drinkers off the hard stuff and into juice bars and healthy living, soon became little more than Prohibition 2.0, as vineyards were uprooted, vodka production slashed, and wine and beer sales taxed to the hilt. Not only did this represent a serious blow to the state's coffers, as taxes on legal alcohol earned it something like an eighth of all its revenues, it again galvanised organised crime, turning it from feared predator to welcome supplier.

I remember a *shestyorka* ('sixer', or gofer) recounting how, when accompanying an older gangster on his rounds in a grimy southern suburb of Moscow selling black-market booze, the locals would not only greet them with open arms, but also encourage them to diversify. Could they get some cigarettes for next time, or would they be able to arrange a medical appointment?[3] This was the start of a process that, in the late 1980s and the early 1990s, saw the more far-sighted gangs becoming virtual one-stop shops for all the goods and even services that the legitimate economy could not provide, whether because of shortage or government action. From this emerged new, more entrepreneurial organised crime combines which burrowed deep into Russia's emerging economies and are still there today.

Fight for the right to party

Laws tend to protect the existing social and political order and impose its values. Often this is generally accepted – few, for example, would seriously complain about illegalising murder and fraud – but at other times it reflects the whim of the monarch, the interests of the elite, or a deliberate attempt at social engineering. China criminalised reincarnation without state approval in 2007, which is not quite as absurd as it may sound, as it was essentially a way to try and control Tibetan Buddhist lamas, who are supposed to be selected through rebirth.[4] Former dictator of Turkmenistan Saparmurat Niyazov, as well as renaming the days and months (April became 'Gurbansoltan' after his mother, and Friday 'MotherDay'), banned opera as 'Un-Turkmen'. In the 1960s and 1970s, successive military regimes in Argentina all but tried to stamp out the tango, the national dance, because it was deemed frivolous and subversive, just as jogging would be in Burundi in 2014.[5]

These are, of course, extreme examples, but it is worth noting that Tibetans are still claiming reincarnations, Niyazov's successor Gurbanguly Berdimuhamedov reversed his bizarre decrees (while admittedly adding some of his own, such as banning black cars as 'unlucky'), the tango is alive and well, and maybe the same could have been said of Burundian president Pierre Nkurunziza, who died at age 55, had he jogged a little more himself. When states try to ban what people think is acceptable, they will usually resist by seeking alternative sources – typically organised crime. This can be corrosive of the state's legitimacy and its 'official morality' on a wider scale. They have tried to ban things throughout history, for a variety of reasons. Sometimes it was to protect their health: the Swedish crown banned coffee fully five times in the eighteenth and nineteenth centuries, convinced it was a dangerous stimulant. Perhaps it was to preserve public order, such as Edward III's ban on football in 1349, intended to reduce the violent brawls the game generated and also to keep young Englishmen focused on the archery practice demanded by the ongoing war with France. Maybe it was to keep them from sin (especially if this also reduced waste and social disorder), such as through sumptuary laws to curb extravagance. Those of seventeenth-century Japan, for example, required peasants to eat barley, not rice, and banned farmers from using umbrellas, and townspeople from wearing silk. Usually, though, it is all about preserving the status quo, whether keeping the workforce sober enough to work, or preventing your elites from bankrupting themselves. Of course, people look for loopholes. Swedes took to buying beans on the black market, or pre-brewed coffee under the counter, and they are now the world's third-largest coffee consumer per capita.[6] For better or worse, football has outlasted many attempts to ban it, and Japanese townspeople would wear silk under plain clothes. No wonder many of the more enlightened thinkers came to appreciate the value of turning a blind eye to some practices, however morally abhorrent they may be considered, in the name of social order. Even theologians concurred that sometimes one had to acknowledge the weaknesses of the flesh: St Augustine wrote, 'suppress prostitution and capricious lusts will overthrow society', while Thomas Aquinas compared it with sewerage works: 'prostitution in the towns is like the cesspool in the palace; take away the cesspool and the palace will become an unclean and ill-smelling place.'[7]

In the modern world, states have become vastly more interventionist, ironically just as – especially, but not solely in democracies – people believe all the more firmly that they have a greater right to make their own decisions, and globalisation has often given them new opportunities to act on them. There is thus a struggle, manifested in lawmaking and lawbreaking, as the boundaries of the acceptable are constantly renegotiated. In this respect, the criminals – supplying drink during Prohibition, pornography before it was (generally, and up to a point) legalised, marijuana, and so forth – are not only entrepreneurs making money, they are also midwives of new moralities. Crime, after all, thrives in that hazy no-man's land between the letter of the law and a community's moral economy. In working, legitimate democracies, this gap ought to be rather narrow, even though there are all kinds of cases where government and lawmakers may be a little in advance of society or a little behind. Even so, there are crimes that almost all of us commit at some time with a pretty clear conscience, such as jaywalking or speeding on that straight, empty road. Even in the most democratic states, though, societies are not homogenous, but constellations of communities, many of whom will have their own notions of what is acceptable. Today's debates over the legalisation of marijuana, the banning of pornography, the morality of destructive and obstructive political protest and the boundaries of 'hate speech' all attest to the variety of perspectives. This is why the smugglers so often survive and thrive, as symptoms of the failures of state-imposed moralities. From coffee and booze, to sex and drugs and rock and roll, in their own ways, in the struggle between official morality and the market, it is usually the former that must ultimately bend.

Sex . . .

In 1964, a cinema manager in Ohio was on trial for showing *Les Amants*, a film with an explicit scene. Justice Potter Stewart memorably admitted that 'I can't define pornography . . . but I know it when I see it.' Although the word's roots are in the Greek word for prostitutes, pornography is more broadly sexually explicit material primarily designed to generate arousal. Yet the term is often value-laden: what may distinguish pornography from erotica is precisely the sense that it is somehow sinful or harmful. Some might consider the 25,000-year-old Venus of Willendorf, a prehistoric statuette of the kind of generous proportions that could politely be described as voluptuous, as the earliest form of pornography, but we have no idea as to its intended purpose (fertility ritual or self-portrait?), nor any reason to regard it as having been considered transgressive or immoral at the time. Erotic petroglyphs from 4,000 years ago have been found on cave walls in China, the Babylonians have left behind sexually explicit statuary, the Greeks and Romans covered everything from walls to pottery with erotica, the Moche people of second- to eighth-century Peru produced inventive ceramics depicting sexual acts of every kind, and the sixteenth-century Japanese nobility had a penchant for explicit woodblock prints. Chinese erotic paintings were even placed in kitchens and elsewhere as a talisman against fire, sex being associated with rain and water. Needless to say, technology was repeatedly harnessed to this industry, as representations of sex became increasingly commodified. Woodblock prints gave way to the movable-type printing press, with the first erotic novels spreading from France in the seventeenth century. The daguerreotype, a primitive kind of photography (the earliest surviving pornographic image is from 1846), was followed by actual photography and then in due course film, video and, most bounteous of all, the internet.

Like it or not, the market existed and still exists, but for most of the time and in most of the world, pornography was legal. Even the infamous Marquis de Sade – and what does it say, when your name becomes the very root of the world 'sadism'? – was repeatedly arrested and committed to a series of insane asylums, yet not for the dark and violent sexual fantasies he penned but for his equally twisted acts. Of course, there were periods of greater intolerance and prurience, often associated with religious fervour. However, it is really only in the nineteenth century that, at least in Europe and North America, the law began to intervene. A watershed in Britain, for example, was the passage of the Obscene Publications Act in 1857, described by Lord Chief Justice Campbell as 'intended to apply exclusively to works written for the single purpose of corrupting morals of youth, and of a nature calculated to shock the common feelings of decency in any well-regulated mind'.[8] Nonetheless, it was over a decade before the first case was brought under this law, in 1868. Immediately, though, definitions became based on what judges or juries might consider 'the common feelings of decency in any well-regulated mind'.

In the United States, a similar process was driven by a Christian zealot, postal inspector and self-styled 'weeder in God's garden', Anthony Comstock, a man whose main concern during his time serving in the armies of the North during the bloody, internecine Civil War, seems to have been the profane language of his fellow soldiers. Through his New York Society for the Suppression of Vice, he managed to persuade Congress to pass the Act for the Suppression of Trade in, and Circulation of, Obscene Literature and Articles of Immoral Use in 1873. This was clearly intended not to reflect but to shape public attitudes; Comstock himself said that he regarded it as his duty to 'attempt to improve the morals of other people by rendering obscene literature and photographs inaccessible'.[9]

Similar laws would follow elsewhere, from Europe to Asia. In China, for example, the illegalisation of traditional pornography also reflected a cultural clash between a prudish and self-conscious new elite and a louche traditional one, fought out over sexual mores and, in what could be considered a pretty universal observation, 'despite – indeed, because of – the democratization of desire and access to sexual representations, individuals continued seeking authoritative positions from which to pronounce judgments on the desires of others'.[10] By now it is the norm that at least some forms of pornography and some levels of access are banned, even if the precise contours of acceptable erotica vary from place to place. The inevitable result has been the rise of an illegal market.

The internet has made most of this illegal market irrelevant by, in effect, making most of the laws equally irrelevant. Gone are the days when pornography meant smutty magazines or well-thumbed erotic novels. Anyone with an internet connection and, perhaps, a VPN – virtual private network software protecting your online identity and allowing you to pretend to be accessing the net from some other part of the real world – can surf oceans of pornography of every kind, from grainy copies of 1970s films to animated My Little Pony antics for the truly niche taste. Beyond its obscenity, it is an industry (estimated back in 2015 at being worth $97 billion globally[11]) rife with intellectual property violations, labour abuses and all kinds of other problems. Yet, insofar as law enforcement pays any attention to it, the focus is on those extreme and exploitative forms that are still generally accepted to be beyond the pale such as child abuse, sexual violence and sexualised 'snuff movies' (which show actual murders). Otherwise, despite there continuing to be periodic campaigns against it, and new proposals for laws and controls, the public does not in the main seem to care. Indeed, there is now even a movement for 'ethical porn', as if it could be free-range and organic. In practice, the law is bending. Just like the bootleggers, the pornographers won, because the public wanted them to.

... And drugs ...

Much the same is true of drugs. Originally, they were a natural, local and organic product. Between seven and nine thousand years ago, an unknown artist was daubing a cave wall in the Tassili-N-Ajjer plateau in south-east Algeria. Among the 15,000 or so engravings and paintings that have been found are a number showing figures holding mushrooms and another, presumably a shaman, with the head of a bee and what seem to be mushrooms sprouting out of his body. The region, incidentally, was home to the *Psilocybe mairei* mushroom,

which contains the psychoactive compound psilocybin. The geo-
metric designs around the figures certainly look like an attempt to
represent a hallucinatory trip. From the peyote and mescaline-packed
San Pedro cactus used by native Americans and South Americans,
to the fly agaric mushrooms consumed by Siberian shamans, the use
of narcotics for ritual purpose dates back to the Stone Age and has
continued since. The white-spotted red fly agaric was likely a key
ingredient of Soma, a sacred beverage in Bronze Age India, and also
of Haoma, its counterpart for the Zoroastrians of ancient Persia.

There is an equally long and rich history of the use of what we
would now consider narcotics for medical reasons. At the end of the
third millennium BCE, Sumerians grew poppies (which they called
'the plant of joy') and from that distilled opium, while coca leaves
were chewed in ancient Peru for their narcotic purposes and to give
labourers the pep to work. In Homer's epic eighth-century BCE poem
The Odyssey, Helen of Troy treats wounded Greek warriors with a
potion she received from an Egyptian queen that 'she cast . . . into
the wine of which they drank to lull all pain and anger and bring for-
getfulness of every sorrow'.[12] This was presumably some variety of
opiate, likely akin to laudanum, an opium tincture first popularised
by the Swiss polymath Paracelsus in the sixteenth century. By the
nineteenth century, laudanum and other opiates were widely used
in Europe and North America as a treatment for everything from
insomnia to melancholia.

There have from time to time been local and temporary pro-
hibitions and injunctions, often driven by political, economic and
religious differences more than anything else. In eleventh-century
Egypt, campaigns against hashish were really about a clash between
other Muslim communities and the Sufis who consumed it. That was
largely limited to burning poppy fields, but in the fourteenth century,
the Ottoman governor of Egypt, Soudoun Sheikhouni, returned to
the struggle with rather more exacting vigour: users risked having

their teeth pulled out, and growers were imprisoned or put to death. Yet still the trade continued.

Narcotics and other addictive products were increasingly being traded across borders and seas. In 1604, King James I of England was deeply sceptical about tobacco, not least because of its origins with peoples he considered near-subhuman, wondering 'what honour or policie can moove us to imitate the barbarous and beastly maners of the wilde, godlesse, and slavish Indians, especially in so vile and stinking a custome?'[13] Nonetheless, he did not ban it, and the debate was driven less by considerations of culture and odour as economics: at the time, Spain was the main source. However, once production grew in British colonial holdings, then it became a commodity to push to new markets, from Muscovy (where it was initially banned and thus a smugglers' market) to India. In China, concern about addiction (and the economic impact of low productivity) led to successive attempts to ban opium in 1729, 1799, 1814 and 1831. None stuck, and while one could blame the British for forcibly keeping China's ports open to Indian opium by sending in the gunboats in the 1839–42 and 1856–60 Opium Wars (the second time in alliance with the French), the fact of the matter is that attempting to deal with a drugs problem by addressing the supply rather than the demand was going to be as futile in nineteenth-century China as it is in the twenty-first-century world.

It was really only in the late nineteenth century that there arose a general consensus in the West that narcotics were a problem and needed to be controlled and banned, regardless of what society may think. Britain's 1868 Pharmacy Act imposed unprecedented controls on what otherwise had been an almost entirely unregulated market, and the death rate from opium overdoses fell dramatically (even if a cynic would note an uptick in alcohol-related fatalities). The first multinational effort to counter the drug trade was the 1912 International Opium Convention, although the 1961 Single Convention on Narcotic Drugs and the 1988 United Nations Convention Against

Illicit Traffic in Narcotic Drugs and Psychotropic Substances dramatically extended the scope of what US President Richard Nixon called in 1971 the 'War on Drugs', a singularly unfortunate expression that dogs us to the present day.

After all, the implication of a 'war' – apart from its militaristic overtones – is that it is something with a clearly defined enemy and a viable victory. Even the most brutal methods can only suppress the use and trade in drugs, but not the underlying social and psychological forces driving people to take them. In China, Mao's dictatorship seemed to 'win' against opium in the 1950s, sending addicts into forced rehabilitation, executing dealers and razing poppy fields. The supply shifted into the Golden Triangle region between Thailand, Laos and Myanmar, though, which blossomed with poppies. As soon as the brutal and unsustainable campaign of repression was lifted, drug use returned to China. Although these days Beijing constantly reports successes in fighting the problem – and continues to execute dealers and traffickers – it nonetheless has a serious problem with methamphetamine, ketamine and heroin use.[14]

According to the UN Office on Drugs and Crime, globally some 296 million people use drugs, with over 36 million people being addicted. Cannabis is by far the most prevalent (in 2021, 219 million used it), followed by opioids including heroin (60 million), amphetamines (36 million), various hallucinogens and psychoactive drugs (20 million) and cocaine (22 million).[15] Even though, for example, cannabis products in Europe and the USA are now two to four times as potent as around the turn of the century, with consequently more serious health implications, at present the trend is towards legalisation. For some, it is because this allows for greater regulation (and taxation), for many it is because they do not see it as qualitatively different from other legal substances such as alcohol and tobacco.

It's estimated that in 2019, half a million deaths were directly or indirectly attributable to the use of drugs.[16] However, according to the World Health Organization, tobacco kills more than 8 million people each year.[17] One cannot meaningfully pretend that this is a direct comparison that really holds water (and tobacco use has generally been declining in higher-income countries, an example of the ways that a combination of punitive taxation and consistent public information can close that gap between state and society), but it does highlight the sometimes arbitrary way we divide the 'good' chemical recreations from the 'bad'. Like it or not, people take drugs, and even many others who do not think that – usually up to a point – they should be able to do so. The continued demand for – and thus trade in – narcotics, along with renewed discussion, especially in the West, of legalisation or at least decriminalisation,[18] speaks to the challenges when state and society collide. We are, to be blunt, not winning the foolishly named 'War on Drugs' – and to a large degree it is again because not enough of us want to.

. . . And rock and roll

What about wider cultural artefacts and movements deemed dangerous or subversive by those at the top, yet avidly sought and consumed by those below? Authoritarian regimes in particular have rightly come to realise that the cultural is the political, even if this can sometimes veer into the bizarre. Nineteenth-century Russian Tsar Nicholas I censored cookery books' references to the 'free flow of air' in the oven, as it sounded a little revolutionary, while twenty-first-century China has banned references to Winnie the Pooh because the internet became full of memes comparing A.A. Milne's podgy bear to General Secretary of the Chinese Communist Party Xi Jinping.

Until the twentieth century, this was primarily a matter of banning plays and books on the grounds that they were obscene or encouraged subversion. Increasingly, though, films, songs and memes that simply present or promote alternative ways of life became fair game for the censors. That which is banned becomes delicious forbidden fruit, and so, inevitably, new criminal markets were born. In the Soviet Union, *samizdat* ('self-publishing') manual copies of banned literature were largely passed from hand to hand. However, even before the so-called *magnitizdat* – illegally taped copies of everything from rock and roll to Bible readings – there was a black-market trade in *ryobry* ('ribs'), poor-quality, home-made records cut into old X-ray plates, as the only available source of suitable vinyl. Many of these were recordings of foreign artists, but more were actually of banned domestic music, whether Baltic folk songs or *shanson* gangster-ballads from the Gulags. The black-marketeers were simply out to make money, but by trading such contraband, they were also subverting the Party's attempts to control its citizens' cultural consumption, and in ways that made them criminals in the eyes of the law, but heroes to most.

This industry could take surreal forms. In one of my first trips to the Soviet Union, I was approached in a hotel lift by what looked like a typical, almost caricature *fartsovchik* black-marketeer: mended, faded foreign jeans, a handily capacious fake-leather shoulder bag, an insincere smile. I was bracing myself for an offer to buy my own jeans, or maybe to change money, when he leaned forward conspiratorially: 'You have . . . Agata Kristi?' At a time when the state bookshops were groaning with the complete works of Lenin, there was even an underground market in works that were either unavailable or simply not printed in anything like the numbers to satisfy demand, from Ernest Hemingway to Dale Carnegie, Alexander Solzhenitsyn to, well, Agatha Christie.

Since then, many other regimes have tried – and failed – to police their people's cultural consumption. The Iranian theocracy banned Barbie dolls for their 'destructive cultural and social consequences' (which, in fairness, many in the West would echo), and in the process created a black market whereby shopkeepers would display the approved locally made 'Sara' doll (in modest Muslim dress) and then sell Barbies from under the counter.[19] While China is the world capital of knock-off counterfeit consumer goods, it also has its own black market in proscribed Western cultural goods, including DVDs of such no doubt deeply subversive films as the Disney animated feature *Lightyear* (because of the scene in which a female space ranger kisses her female partner), the superhero actioner *Spider-Man: No Way Home* (because the distributors refused to cut scenes showing New York's Statue of Liberty) and *Back to the Future* (because references to time travel and the 'disrespectful portrayal of history' are banned).

Even North Korea, arguably the most ruthlessly policed and isolated modern state, where TVs and radios are fixed to government frequencies and the only tablet computer is a domestically produced one that records every app opened and the user's browsing history, has not been able to hold the line. Illicit street markets, known as 'Frog Markets' after the way sellers will jump up and run when the police raid them, largely sell food and similar essentials, but also have side-orders in USB sticks (used for copied films and music) and South Korean Choco Pie snack cakes (effectively banned since 2014). 'Supreme Leader' Kim Jong-Un may be notorious for his luxurious lifestyle, but since 2021, he has been exhorting his people to eschew 'alien ideology, culture and lifestyles' with little evidence of success.[20] Instead, as the North Korean phrase has it, in the black markets, 'you can find anything but a cat's horn', whether you're looking for a bootleg copy of the latest James Bond film or, arguably even more dangerous for the regime, K-Pop from over the border.

Gangsters as revolutionaries

Obviously, the smugglers and the black-marketeers are in it for the money, exploiting the markets handed to them by humourless and hidebound authoritarians and well-meaning liberal regimes alike.

They are able do so, though, because society as a whole, or at least a sufficient critical mass within it, refuses to accept the constraints placed upon them by the powers that be. In this respect, then, if in no other, the criminals are not just lawbreakers, they are rebels and even, dare one say it, on the side of freedom and the people. If the state will not oblige, then why not turn to the criminals?

The criminals thus again have become the indicators of the gaps between what society thinks it should have, and what the state is willing to let it have. When that gap is large enough, then the gangsters are all too willing to fill it, and deviant behaviour can become redefined as respectable or legitimate. Furthermore, criminals can find for themselves a place in every corner of society, from back-street drug dealing to providing risqué antiquities for the rich and cultured. Whenever there is a market unmet in the upperworld, the underworld will adapt to meet it, and a process that might once have taken place on a local or national level is increasingly global. The goods the criminals source, the markets they service and the financial flows that ensue criss-cross the world, taking fullest advantage not just of new means of transport and commerce, but the degree to which law enforcement is still largely confined within national borders. Organised crime can and does cut deals with its peers around the world without concern for World Trade Organization rules or the harmonisation of standards; it can and does take advantage of inter-state rivalries (when the Iranian Revolutionary Guard Corps waves opiate traffickers through on their way from Afghanistan to the West, they are not just taking a cut, they can feel they are striking a blow against their enemies); it can and does play off the differences between national law codes and rules on intelligence-sharing. No wonder that it is the criminals who are among the most enthusiastic internationalists around.

PART THREE
THE AGE OF GLOBALISATION

CHAPTER 11

DRUG TRAFFICKERS, APOSTLES OF THE MARKET

In 1996, an unlikely trio of shady characters were sure they were onto a good thing. There was Ludwig 'Tarzan' Fainberg, a Russian dentist-turned-gangster entrepreneur, at the time running a topless Miami nightclub called Porky's; there was Juan Almeida, a high-end car dealer whose clients included a fair proportion of neighbourhood criminals looking for swanky wheels; and there was Nelson 'Tony' Pablo Yester-Garrido, a Cuban immigrant and underworld enforcer with a reputation for violence. The Cali drug cartel wanted a submarine, and this charming trio thought they could swing a deal with a Russian admiral to buy a Project 641 Foxtrot-class attack submarine for $5.5 million, and then sell it to the Colombians for $35 million.[1]

Seventy metres long, powered by three diesel and three electric engines, a Project 641 had the range to travel from Latin America to Europe and back before needing to be refuelled. The thought that these three adventurers could broker such a deal – and that the Colombians could maintain and crew it – may seem extraordinary. However, the 1990s was a decade of chaos in Russia and the military were struggling with a collapse in their morale and budgets alike. It did not seem quite so fantastic a thought that the submarine could somehow be made to go missing. The drug cartels were likewise not lacking in resources and ambition. In the words of a US Navy officer afterwards, 'If you're going to spend $35 million on the boat, you can probably afford whatever it would take to make it work.'

As it was, this particular deal didn't happen, thanks to FBI wiretaps and a falling-out between thieves, which the trio themselves later openly admitted in a gonzo documentary called *Operation Odessa* (2018). Even if they could not buy submarines off the shelf, though, the cartels still thought it had been a good idea. So instead, they began building their own, going beyond the semi-submersible smuggling boats they had already been using, and constructing true, ocean-going submarines. In 2010, for example, Ecuadorian police seized a 31m-long Kevlar and fibreglass diesel-electric submarine that could have carried 10 tonnes of cocaine, worth up to half a billion dollars, all the way to Europe. Since then, the numbers and sophistication of these artisanal 'narco-subs' have only increased, and even the arrest in January 2022 of the reputed master craftsman of this cottage industry, Óscar Moreno Ricardo, is unlikely to change this. The alleged '*Rey de los Semisumergibles*' ('King of the Semi-submersibles') Moreno Ricardo was arrested in Medellín by a joint taskforce of the Colombian police and US Drug Enforcement Administration.[2] However, there are many other journeymen in Latin America who have also been busy building these boats, and a DEA officer who had been involved in the hunt for Moreno Ricardo was matter of fact: 'The next one might not be quite as good or built quite as quick, but they're on the way. Hell, they might even be better.'

After all, Ricardo had nothing to do with the redoubtable *Che*. On 29 October 2019, this 21.5m-long fibreglass semi-submersible, of which no more than half a metre protruded above the waves, set out from the Amazonian coast, having been built in a hidden workshop near the Brazilian city of Macapá. It carried Agustín Álvarez, a former Spanish amateur boxing champion, and two Ecuadorians, as well as 3 tonnes of cocaine. Stuck in a cabin so small that two of the three men had to lie down at any one time, living off energy bars, rice, sardines and biscuits, with a plastic bag as their toilet, they nonetheless piloted across the Atlantic in a 27-day, 5,500km odyssey. It anticlimactically ended in arrest when, after two attempts to rendezvous with cartel boats sent to offload the cocaine had failed and their fuel ran dry, they were forced to scuttle *Che* off the Galician coast.[3]

Connecting the world

Considering that it is estimated that fewer than one in eight boats are ever intercepted, why on earth would the drug gangs *not* use them?[4] The *Che*, for example, cost less than a million dollars to build, but the 153 bales of cocaine it carried had a value of more than $107 million. The drug trade is, after all, vastly lucrative – worth more than half a trillion dollars a year – and global, even if largely moved by rather more conventional means than these submarines. It is hardly surprising that this kind of money generates all kinds of other ambitious and imaginative schemes, from the marijuana-carrying drones crossing the US–Mexican border, to the two statues an Iranian man tried to import into Thailand that turned out to be made entirely out of crystal methamphetamine, worth $1.6 million.

Of course, people smoke, shoot up, swallow and snort drugs everywhere, often local or home-grown. Cocaine is widely used in Latin America, opiates in the Golden Triangle as well as the Afghanistan–Pakistan–Iran Golden Crescent, and marijuana and methamphetamine wherever it is grown or cooked. However, the real money is to be made in trafficking. Most narcotics come from specific regions, usually defined by the right combination of appropriate climate and amenable or absent government (over 80 per cent of the world's heroin comes from Afghanistan, almost all cocaine from Latin America), but head to the lucrative markets of Europe, North America and, increasingly, the rising Pacific rim. In 2017, for example, 17 kilos of opium poppy, enough to make a kilo of heroin at export quality (50–70 per cent purity), cost $2,550 in Afghanistan; by the time it had been refined into the hard drug, it may have been worth around $15,000–20,000. However, the street price in, say, Ireland of that kilo, after it had been cut with starch, baking soda, talcum or the like (uncut, it would be lethally pure), was around $155,000, more than 60 times the value it had as Afghan opium poppy.[5]

While these days marijuana may come from discreet suburban 'grow houses' thanks to hydroponic techniques, and synthetic drugs can be assembled in a local meth lab (albeit quite possibly requiring imported 'precursor chemicals'), the bulk of drugs still come across borders, and thus force the traffickers to sell locally but think globally. This creates world-spanning markets served by equally complex and far-reaching networks, which organise their crimes so as to maximise security and profit. Drugs have been smuggled in all sorts of different ways, from cocaine hidden inside hollowed-out pineapples (a surprisingly common trick) to the 45 kilos of heroin artfully woven into a rug that was seized in Leipzig in 2014. In 2017, Kuwaiti police even intercepted a homing pigeon coming over the Iraqi border wearing a tiny backpack stuffed with 178 ketamine pills.[6] However, each individual trafficking operation, from the condoms of drugs swallowed by a 'mule' about to take a flight, to the packages hidden in industrial products, loaded on the back of a lorry, are almost invariably simply part of these sophisticated global supply chains that connect impoverished conflict zones to the most prosperous parts of the globe.

The sourcing: narco-bandit kingdoms

It's no coincidence that the US 'War on Drugs' often did come to look like a real war ('If we cannot destroy the drug menace in America, then it will surely in time destroy us,' warned President Nixon apocalyptically in 1971[7]). Western soldiers torched opium fields in Afghanistan, US-backed local forces drenched Latin American coca fields with herbicides, and 28,000 US troops invaded Panama in 1989 to topple General Manuel Noriega, despite his past role as a CIA asset, because of his role as a narcotics kingpin. Sometimes, they found themselves facing non-state or state-like actors with the organisation and firepower to make this an unexpectedly even match. In Afghanistan, the United States spent $1.5 million a day fighting its drug war, deploying everything from elite special forces on the ground to F-22 Raptor stealth fighters, and still lost.[8]

Most drugs – or at least the precursors from which they are made – need space in which to be grown, and then processing, especially if it is to be done on a large scale, may require substantial and obvious facilities. The kind of small-scale processing that used to take place in Afghanistan until it became more industrial could be run from a large house or similar, often in a location inaccessible by motor vehicle. Yet it could only produce a few kilos of heroin at a time.[9] Larger and more efficient facilities require road access, electric power and piped water. In an age of aircraft, drone and satellite surveillance, of sophisticated police intelligence analysis, even simply of checking unusual levels of power usage (such as might indicate a cannabis 'grow house' using heaters, hydroponic tanks and bright lights), it is convenient to operate from territory run by governments willing to turn a blind eye, or in which the government treads lightly or not at all. The alliances that so often form between organised crime and insurgencies as a result have not only enriched the criminals but also the rebels, who may either get into the business themselves or else simply 'tax' their underworld colleagues in return for unhindered production and trafficking.

It's a vicious circle: instability and insurgency facilitate the narcotics industry, which in turn generates more disorder and arms the insurgents. Latin American Marxist rebels such as Peru's Sendero

Luminoso ('Shining Path') and Colombia's FARC (the Revolutionary Armed Forces of Colombia) funded themselves thanks to the
cocaine industry, just as the militants of the Kurdish PKK (Kur-
distan Workers' Party) in south-eastern Turkey and northern Iraq
took their cut from the heroin traffickers looking for secure routes
towards Europe. In the 1990s, as the Balkans exploded into civil war
and inter-ethnic violence, the ethnically Albanian Kosovo Liberation Army may have received half of all its funds from taxing this
same trade.[10] Afghanistan's rebels, from the Mujahideen fighting the
Soviet invasion in the 1980s to today's warlords, likewise depend on
either direct involvement in the opium trade, or taxing it in the territories they control. Today, in Africa's Sahel region (the impoverished
strip of nations bordering the Sahara Desert to the north, Burkina
Faso, Chad, Mali, Mauritania and the Niger), corruption, instability
and rebellion combine to make this one of the fastest-growing drug
hotspots in the world. While the drug most commonly seized there is
cannabis resin, the real growth is in cocaine. The region has become
a key trans-shipment route from Latin America to Europe, largely
handled or protected by insurgent armies. From the brutal civil war
in Syria (where both the government and many rebel groups produced and dealt in Captagon, a mix of caffeine and amphetamine
known as the 'poor man's cocaine') to the conflict in Yemen (where
heroin trafficking funds the Houthi rebels, whose fighters also chew
the stimulant leaf khat), rebellion, war and drugs form an unholy but
also lucrative and energising mix.

Sometimes, there are bandits who in due course became governments. The modern world tends to be less tolerant of this primordial
state-building, though, and even examples of pseudo-states such as
Somalia's Puntland are few and far between. Modern states need to
be welcomed into the club of nations – expressed as much as anything else through the global institutions that govern everything from
inter-bank connections to air travel – to be able to function.

The trafficking: from A to B

The individual farmers producing opium poppy, or coca, or ephe-
dra, are rarely operating at the scale at which they can process their
crop, let alone traffic it around the world. Instead, they are typically
at the mercy of the gangs operating at the next stage of the business, who buy up the crop and assemble economically viable stocks
either to process themselves or sell on. Sometimes, this is little more
than extortion at Kalashnikov-point, but again the wilier criminals
understand that the carrot may be more effective than the stick. In
Afghanistan, for example, it is not necessarily the case that opium
is the most lucrative crop to grow, but with a guaranteed market
and quick turnover, it gives the farmers the best chance to get the
credit they need to maintain or expand their enterprises. Indeed,
despite all kinds of efforts to create working micro-credit schemes
across the country to help wean farmers off opium, it is actually
the traffickers themselves who have cracked this and gladly use
part of their huge profits to invest in those who would grow more.
And there is still always that Kalashnikov to compel production, if
needs be.

So whether they are tribal warlords, insurgent armies or
organised crime groups, traffickers consolidate stocks of the crop.
Sometimes, they process them into more valuable and compact narcotics themselves. Most Afghan opium, for example, is processed
into heroin inside the country precisely to maximise profit, but also
ease onward export. Others sell on to other gangs able to perform
this next stage in the process. After all, processing is often a complex
operation, requiring not just space and skills, but also a variety of
precursor chemicals, most of which have legitimate uses, but which
are often also purchased on the black market because otherwise they
offer a way for the police to track narcotics manufacture.

Then it needs to be moved to market. Sometimes, the same gangs will handle that, too, like the Latin American gangs with their submarines. The Triads, for example, take fullest advantage of their powerful position in not just the Chinese but wider South-east Asian underworld, as well as their presence in Chinatowns around the globe, for just such integrated operations. Triads based in Hong Kong offer potential drug mules, typically twentysomethings with no criminal record, classic examples of the rising new middle class that is such a feature of international tourism, not just cash but free air fares and hotel accommodation in return, so they can combine trafficking with some sightseeing.[11] More often, though, what emerges is a supply chain of individual gangs and entrepreneurs handling their own portion of the world-spanning routes taking the drugs to market.

A market, not a gang

Consider, for example, the so-called 'Northern Route' moving opiates from Afghanistan to western Europe via Russia. From its high point when it handled perhaps a quarter of all the heroin reaching western Europe, it has been much attenuated since the 2022 invasion of Ukraine, which essentially broke the close working relations between Russian and Ukrainian gangs.[12] In its heyday, it was essentially a loosely braided array of individual routes. One such saw warlords in the northern Balkh province of Afghanistan gather opium, which was sold over the border into neighbouring Uzbekistan. High fences topped with barbed wire and overlooked by watchtowers mark the border, but barges ply the Amu Darya River between regional capital Termez and the Afghan port of Hairatan, and a surprisingly modest bribe is enough to smuggle the opium through. Of course, in many ways the bribe is a token thank-you, because this leg of the journey, and the subsequent processing of opium into heroin, took place at a factory just outside Termez owned, through proxies, by a senior figure in the local branch of the DXX, Uzbekistan's much (and rightly) feared secret police. No one was going to mess with his business. He paid the warlords sometimes in cash, but mainly in kind, sending them everything from ammunition to consumer electricals. From Termez the heroin would be flown on a military aircraft – no pesky customs checks for them – to Tashkent. Thence it would fly north to the Russian city of Yekaterinburg, east of the Urals. Why not Moscow or St Petersburg, or a destination closer to the main trafficking routes into western Europe? The answer is that a classmate of that DXX officer – back when they were training together in the Soviet KGB – ended up as a well-connected businessman for both upperworld and underworld economies there. It's good to deal with someone you know and trust, when it's a multimillion-dollar enterprise and you can hardly turn to the courts if something goes awry.

Much of that heroin ended up being sold across central Russia, bought up by the local gangs which serviced the depressingly buoyant local market. About a third, though, was sold on to a gang based in the western city of Tolyatti, 'Russia's Detroit', named for an Italian communist leader when a massive car plant was built there in cooperation with Fiat. The man from Yekaterinburg had for years held several car concessions, which had involved negotiating some complex protection rackets, and from that a fruitful cooperation with an offshoot of the city's once-notorious Neverovskaya organised crime group. Another former 'Neverovets' had since set up business in Lugansk, which between 2014 and the beginning of 2022 was the capital of the 'Lugansk People's Republic', a wholly unrecognised rebel pseudo-state under Moscow's umbrella, whose economy was essentially kept float by secret subsidies from the Kremlin and criminal activities of every kind, from coal smuggling and credit-card fraud to heroin trafficking. Until 2022, Ukraine's criminals were all too willing to cooperate with their Russian counterparts, even as their respective countries were at daggers drawn, so he and a partner based in Kyiv would together stump up the cash to buy the heroin, and most would then be sold on to Polish, Slovak and Romanian gangs, taken across the border by truck, and then distributed around the EU.[13]

The reason for this lengthy travelogue is to illustrate the extent to which international narcotics trafficking is not carried out by individual gangs or even networks, but a *market*. By planes, trains and automobiles, over more than 4,000 miles, the supply chain connected Afghan warlords who had likely never travelled more than 50 miles from their home province, corrupt political policemen, amoral entrepreneurs for whom business is business, whatever the commodity, outright gangsters and underworld facilitators. It involved swaps and payments, and what may seem perverse leaps of faith. The question is, how can this be organised?

The thoroughly modern narco

The Monstruo 2010 really belongs in a film franchise. It is one of the so-called 'narco tanks', a customised brute assembled in an underground workshop for the Los Zetas Mexican drug cartel. On the basis of a large Ford SUV chassis, it was plated in inch-thick steel, with its windows replaced by small bulletproof-glass ports. It had a turret and could carry 20 armed men, but in addition featured an array of gadgets that take it away from Mad Max and towards James Bond: a metal battering ram, below a front grille electrified with up to 700 volts; the capacity to spray an oil slick or drop nails behind it; even satellite communications gear able to intercept police radios. Admittedly, with all that extra weight, it could only trundle along at a flat-out maximum speed of 25–30mph, and it was seized by the authorities in 2011. It is thuggishly unsubtle (likely in part the point), which is perhaps why this kind of improvised vehicle has increasingly been phased out by less obvious 'narco tanks': SUVs and pick-up trucks with hidden armour and weapons, so as to balance firepower with a little more discretion.[14]

The rise and fall of the Monstruo-type vehicle was used by a veteran of the US Drug Enforcement Administration as a metaphor to explain to me how highly sophisticated organisations can emerge from large numbers of usually highly unsophisticated people. 'At first, you got the natural macho impulse to go big and bad, bang on one more gun, make the armour thicker, until you end up with something that looks mean as hell, but no one can for a minute mistake for anything else,' he said. This kind of 'narco tank' may be of value in the rolling turf wars between cartels, but it's also obvious to the authorities, who have an incentive and the means to take them off the streets (they seized over a hundred). 'So, the macho guys have to start listening to the smart guys, who talk about cost-effectiveness, and low profiles. Having seen their tanks taken or broken down on a dirt track, this time they listen.'

His point, ultimately, was that drugs gangs – whether opium-trafficking warlords in Afghanistan, cocaine cartels in Latin America, or Chinese fentanyl dealers – follow a trajectory that moves, often in a few years, from bandit to businessman. Initially, they need to be able to threaten and use violence to corner markets, fight off state and rivals alike, and enforce their rules and deals. However, even the most powerful or vicious gangs cannot reliably and sustainably project their muscle internationally: they need instead to find partners, whether as sellers, buyers or middlemen. Increasingly, just like states, these organised crime gangs come to appreciate the relationship between profit and power. At first, muscle allows them to start making money, but over time, it will be the ability not just to make money, but to raise and manage it effectively, that will be crucial to their survival: it costs money to hire and arm gunmen; bribe politicians, judges and the police; engage the best lawyers and accountants. Just as the state that can tax and administer most efficiently can invest more in its security, so too the drug gang. Maybe that means bringing more and more of those 'smart guys' into the inner circle, but it also means restructuring the organisation and its operations alike, often as if it were just another corporation.

Like upperworld corporations, they face the dilemmas of whether to specialise or diversify (many are now 'polydrug gangs', one-stop shops for all your narcotic needs) and whether to integrate horizontally or vertically (merging with or taking over other, comparable gangs or instead moving up or down the supply chain, to capture more of the profits made along the way). The huge sums of money involved need to be managed properly and carefully, not just laundered, but reinvested. Originally, profits over and above those needed to maintain the operation and satisfy its principals' desires for property, bling and firepower would typically end up in 'non-productive sectors, such as real estate and the entertainment industry (gambling, brothels and similar businesses)', often with the aim of either making a quick profit through speculative purchases or laundering the money.[15] However, there are only so many sportscars and slot-machine arcades one can buy, and after a certain point the drug dealers (or at least their money managers) start to think more seriously and strategically. Thus, drug dealers from Marseilles invested heavily in two apartment complexes in Dubai, and an Indian pseudoephedrine smuggler put money into the film industry.[16]

Those profits also need to be maximised, if needs be by managing the market. In 2009, for example, British and US forces in Afghanistan launched a campaign against the opium production that was helping bankroll insurgents. Despite real success, it had almost no impact on global prices for heroin because it emerged that the gangs had stockpiled 10,000 tonnes of opiate, most in neighbouring countries, in order to prevent previous years' over-production from flooding the market and driving down the price. Fortuitously for them, that meant they had enough in hand to supply the world's heroin addicts for the next two years, by which time the traffickers had worked out how to work their way round (or challenge) this campaign.[17] All this demands not just foresight but also cooperation with rival gangs, even the creation of cartels or monopolies.

The real point is not about drugs themselves. They are currently the dominant product in the global illicit market, but where they go, other commodities have followed. Trade and travel across borders doubled between the mid-1980s and 1990s, and despite the temporary dip caused by Covid-19, the trend has largely continued. There are some 65 million shipping containers sitting in ports or making their way around the globe onboard ships or loaded onto truck flatbeds, more than an order of magnitude beyond the capacity of customs to search. Although all containers are 'screened', at least in most developed countries, this is largely little more than a check of the paperwork. Only 3.7 per cent of containers coming off ships in the USA are X-rayed or manually checked, depending on the place, the level of backlog and the source (an American Customs and Border Protection officer once told me that a container coming from Colombia whose manifest says it contains coffee will almost always get X-rayed, because so many traffickers believe the urban myth that it masks the smell of drugs from sniffer dogs' noses), and just 1.5 per cent reaching the EU.[18] As societies, we have made decisions about priorities: how much money do we want to spend on our customs agencies (as little as we think we can afford) and how much cost and delay do we want to impose on our trade (again, as little as possible). The corollary is that we are implicitly accepting that we will do only so much to control the arteries of international trade and travel that make the modern world what it is, and on which the upperworld economies also rely. That, furthermore, is for an inert criminal commodity: just think how hard it is to throttle an illegal trade that can travel on its own two feet.

CHAPTER 12

PEOPLE AS CUSTOMERS AND COMMODITIES

'Hey, this is kind of like Uber. Like this is a rideshare thing. I'm just going to go and pick somebody úp.' It was an appealing rationalisation for the Arizona Christian University students who had taken to earning $1,000 a time to pick up illegal migrants from border towns and make the night drive to drop them off in the state capital, Phoenix.[1] They were typically recruited on the Snapchat messaging app and were usually football players, and over time a micro-criminal organisation had emerged, with assignments being distributed by one of the team, relying on the fact that in practice, drivers in such small-scale cases were very rarely actually charged.

As with the narcotics trade, the trafficking of people – whether eager prospective migrants, like the customers of this 'rideshare thing', or victims being forced into lives of virtual slavery – is at once organised and disorganised, complex global economies shaped by sophisticated networks, yet often carried out by miscellaneous collections of individuals who may have little real sense of the role they play in the whole. It also raises difficult ethical questions which again speak to the degree to which organised crime provides a service to those who reject the illegalisation of their activities. After all, while it is hard not to consider the trade in people among the most pernicious of all, one must draw a distinction between the human traffickers who are essentially dealing in slaves and the migrant smugglers who are offering people the chance to make a new life for themselves away from poverty, war or oppression.

Either way – and it can often be hard to tell these two phenomena apart – this is a world on the move. According to the United Nations World Tourism Organization, in 1950, there were 25.2 million legal international arrivals (so one person making three trips would count as three); by 1980 this had increased more than ten-fold, to 278.1 million. Another thirty years, and in 2010 it reached 950.8 million, and by 2018, before Covid, it had reached 1.4 billion: more than 55 times the 1950 figure.[2] Among these travellers were drug mules and fugitives, illegal migrants and criminal emissaries, but what can we do? Cheaper, faster and ever more reliable travel has contributed not just to the increasing sophistication and globalisation of economies but also increasingly mobile populations, not just tourists and traders, but those coming to work, settle and raise families. Between 1970 and 2017, the number of international migrants trebled from 82 million to around 244 million, comprising 3 per cent of the world's population. Many were legal, but many were not. It is, after all, a relatively recent phenomenon that states seek routinely to control who come to live in their lands. The Page Act of 1875 was the first federal immigration law in the United States. Even so, it only prohibited the entry of 'undesirable' immigrants, which to Representative Horace F. Page meant 'cheap Chinese labour and immoral Chinese women'. (The 1903 Immigration Act specifically excluded anarchists, beggars, epileptics, and the importers of prostitutes, the latter clause raising the question of whether this was an act of immigration control or protectionism.) France only began controlling immigration in 1932. Emigration was sometimes even more restricted, by states unwilling to lose members of their workforce. Japan had been trying to limit outflows since 1639, for example.

The slave trade

What this has meant, though, is that what was once legal – either voluntary migration or, reprehensibly, slavery – has now become controlled, but neither practice has stopped, simply been handed to the criminals. Humans are still a commodity. They may be child soldiers, coerced into fighting for some warlord such as Joseph Kony, the former Catholic altar boy whose murderously mystical Lord's Resistance Army has terrorised northern Uganda, South Sudan, the Central African Republic and the Democratic Republic of the Congo since the late 1980s. They may be starry-eyed would-be migrants looking for a new life. They may be sex workers trafficked into service or indentured workers who find themselves without documents, rights or salaries, picking cockles off sandbanks, cleaning houses or building sports stadia, for a pittance at best, the day's food at worst.

Slavery was central to almost every ancient society. The very first primitive hunter-gatherer societies typically had little use for them, as they were just more mouths to feed, but as society became sedentary, as agriculture became of growing importance, and towns and cities sprouted, then a cheap labour force which could dig canals, plough fields, build homes and monuments, and serve their masters became not only possible, but necessary. Slavery has waxed and waned in its scale and importance since, but never really gone away, nor done so quickly: the last country in the world to abolish it was Mauritania, as recently as 1981 (and even now, there are those who claim the institution is criminalised more in principle than in practice).

But even if slavery is now illegal across the globe, there are more enslaved people than at any time in history: up to an estimated 50 million.[3] These are so-called 'modern slaves', whose status is (generally) enforced not by the law, but by violence and artifice. Still, that is perhaps one in 150–200 of the global population, above all engaged in physical or household labour or subject to forced marriage. However, this tragic statistic only covers part of the wider issue of the treatment of people as property, as a commodity and a resource. For all that upperworld society has notionally turned against slavery, it has proven unable or unwilling to enforce this commitment. To put it bluntly, we still buy cheap consumer goods that may have been put together by child labourers in Bangladesh or prison-camp inmates in China, whose only 'crime' was to be of the wrong ethnicity, faith or political opinion. We still employ 'illegals' to pick our crops, work in our restaurants, and sweat on our building sites, without granting them the rights of citizens, and we still went in record-breaking numbers to the 2022 FIFA World Cup in Qatar, despite hundreds or maybe thousands of migrant labourers on coercive contracts having died in building the facilities.[4]

A history of exploitation

This is one of the key distinctions between 'modern' and 'old-fashioned' slave societies. Today, behind a façade of labour contracts, au pairs, cleaning agencies and gangmastering, forced and coerced labour out of sight remains out of mind. In the past it was much more obvious. In much of West Africa, even before the Atlantic slave trade, they represented often around a third of the population, largely fellow Africans; in the Roman Empire, it was between a fifth and a third, varying by era and location; possibly three-quarters of the population of the Tatar Khanate of Crimea in the sixteenth century was slave, mainly captured from Muscovy to be worked, traded or ransomed. While slavery was open and legal, there was little room for organised *crime*, so much as organised raiding and trading. There were some exceptions. The notorious third-century Roman bandit chieftain Bulla Felix would detain waylaid artisans with a skill useful to his group, forcing them into temporary service before letting them go.[5] The story is that he sent them on their way with a parting gift, too, although that does sound more like the kind of humanising touch folklore subsequently adds to ennoble those who manage to thumb their nose at the mighty. Nonetheless, it does emphasise not only the scale and discipline of this group (which was said to number 600 desperados) but also the extent to which in its own way it operated as an active economic community rather than just some parasitic and predatory army. If anything, gangs would more often run sidelines making money by returning runaway slaves, drawing on their networks of informants and smuggling connections. The Sumerian Code of Ur-Nammu from around 2100 BCE sets the reward for returning a runaway slave (two shekels, which is, incidentally, the same fine for knocking out another man's tooth), while in the Ottoman Empire, a professional slave-hunter known as a *yavaci* would either track them down himself, or act as a broker. Anyone seizing a runaway would then exchange them for a so-called 'good news' fee from the *yavaci*, who would in turn recoup that and a fee of his own from the slave's owner.

Later, other mechanisms would be developed to try and extract the cheap, often unskilled labour societies needed, from serfdom (arguably little more than land slavery) and *corvée* labour taxes to Stalin's Gulags and the analogous Chinese Laogai work camps and prison farms. In part, this reflected a growing ethical discomfort with the institution, in part a pragmatic reflection of the way that slave labour is not always the most cost-effective. Of course, this process took place at different speeds in different places. Slavery had never been formally legalised in England, but it took until 1807 for the international slave trade to be outlawed, and even when the Slavery Abolition Act was passed in 1833, it excluded India, even as the Royal Navy's West Africa Squadron had begun hunting slavers on the high seas. Later, the 1863 Emancipation Proclamation represented the culmination of a piecemeal process in the United

States which had been taking place for almost a century. Since as late as 1850, the Fugitive Slave Act, the notorious 'Bloodhound Bill', required that escaped slaves had to be returned to their owners, even if they made it to states which had banned the practice, all part of a messy and mutually unsatisfying compromise between the North and the South.

Nonetheless, by then the pendulum had swung decisively, and where once those who would free slaves were the criminals, increasingly it was the slavers. Slavery has adapted to its new criminal status, though, with 'modern slavery' being defined as the exploitation of people through deception, threat, violence, coercion, or the abuse of power. The forms, from forced prostitution to child labour, may be those of the ancient world, but increasingly, this has become the business of contemporary organised crime, because there is still a depressingly buoyant market for cheap and disposable labour, sexual victims and wives who can be bought, without the tiresome need to woo them (22 million of the estimated 50 million 'modern slaves' are accounted for through forced marriage).

Are there really now more slaves, even though it is illegal? Comparison is difficult. There may be, as mentioned, 50 million in the world today, one in four of them children, but this is another crude estimate. However, we have even less of a reliable sense of how many there were in the past. What data we have tends to focus on the transatlantic trade which, however horrific and massive, represented only a fraction of the global tally. What of the African slaves owned by Africans, of the Asian slaves held by Asians, of, indeed, the European slaves held in Muslim states? Between 1800 and 1875, for example, an estimated 1.35 million slaves were imported from the Caucasus and Crimea to the Ottoman Empire, while yet more were bought or captured from Africa.[6] Furthermore, today's notion of 'modern slavery' is much more capacious, and embraces all kinds of practices that were depressingly common in the past, from wife-selling to serfdom. Meanwhile, the world's total population has grown dramatically. In 1800, when the transatlantic slave trade was still on the rise, the estimated global count was a billion souls, which has swollen to some 8 billion today. On that basis, even though only 0.4 per cent of all trafficking victims are ever identified,[7] the proportion of the world's population which can be considered in bondage has surely diminished, at least.[8]

Modern slavery

Nonetheless, it still continues, and it is big business, generating an estimated $150 billion in profits annually even back in 2014, according to the International Labour Organization,[9] more that the total GDP of Hungary then. Despite the widespread assumptions that it is primarily connected with the sex industry, 'only' an estimated 6.3 million people are in that terrible situation at any point in time, more than 75 per cent of them girls or women. It is really devoted to providing cheap labour of every kind. According to the International Labour Organization and the Institute of Migration, there are some 27.6 million people in forced labour, more than 3.3 million of whom are children, and 11.8 million women and girls. Of the forced labourers, more than half are to be found in Asia and the Pacific (15.1 million), followed by the slightly odd pairing of Europe and Central Asia (4.1 million), Africa (3.8 million), the Americas (3.6 million), and the Arab States (0.9 million).[10]

Of course, many never cross a state border. Again, there is an easy assumption that slavery, especially of the 'modern' kind, is a transnational phenomenon, but of the total 50 million, probably just under half are trafficked internationally. The rest (and this is especially true for forced marriages and child labour) tend to remain within their home countries. Some 37 per cent of the victims of trafficking within the EU are actually citizens of EU member states, for example.[11] These may be street kids who have been forced into criminal work, women forced into abusive marriages by their families, or vulnerable adults who have been 'cuckooed', forced into allowing their homes to be used as a base for drug dealing. Further afield, the market is often for cheap labour that can be treated almost as disposable. In an age when people rightly expect decent pay, proper benefits and reasonable amounts of time off, when health and safety laws preclude sending child labourers into unstable mines to breathe in cobalt-laden dust (as happens in the Democratic Republic of Congo[12]) or forcing prisoners to labour in chemicals works without proper protection against mercury vapours (as happens to Uighurs who fall foul of the Chinese state[13]), then there is an incentive to use coerced labour.

Where people are trafficked internationally, that is especially where the organised gangs enter the process. Some victims have been duped, but many are fearful and recalcitrant: they need to be controlled, coerced or coached. Whether tightly knit groups or loose networks, or small outfits running a single brothel or other enterprise, the criminals need to be able to manage their victims, to get them across borders and supervise them during stops to change means of transportation or simply take a break. This will again often mean engaging the services of other criminals: corrupt border officials, specialists able to get false documentation, underground doss houses where victims can be stored, possibly under someone else's guard, while preparations are made for the next leg of the journey. Just as with drugs, the trafficking of people is often less about specific organised crime gangs – although there are certainly those which manage the whole process, from recruitment to exploitation – as much as an organised criminal economy.

The underworld travel agents

On the other hand, there are also the people smugglers, service pro-viders who, for a fee, help willing migrants illegally enter another country. A quick hop over the US–Mexican border may entail paying a so-called 'coyote' $4,000; conversely, a 'snakehead', as Chinese migrant facilitators are known, could charge anything from less than a thousand pounds to almost £40,000 to be smuggled all the way from China to the UK.[14] Of course, people traffickers and migrant smugglers overlap, with some naive migrants who thought they had paid their full fees to move countries finding themselves faced with new demands for money and, undocumented and vulnerable, forced into indentured work to pay off these spurious new 'fees'. They are, after all, unlikely to turn to the police, not least as many will come from countries where a man in uniform is to be feared and avoided. What is striking, though, is how far this particular organised criminal sector structures itself precisely as a service industry.

The majority may be cynically exploiting the desperation of their customers to make it to a new home, peddling false narratives of the easy lives and job opportunities awaiting them, while operating on the cheap. Tales of migrants suffocating inside sealed refrigerated lorries or drowning when shoddy or over-packed boats sink in rough seas are depressingly common. Nevertheless, others will offer guarantees, testimonies, and go so far as to advertise their services. 'We have trips by rubber boat almost on a daily basis, on a boat . . . going to Farmakos, Mytilini, and Chios; price USD 900,' offered one smuggler selling transfers from Turkey to Greece, even offering insurance.[15] 'With the beginning of the new season we have a range of journeys on offer. Turkey Libya Italy, $3,800. Algeria Libya Italy, $2,500. Sudan Libya Italy, $2,500 . . . The boats are all wood . . . If you have questions, contact me on Viber or WhatsApp,' went another post, on Facebook.[16] Some offer a two-for-one warranty, a free second attempt into the destination country if the would-be migrant is intercepted and deported the first try. Of course, many lie, or sub-contract actual crossings to less scrupulous gangs such as those packing migrants into small boats crossing the English

Channel that are deliberately overloaded, counting on the French or British authorities to rescue them if and when their vessel overturns. Others, by contrast, will not only try and do right by their clients, they even offer other services, from helping secure fraudulent student visas to assisting them transfer their assets abroad. These are likely to be those recruiting from specific locations or communities where there is much competition, and so they depend on word-of-mouth and personal recommendations from satisfied customers to attract new business. It is usually where the criminals have established some kind of monopoly and can defy market forces – as may be the case these days in Egypt and Libya – that conditions tend to be most abusive.

Yet this is a business which is largely organised through specialist gangs, not something that has been taken over by the big organised crime players. Even the transnational Triad organised crime networks, which are often assumed to play a key role in the smuggling of Chinese migrants, largely leave it to individual criminal entrepreneurs or loose business networks.[17] They seem to believe there are too many dangers (not least from the potentially wagging tongues of all those clients) and too much specialist knowledge required, so it is not worth getting involved. Besides, it depends on careful image management, hard to reconcile with drug trafficking and the like, as these snakeheads generally prize themselves on their reputations. The most famous – or notorious – of them all, Cheng Chui Ping, or Sister Ping, was feted in her home city of Fuzhou as the woman who helped thousands of her countrymen flee poverty. When she was arrested in Hong Kong in 2000 and extradited to the USA, there were those from her birth village who offered to do jail time on her behalf. Many of her clients, after all, returned wealthy by Chinese standards of the time, or sent back money that made all the difference to their communities. As Chinese-American journalist Justin Yu wrote at her trial, 'In China, a human life isn't worth 10 pennies. Ten thousand people come and 100 people die? Bad luck. If they make it, their families get rich. Their villages get rich.'[18] She had reportedly made more than $40 million in her 20-year criminal career, employed heavies from the Fuk Ching Chinese-American gang not just to guard her charges but also make sure they paid their fees in full, and was responsible for the deaths of ten people who drowned when the smuggling ship *Golden Venture* ran aground off New York.[19] Nonetheless, she was still a legend thanks to her perceived success rate and professionalism: the only complaint of one client, who paid $18,000 for a flight to Guatemala on a tourist visa, a walk into Mexico, a night crossing of the US border in a cargo van and then a flight to Newark, New Jersey, to work in a relative's restaurant, were the 'insects biting us in the jungles while we were walking to Mexico. But I was a country boy, and I was used to this,' and besides, as it was Sister Ping's operation, 'the services were quite good. We got plenty of food and water on the way.'[20]

Of course, China is a very different country these days, and the appetite for long, expensive and illegal migration ventures to work in marginal economic activity is distinctly reduced. One US immigration officer once joked to me that it wouldn't be too long before impoverished Americans from the Rust Belt were trying to get themselves smuggled into China. This is a market that bends to economic trends and the disparities of rich versus poor countries, but can also quickly respond to emerging opportunities. Thus, forces from climate change (which is expected to cause serious hardship for 143 million people in the Global South by 2050[21]) to wars (part of the reason for Europe's welcoming approach to Ukrainian migrants after Russia's 2022 invasion was precisely to avoid creating an illegal market) all shape the changing geography of migrant smuggling.

Whatever the origins and destination, the actual movement of the migrants is again typically not handled by a single gang, except when very short-range, but rather in a chain, with the original agent in many ways acting as an underworld travel agent, arranging for the migrant to be passed from one local and specialised gang to the next. For example, a would-be migrant from land-locked Niger in West Africa may start by being transported on the back of a pick-up truck through Afrod, an informal trade network run by ethnic Tuareg transport entrepreneurs that runs across the Sahel regions they inhabit all the way to Libya or Algeria.[22] If they make it across the Sahara – and not all will – then if they are lucky, another gang will get them on a ship to Italy, but now that Rome is cutting deals with local governments to crack down on this route, it may instead be Greece or Turkey. They may not necessarily be met on arrival, but instead have instructions on how to walk or even take public transport to a meeting point (perhaps a place outside town marked by something like a plastic bag hanging from a tree), where the next group of smugglers will take over, perhaps arranging them to be secreted inside a truck heading deeper into Europe (with or without the driver's knowledge), or dispensing prepared documents to allow them to make their own way. For every exotic case, like the individuals sewed into car seats or somehow squeezed behind a van's dashboard, there are thousands of eager or desperate migrants themselves willing to sneak across a border, throw away their identity documents (so as to reduce the chance of deportation back to their home countries), silently huddle in the back of a truck or gamely jump into a wobbly rubber boat without a life vest, all because that is what they were told to do by the criminals to whom they paid thousands. They want that dream, and they see those who offer to provide it as not exploiters, but service providers. Again, criminals meeting market demands gain a certain legitimacy, and this applies as much to those holding out the promise of a life free from war or hunger as those, say, offering what at least looks like the latest must-have luxury.

CHAPTER 13

KNOCK-OFF MAGNATES AND COUNTERFEIT CONSUMERISM

A British customs officer seconded to an African country as part of a joint operation recounted a conversation he had in a hot and noisy bar, while playing the role of a potential buyer. He was negotiating over a consignment of fake designer clothes, produced in South Korea and Thailand, and then smuggled through Africa. Suddenly, though, the shady 'import-export facilitator' he was talking to made a throw-away comment that changed everything. 'I am offering you a good price, very good, because I am liquidating my stock. Clothes are easy enough, but I am moving into a serious market, very serious: drugs. No, no!' he hurriedly added when he saw the officer's reaction, 'not those drugs! Medicines. Very nice, very profitable.'

Very profitable, yes – very nice, certainly not. Counterfeit pharmaceuticals, from antimalarials to antibiotics, make up anything from 30–60 per cent of the total African market. If your 'Rolex' turns out to be a cheap mechanism in a gaudy shell, you may be embarrassed, out of pocket, and late for an appointment, but nothing worse. But your medicine? The World Health Organization estimates that at least 100,000 people die in Africa every year because of counterfeit pharmaceuticals, and millions more suffer unnecessary pain or complications.[1] When people are desperate, they will buy what they can afford and hope for the best. This is, of course, the most serious and potentially deadly end of the counterfeit business, though. The modern world's relentless juggernaut of fashion, its globalised supply chains, its sweatshops and factories, have generated a massive industry worth an astonishing $650 billion in counterfeit goods of every kind according to the World Customs Organization.[2] (That's almost equivalent to the total annual GDP of Switzerland.)

Counterfeit culture

This is nothing entirely new, of course. In ancient Rome, the senator Seneca the Elder reported the presence of workshops forging Greek jewellery, textiles and glass because that was regarded as more desirable.[3] The irony is that the quality of the workmanship was likely comparable to the original – but it was the alleged provenance that elevated the value. In another example, as Marco Beretta has argued, glass imitation gems could often be highly prized and valued, not necessarily because the buyer was fooled, but because of the artistry behind the illusion.[4] Nonetheless, the real expansion in the scale and value of the market for fake cultural artefacts, especially historical ones, is another product of modernity. In Europe and North America, it coincided with the industrial revolution, and the rise of a new monied class looking for ways to demonstrate their taste and education, and to connect themselves to an aristocracy that had long been able to enjoy the plunder of empires. This was also an era of greater travel, especially the custom of the Grand Tour, a rite of passage for upper-class young European men (and a few adventurous women), who would spend months or even years making their way through Europe. The aim was to expose them to the cultural glories of classical antiquity and the Renaissance. A cynic might wonder if they were as likely simply to return with a new set of prejudices and sexually transmitted infections but, coinciding as it did with a boom in archaeological excavation, it certainly contributed to the popularisation of private collections of art and antiquities.

As a new middle class also began to rise, and the railway made travel cheaper and easier, this custom also became more widespread, and, as ever, demand begat an illicit market. Italian chancers would sell marble offcuts as fragments of Michelangelo works, and in nineteenth-century Mexico, individual artisans began producing supposed Aztec and Mayan figurines that were often wholly fantastical, relying on the fact that even experts at the time had little idea what the real ones would have looked like. The craftsman had free rein to create whatever he thought he could flog to the ignorant tourist or archaeologist alike.[5] The rise of a Chinese middle class in the twenty-first century has likewise encouraged tourism and with it a growing market for bogus finds and trinkets geared for them – in the words of an Italian police officer involved in cultural crimes, 'Nothing too big, nothing too obvious, but the irony is, we're seeing fake Roman pottery shards and [Renaissance] jewellery being made in Chinese factories for Italians to sell to Chinese tourists.'

Above all, though, the industry of cultural crime, just like common counterfeit of consumer items, has been totally reshaped by the industrial revolution and globalisation. The result is an everyday trade in counterfeit commodities and pirated intellectual property: the fake designer trainers, the replica Cartier watch, the illegally downloaded blockbuster film. It is the very processes behind the rise of consumerism as a whole that fuel these crimes. Every advert telling the potential customer that here, *here*, is a product that will bring them health and joy, make their lives easier and their days brighter, is also fuelling a sense of desperation and entitlement that leads people eagerly to buy under the counter. At the same time, the architecture of new kinds of business has emerged: quick, cheap industrial production, easy global distribution, frictionless e-commerce, virtual payments, the capacity to flout intellectual property laws by working out of foreign jurisdictions. Again, the law and its enforcers are playing catch-up with social pressures, and although they are not always losing on every front, their capacity to control a market that is driven by eager consumers is stretched to the very limit.

Counterfeit couture

There has been, one could say, a true democratisation of the market for counterfeit, and today 5–10 per cent of all global trade in consumer goods is fake, from pirated films and software to knock-off handbags. Indeed, while the Organisation for Economic Co-operation and Development believes it represents 2.5 per cent of all global trade,[6] Europol estimates the total flow of counterfeit and pirated goods coming into the EU alone as being worth up to €119 billion, representing almost 6 per cent of total imports.[7] After all, people want what they want, and in the modern world they too often come to consider it as their right. What if they would rather not – or can't – pay the asking price? They might balk at being sold something obviously stolen, but who can resist a bargain? What is the harm in that?

Of course, there are harms, but once again, out of sight is depressingly often out of mind. The child-labour sweatshops in Istanbul's Küçükpazar neighbourhood, where Syrian, Pakistani, Iraqi and Turkmen children, many of them refugees, cut and sew counterfeit clothing in the shadow of the historic Süleymaniye Mosque, are a long way from the market stalls where the products are sold.[8] The loss of government revenue may well eat into the funds available for social care or national defence, but who notices that when they buy notionally 'duty free' – counterfeit and untaxed – cigarettes at a car boot sale?

'Branding' is not new, but in the bygone age of the handmade and the bespoke, it was that much harder to be able to get away with counterfeit, and the profit margin between something that was special and something that *looked* special was that much narrower. Today, the difference in production cost between a designer T-shirt sold for an extravagant amount and that of a pretty decent replica mass-produced in a similar factory may be negligible, with the difference accounted for by advertising, endorsements and an enthusiastic willingness to charge whatever a gullible market can bear. An earnest entreaty by US customs warning that 'each time you buy a counterfeit good, a legitimate company loses revenue',[9] is accurate to a degree, even though it is unlikely that many people willing to pay even £400–600 for a high-end 'superfake' Chanel Coco Charms Flap Bag would necessarily have bought the legitimate one for over £4,000. However, given that few people will likely be moved by the plight of the poor, exploited designer houses such as Chanel (net income in 2021, $4 billion) or Gucci ($11 billion), this has largely fallen on deaf ears.

Most counterfeit is still made in China, largely unhindered by the police that so assiduously crack down on people wearing pyjamas in public (in 2019, officials in the eastern city of Suzhou deemed this 'uncivilised'[10]) and those celebrating Christmas (in 2021, this was characterised as 'Western spiritual opium' and a 'Festival of Shame'[11]). Other main sources include Turkey, Singapore, Malaysia and, indeed, the USA, but in practice counterfeit goods are produced wherever circumstances permit, and trafficked around the world in every conceivable way, from container-loads of knock-off trainers to individual items dispatched through the post. A mass market, a hunger for brand names, industrial-scale production and global supply chains have come together to create a market that is almost impossible to police. Indeed, even a quick web search will throw up sites openly presenting themselves as retailers in counterfeit branded items.

Furthermore, the evolving patterns of supply and demand also highlight changes in economic distribution and consumerism. China, the world's greatest source of counterfeit, is increasingly also a consumer, as people can afford more – yet aspire to even more than that. This has even become something of a knock-off culture, known as *shanzhai*.[12] Literally meaning 'mountain fortress', evoking the mythical medieval bandit-heroes of the *Water Margin*, it has revolutionary overtones somewhat at odds with a reality of counterfeit designer goods and mobile phones. Nonetheless, in the words of a philosophy professor at Zhongshan University in Guangzhou. '*Shanzhai* culture is a rebellion against the monopoly sectors' that 'shows the desire by poor people for a better life and fashionable things'.[13]

Digital duplication

Shanzhai has spread beyond the physical into everything from culture – in the wholly unofficial *Harry Potter and the Porcelain Doll* (2002), the pseudo-Harry takes on the strangely renamed Yandomort – to software. After all, copying the intangible is even more productive, and provides a lucrative stream of income for underworld businesses of every kind. Those heavy-handed (and much derided) warnings on DVDs and the like, stating that intellectual property piracy funds terrorism, may look over-the-top, but they are true. Again, despite efforts by government and industry bodies (such as the charmingly anachronistically named International Federation of the Phonographic Industry) to convince us otherwise, there is a widespread assumption that copying music or pirating software is an essentially victimless crime, or else only harm fat-cat corporations and high-rolling musicians who otherwise would be squandering the money on cocaine, fast women and faster cars.

The result? Almost a quarter of global internet bandwidth is being taken up by the illegal downloading of copyrighted materials, more than a third of all music consumers still pirate music, and a similar proportion of software installed on machines around the world is unlicensed. There is a vicious circle at work. These practices cost the relevant industries money; the film industry loses anything up to $97 billion annually to digital piracy, for example, and television almost as much. Instead of taking this out of their payments to big-ticket actors, their special-effects budgets or their shareholder dividends, they tend to push the cost onto their consumers. They, in turn, look at the cost of a cinema ticket, a download, a subscription or a DVD (or indeed a book: the rise of the e-book has created its own huge new market in illegally downloaded works) and decide that the corporations are nothing but shameless profiteers. They feel justified in their piracy, and so it goes. In an admittedly small-scale survey in the UK in 2018, 53 per cent of respondents who consumed pirated content accepted that it was wrong – but did it anyway.[14] In 2024, an international YouGov survey found 27 per cent admitting to using pirated content, with 62 per cent of them citing the price as their excuse.[15]

If anything, the situation is even more egregious with pirated software, despite the potential problems with being unable to update it, possibly suffering glitches, and being infected with malware ('malicious software'). According to data from BSA, the Software Alliance, 37 per cent of all software worldwide is unlicensed, and not just that used by private citizens.[16] Certainly back in the 1990s, most Russian police stations' computers – when they had any – seemed in my experience to be running cracked, unlicensed copies of Windows. This 37 per cent figure masks a considerable global variation, though. In the majority of countries, including China and Russia but especially the poorest, the figure is over 50 per cent, whereas in most of western Europe and North America, it is substantially lower. However, it also raises a wider question of equity. Again, piracy jacks up the costs to legitimate users, mostly in the wealthier countries. Quite how one interprets this is one of those philosophical or political Rorschach inkblot questions. Is this an unfair burden on the honest, or an example of progressive taxation, making those who can best afford it, pay for those who cannot? (Of course, it also makes it that much harder for the less wealthy to afford to be legitimate users.)

The bare essentials

Even more complex moral questions arise in some of the other sectors with serious counterfeit problems, such as medicines and foodstuff. An explosion in 'American sweet shops' in the UK in recent years, some of which have turned out to be selling cheap, locally sourced supermarket chocolate bars slid into imported brand wrappers (and, indeed, evading tax on a massive scale), has highlighted the relatively trivial end of food and drink counterfeiting. This is more properly substitution, and along with adulteration – the addition of some alternative and typically cheaper substance – is usually harmless. In 2022, a Spanish company was accused of the largest wine fraud in history, worth €14 million a year, by passing off some 40 million bottles of cheap table wine as fine vintages simply by swapping the labels. Reportedly, for example, they sold more than 22 million bottles labelled as coming from the Denomination of Origin Terra Alta – which is 5 million more than the whole region produces.[17] (As of writing, the case is still in court.) Nonetheless, what is perhaps telling was that so many could be sold with so few drinkers apparently being any the wiser. This is key to so many food scams: we are often less discriminating than we might assume. This kind of fraud is typically perpetrated by companies, large and small. In 2013 and 2014, for instance, Taiwan was rocked by a series of scandals in which companies were found to have been adulterating their cooking oil with everything from cheaper cottonseed oil to the illegal colouring agent copper chlorophyllin.

Sometimes, though, these scams have rather more serious implications, leading to illness or worse, which is one reason why Interpol and Europol have a permanent joint project, Operation OPSON, combating the issue. In 2011, more than a hundred people died in West Bengal from drinking locally made booze that had been mixed with something to sweeten it and give it more of a kick – that some-thing turned out to be methanol, the main ingredient of antifreeze. Chinese factories have been caught adding carcinogenic industrial salt and other toxic additives to soy sauces and seasonings packaged to be sold under famous and reputable brand names, while others have sold packets of 'grain' and 'rice' actually made out of potato starch mixed with synthetic resin. Much of this has been sold to African markets, and the presumption is that this is both because there are consumers desperate for cheap buys but also because local consumer protection and customs authorities may be less rigorous or more corruptible. Nonetheless, in December 2016, Nigerian customs seized more than a hundred 50kg bags of 'Best Tomato Rice' that was actually just plastic beads. They were being smuggled into the country just as the price of this staple was rocketing ahead of the Christmas and New Year holidays. As a Nigerian official noted, 'Only God knows what would have happened if people consumed it.'[18]

Counterfeiting can certainly kill. Cars with substandard counter-feit parts crash or burn, machinery with counterfeit bearings, drives, pumps and valves stalls or explodes, and what about aircraft? Ever since 1989, when a DC-10 crashed in Chicago after an engine fell off the wing because the substandard, knock-off bolts securing it had rattled loose, the aerospace industry has realised there is a problem. Most countries and airlines have stepped up their controls intended to prevent the knowing or accidental use of substandard counterfeit parts, but when a South African Airways flight in 2019 was forced to make an emergency landing, allegations were made (since denied by SAA) that this was because of the use of fake components.

Even setting aside the counterfeit medicines, adulterated foods and knock-off spares, it would be a mistake, however easy, simply to see all this as a response to exploitative consumerism. It may seem that it really doesn't matter if someone buys a $10 fake Rolex (which may be a perfectly functional watch) and not a $6,000-plus original (and sometimes it's very plus: half a million dollars for a GMT-Master II Ice?). They probably would not have bought an original, and in any case, how concerned ought we to be for a company that registered $13 billion in revenue in 2021? Yet it does matter. The products are generally made in factories, which in turn have to avoid being closed by the authorities. At best, this fuels corruption, which tends to metastasise: if an official takes a bribe to turn a blind eye to a workshop making fake designer goods today, they are more likely to do the same for a meth lab tomorrow. Otherwise, production, warehousing and even trafficking happen in the uncontrolled spaces of the world, raising money for local strongmen, bandit chieftains, insurgents and pariahs. Thus, weapons were smuggled through the ethnic Russian breakaway Moldovan region of Transnistria in the 2000s, counterfeit cigarettes were made in the self-declared 'People's Republics' of the Donbas in Ukraine in the period 2014–22, and North Korea peddles fake Viagra.

This is a trade which works best globally and at scale, goods produced in places where costs are low and the authorities amenable, and shipped to where demand is strong and prices high. This globalisation has in so many ways made the modern underworld. It also creates a vicious circle: the scale of counterfeit being shipped around the world both overtaxes the capabilities of those customs officers and other men and women intended to keep the trade lanes clean, and also encourages the emergence of loopholes and the corruption of the control agencies. This, in turn, creates under-controlled routes that can then be misused for even more nefarious purposes. After all, as we will examine next, the criminals have seized all the opportunities of global trade and traffic with gusto and greed, whatever the cost, even to the world itself.

CHAPTER 14
SELLING THE EARTH

In 2019, the MV *Manukai* was approaching the port of Shanghai when its Automatic Identification System and GPS tracking data suddenly started to glitch, flickering offline, then locating the ship miles away. There didn't seem anything wrong with the hardware and, along the Huangpu River, other ships' transponders also seemed to be malfunctioning. It turned out that unregistered ships had cloned their identities to try and sneak past undetected with clandestine loads. What was worth such high-tech deception, something that had already led to one serious accident? Sand. China's runaway building boom had led to severe shortages of fine sand, of the sort that can be dredged from the bottom of a river like the Huangpu – and the mighty Yangtze, into which it flows. Innocent-seeming ships would lower pipes to the riverbed at night to suck up thousands of tonnes of what Chinese builders have come to call 'soft gold'. With a full hold worth over $85,000, although the police keep catching such sand-thieves, the business has been lucrative enough that gangs using electronic warfare continue to ply their trade.[1] Nor is this business confined to China. Construction globally uses more than 40 billion tonnes of sand and gravel every year, and its extraction is a $70 billion industry.[2] Its illegal side is visible everywhere, especially in India, where struggles within and against the 'sand mafias' have cost hundreds of lives. Beaches are disappearing, river and marine ecosystems being disrupted, even coastal currents are being redirected. But the sand must flow.

These markets increasingly extend to any resources for which there is an under-policed supply and a suitably lucrative demand, natural resources plundered by organised criminal enterprises at terrible cost to local economies and the global environment. Siberian forests are cut down illegally, again to fuel China's construction boom. 'Blood diamonds' and other conflict minerals fund insurgencies and civil wars. Endangered species are wiped out for high-status food or folk medicine, or as trophies to adorn a hunter's wall. Such are the profits to be made, that often this is done at scale, heavily armed, and with extensive corruption to ease the way.

Illegalising ecocide

Humanity has long pillaged the Earth with little thought of the consequences. The deep forests of the Mediterranean basin were cut down by the Romans for fuel and materials to build everything from homes to warships, just as the Chaco Anasazi of what is now Arizona and New Mexico essentially deforested themselves to death, their civilisation collapsing around 1200 as a result of self-inflicted ecological disaster. In a particularly grandiose example of man's need to reshape the environment, the need for agrarian production – and a large tax base – has meant that over the millennia, China's geography has been remodelled in the name of farming, in effect destroying whole ecologies. As Robert Marks put it, 'The overriding trend over the past 4,000 years is of the simplification of natural ecosystems into a particular kind of Chinese agro-ecosystem.'[3] Mining and smelting have throughout history fouled waters and airs alike with toxic contaminants. Animals have been driven to extinction through hunting or the destruction of their natural habitats: 42,100 species of plants, animals and fungi are on the International Union for Conservation of Nature's Red List of Threatened Species, 28 per cent of all the ones of which we are aware.[4]

Once again, what has changed is that we are now more likely to ban especially destructive and wasteful practices. This is fine as far as it goes, but it has created lucrative illegal markets on both global and regional levels. It is the usual dilemma: by banning, taxing and restricting, we can and do make a difference in combating practices we regard as dangerous, destructive or simply despicable, but inevitably this creates opportunities for some to make money exploiting or flouting these controls. A particular downside is that the people doing this are often organised criminals, warlords and insurgents, whose profits can be reinvested into even more socially dangerous activities. These are the kind of thorny moral and political dilemmas with which we must wrestle in today's complex world: ban and make a bit of a difference, but in the process empower and encourage organised crime.

And these dilemmas are global. Environmental crimes are by definition almost always transnational, in their effects if not their commission. An illegally felled tree ends up in a factory and then as a floorboard on the other side of the world and is part of the process of deforestation that is contributing up to one-fifth of the greenhouse gas build-up that, in turn, is driving global climate change. A shark illegally fished in what are meant to be protected waters of the Galápagos Marine Reserve off Ecuador ends up as shark fin soup in Hong Kong, but also means that there is one fewer apex predator to eat the smaller predators, who therefore consume more of the smaller fish that, in turn, eat the algae that grows on coral reefs – which, in turn, begins to kill off the coral. A ruby illegally exported from Myanmar helps fund its army, the Tatmadaw (which could be considered the country's primary organised crime gang), and generates capital then reinvested into producing methamphetamine that then ends up on the streets of Sydney or Seoul.

Besides, the World Bank has estimated that illegal logging, fishing and wildlife trade alone – only a small part of the total range of ecological crimes – cost source countries, typically lower-income ones, $7–12 billion each year in lost potential revenues. This undermines their stability and efforts to develop themselves, and places a greater aid burden on the rest of the world.[5] By contributing directly and indirectly – through poverty, crop failure and impoverished states – to conflict and despair, it also fuels other criminal activities, such as people smuggling and trafficking. Everything connects.

Blood diamonds and conflict minerals

The workshop in Europol's shiny headquarters in December 2018 had been both wide-ranging and pretty downbeat, as a collection of scholars, police officers and prosecutors chewed over the vicissitudes of what was being called 'Eurasian organised crime'. The day was over, though, and the conversation over drinks meandered between the professional and the day-to-day, sometimes zigzagging unexpectedly from the one to the other. Talk had moved on to cars, and one magistrate's decision to buy an electric one. One of the cops, an Italian who had served as a liaison officer at an embassy in Africa, shook his head: 'It's not just that one of them needs something like six times as many rare minerals as a regular car, it's that if you're lucky, it's the Chinese who provide them.' And if you're unlucky, I unwisely asked? 'It's the warlords.'

Individuals can strike it lucky and find a seam of gold here or an emerald mine there, but properly exploiting diamonds and rare earths takes investment capital, international contacts and economies of scale. The product is in demand and hard to track, making it perfect for a succession of corrupt governments, rebel movements and warlords to exploit. During the early stages of the Angolan Civil War (1975–2002), perhaps a fifth of the country's diamond exports were illicit, almost all funding the UNITA rebel movement's operations. This led to the UN-sponsored Kimberley Process in 2003, a certification scheme for rough (uncut) diamonds meant to prevent their being sold by criminal actors and in contravention of sanctions. It was a step forward, but there have since been repeated criticisms of the scheme as having too many loopholes and being too easy to bypass.

Since 2012, for example, the Central African Republic has been wracked by a confused and bloody civil war, and the various insurgent forces have turned to gold and diamonds to fund their operations. At peak, this accounted for more than 80 per cent of its diamond exports. Likewise, Zimbabwe has been under a range of US and European sanctions since 2003 because of its corruption and human rights record, which also affected its diamond industry. In 2008, the Zimbabwean military took over the Marange diamond fields, using forced and child labour to extract gemstones from the region. The Marange fields were sanctioned, but between 2008–10, diamond exports from Guinea in West Africa mysteriously ballooned to something like three times the country's reported production capacity. It turned out that hundreds of thousands of carats of diamonds were being smuggled by the Zimbabweans to Guinea for 'laundering' and export. That loophole may have been closed, but leaked documents from Zimbabwe's notorious Central Intelligence Organisation showed that dictator Robert Mugabe's 2013 election victory was won not only through violence and intimidation, but also a war chest of more than $1 billion from illegal diamond exports.[6] In fairness, the Kimberley Process has made a real difference: so-called 'blood diamonds' from conflict zones are still making their way onto international markets, but nowhere near as many, and nowhere near as easily and cheaply.

However, even as diamonds are being brought under control, many other 'conflict minerals' are still widely exported, from gold and jade to the '3Ts': tin, tantalum and tungsten. Again, gold and the 3Ts have been mined in the Central African Republic and the Democratic Republic of Congo and exported by insurgents, ending up in electronic components in everything from microwave ovens to mobile phones. Just as most opium poppies are grown by small-holders who are then forced to sell to local strongmen who collect industrial-scale loads by extorting from a whole district, so too many of these minerals are mined by small-scale 'artisanal' crews who tend not to be working land they own and as such have no legal title to what they collect with shovel and pick, leaving them vulnerable to the warlords.

Again, efforts are being made, not least by major Western electronics manufacturers, to ensure their supply chains do not stretch into war zones, as much for the reputational as the legal risks. Apple, for example, regularly removes smelters and refiners from its supply chain precisely for this reason. However, China's growing grip on the world's rare earths and other crucial minerals is not only a geopolitical concern for the West, it is also undermining what efforts are being made to address the use of forced labour. Chinese companies, for example, source cobalt from 'artisanal' mines in the Congo, in which an estimated 40,000 children labour in deeply exploitative conditions, and as of writing are negotiating with the Taliban in Afghanistan for access to that country's rare earths.[7]

There is even conflict oil. When Islamic State was at its peak from 2014–17 and dominated swathes of Iraq and Syria, it supplemented its trade in drugs and antiquities with petrochemicals from fields and refineries under its control. However, the real illicit business has been in West Africa. Since oil was discovered in the Niger Delta in 1956, what could have been a boon for Nigeria became in many ways a curse, fostering corruption and massive oil theft by everyone from the insurgent Movement for the Emancipation of the Niger Delta (MEND) to members of the government. What became known as bunkering – stealing oil from storage facilities and pipelines – accounted for, at peak, an estimated loss equivalent to 470,000 barrels per day of crude oil, worth $700 million every month. Little attempt was even made to hide this trade. In 2022, for example, a 3-million-tonne capacity supertanker reportedly sneaked into Nigerian territorial waters. According to the Nigerian Navy, it was detected, intercepted by one of their patrol boats while trying to dock at a facility to take on stolen oil; but according to the Nigerian opposition, it had already accomplished that task. Either way, it then sailed all the way to Equatorial Guinea before it was stopped. This specific case never went to court: some say this was oil theft, others little more than extortion by the Nigerian Navy. Nonetheless, it says something that it is considered plausible that a ship that is a third of a kilometre long, with an average speed of 6.2 knots (just over 7 miles per hour), could have managed to evade the Nigerian Navy – one of the most powerful in Africa – for long enough to fill up on illegal oil and was only later detained by the navy of Equatorial Guinea, a hundred miles away.

It may not be a conflict resource, but wood is another commodity with an illegal market that is both globally trafficked and globally destructive. Deforestation can result from indirect market pressures. Indonesia's rainforests are being encroached upon by the demand for palm oil, for example, while the market for beef and thus clearance to create cattle ranching land has eaten into Amazonia. However, this is accelerated by criminal markets. Illegal logging is an industry whose value has been estimated at potentially more than $150 billion a year, which would make it equivalent to human trafficking by value.[8] Reportedly, some 90 per cent of the logging that is shrinking the rainforests of Amazonia at a terrifying rate is illegal (although the former Jair Bolsonaro government was reportedly considering an imaginatively cynical way to meet its official target of cutting illegal logging, by simply legalising *all* logging).[9] Likewise, China's housing boom contributed to a rapid increase in illegal felling of the forest of the Russian Far East.

The toxic economy

Illegal logging has savage environmental impacts, destroying species' habitats and thus local biodiversity, accelerating soil erosion and desertification, as well as coastal flooding. In West Africa, for example, deforestation has changed weather patterns, doubling the risk of flash floods for the fast-growing cities along the coast.[10] These are only by-products of crimes committed without thought of their ecological consequences, though. The growing regulation of polluting and dangerous materials and practices has created its own illicit markets.

As we began to realise the danger in depletion of the ozone layer, countries looked to phase out gases which depleted it such as the CFCs (chlorofluorocarbons) found in all kinds of cooling systems, from refrigerators to car air conditioning. The 1987 Montreal Protocol on Substances that Deplete the Ozone Layer banned them worldwide, in what former UN Secretary General Kofi Annan called 'perhaps the single most successful international agreement'.[11] It was indeed effective, preventing the equivalent of perhaps 10 gigatons of carbon dioxide (CO_2) per year from reaching the atmosphere, equal to around a quarter of global annual emissions.[12] However, there were many less-scrupulous companies and individuals who did not want to spend money on replacing or upgrading their systems, and a black market in CFCs was born. A very lucrative one, too: in the 1990s, a 30-pound cylinder of CFC-12, a conveniently inert and odourless gas, could be bought in China for around $40 and fetch up to $600 on the US black market. As one smuggler involved in the environmental contraband trade exulted, 'This is better than drug smuggling.'[13] In the 1990s, CFCs worth half a billion dollars were traded illegally each year, and while their use has since dwindled in richer countries, they are still widely employed in poorer ones, where there is a lively trade in these destructive gases.

Those not willing to go to these lengths might instead have reluctantly decided to replace their old, CFC-reliant refrigeration systems with new ones. What to do with the scrap? Most of it was disposed of responsibly, but all too much ended up added to the toxic and environmentally damaging waste dumped at sea or in lower-income countries by companies that were nothing more than organised crime fronts. This has long been a problem. Back in the 1980s, the cost of properly disposing of a tonne of hazardous waste in the US was at least $250, while having it shipped to Africa and dumped there cost generally no more than $40.[14] Since then, the increasing burden of regulation on safe handling and disposal has pushed up the legitimate price, while doing little to the illegitimate one. In 1992, for example, the Bangladeshi government bought more than 3,000 tonnes of fertiliser from the United States, which was then distributed to farmers around the country. Many had already started spreading it on their fields before it was discovered that it actually contained industrial waste: the dust from copper smelting, rich in lead and carcinogenic cadmium. Eventually, the sellers were convicted by a US grand jury, but the $1 million fine they were forced to pay was less than they had saved by not disposing of a thousand tonnes of waste legally and responsibly.[15] By the 2020s, the gap had only grown, making this filthy business all the more lucrative, where the dangers are minimal compared with the profits.

Since then, a growing new dimension to the problem has been e-waste, all those discarded, dated or damaged devices generated by the multiplication of the electronic gadgets we use and the galloping pace of upgrades and new capabilities. They can be refurbished, resold or their materials salvaged for recycling, but this is often not commercially viable, and so this is the fastest-growing source of global waste, accounting for almost 62 million tonnes in 2022. Although China accounts for most overall, per capita it is the high-income, developed nations of the West that generate most e-waste. What is done with it? A growing amount is shipped to landfill sites in low-income nations. There it is meant to be sorted and either resold or recycled, or disposed of carefully and safely. Wouldn't that be nice? Much, to be sure, is picked over for reclamation, even if often by desperately underpaid workers who expose themselves to frequently dangerous levels of toxic substances used in these gadgets, from the mercury in batteries to the cadmium in printer toner dust. Yet much is simply dumped at land or sea, the cocktail of compounds and minerals leeching into the waters, dispersing in the air and polluting the land. Crime pays, and pollutes.

Living gold

The Russian TV series *Zapovedny Spetsnaz* (2021–3) roughly translates as 'Nature Reserve Special Forces'. The protagonist is a former Russian commando turned wilderness warden, tackling – with the aid of a female shaman able to call on the spirits of nature – heavily armed poachers, gangsters and exploitative businesspeople intent on plundering the natural assets of Lake Baikal. This may sound pretty fanciful, but it is based, however loosely, on the real experiences of the rangers who since the 1990s have had to take on a whole array of environmental pirates. There was the so-called 'caviar mafia', for example, which first challenged law enforcement head on with gun and bomb for control of this lucrative business, then relied on bribery.[16] More recently, a particular problem has been the hunters after the dwindling stocks of Amur leopards and Siberian tigers. The latter is a splendid beast, the largest of the surviving species of tiger, and a formidable predator – except when picked off by poachers armed with military sniper rifles, telescopic sights and night-vision goggles.

The bones, penises and other body parts of a dead tiger are, after all, worth anything from $4,500–9,000 once smuggled across the border into China, for use in traditional medicine.[17] Border guards can be bribed to turn a blind eye, whole carcasses hidden amid consignments of mutton, bones ground into powder and carried out packed in talcum tins.

Interpol has estimated that the underworld's trade in wild animals – albeit often just their meat or their parts – is the third largest illegal business in the world. Ivory is still prized, and an elephant is poached for its tusks about every 15–30 minutes. Rhinoceros horn is used in Vietnam to banish hangovers and fevers (regardless of the absence of scientific evidence to support this) and in Yemen for the handle of the curved *jambiya* dagger presented to boys when they reach the age of 12; on average, three African rhinos are killed for their horns every day.[18] African pangolins are being exported illegally to China for both their meat and their scales, used in traditional medicine to promote the circulation of the blood and lactation in pregnant women (needless to say, again with no scientific basis). Then there is simply the yen for exotic pets, the more endangered the better.

Overall, though, it is the combination of ancient custom and modern methods which is most harmful to the world's biodiversity. Although it adds no flavour to the broth, shark fin soup has been a Chinese tradition for 600 years, because the difficulty in catching the predator and its power and ferocity made it a fittingly rare ingredient for the imperial table and thus fashionable within the elite.[19] As a result, even though nearly 60 per cent of the world's species of shark are endangered, some 70 million of them are fished out of the water every year just for their fins. These are hacked off on the deck of the ship, and the shark is thrown back into the water to die a slow and painful death as it sinks to the bottom. 'Finning' has been banned by many countries, but given that a kilo of shark fin is worth up to $600 in the Asian market, the incentives are clear. Although the trade is arguably morally bankrupt, it is not always carried out illegally. Perhaps a third is done clandestinely in waters meant to be closed to the practice, though, and fins are smuggled into jurisdictions which have banned the trade, including a number of US states. Taiwan banned the removal of sharks' fins at sea in 2012, but China has done no more than take shark fin dishes off the menu for official government functions.

Everywhere and nowhere

All this said, it is easy to be excessively downbeat. In the 1970s, international trade bans did much to address the poaching of elephants and rhinos, and the 1975 Convention on International Trade in Endangered Species (CITES), while not a perfect answer, did place the question of wildlife crime squarely on the global agenda. This has also put pressure on governments whose instincts have often not been especially eco-friendly to change their policies, such as in Beijing's decision to close its domestic ivory market in 2017. Likewise, the degree to which other ecological crimes, from waste dumping to conflict minerals, not only pose wider risks but also encourage corruption, violence and exploitation is more clearly recognised now. We may not have all the answers, to be sure, but arguably we are asking the right questions.

The scholar Rosaleen Duffy has provocatively suggested that the pendulum may actually have swung too far, with an excessive securitisation of the problem.[20] NGOs looking for ways to win the attention of governments, security industries eager to 'greenwash' themselves, and political establishments prone to view everything through the prism of the day – which for Washington meant until recently international terrorism – all contributed to seeing these problems as demanding a militarised response. In fairness, there is a place for these kinds of measures, and on a purely emotional level it is hard not to feel satisfaction when South African 'bite dogs' take down a poacher, or when gun-toting Italian Guardie di Finanza (Financial Police) swoop on another Mafia clan's illicit waste dump. As the 'Global War on Drugs' should have shown us, though, there certainly is a limit to how far surveillance drones, well-armed rangers and draconian legal penalties can prevent environmental crimes, so long as there is still an economic rationale for these criminal businesses. Indeed, tighter controls can actually generate scarcity for goods and services, which drives up the value in the underworld marketplace.

Addressing this dimension of the issue is harder. The problem is that these are crimes which are at once obvious and unseen, everyone's and no one's. A softwood plank from an illegal logging operation looks just the same as one from a carefully managed forest; a gold ingot is a gold ingot; and once that broken fridge or ancient mobile phone is out of one's house, who gives a second thought where it goes? So long as a waste disposal firm looks legitimate, if it is offering a good price, why should a business not engage it, trusting that it won't simply offload a thousand tonnes of scrap into the ocean? Who is going to wonder if that ring's emerald centrepiece was mined by virtual slave workers controlled by Colombian paramilitaries? At the same time, just like a butterfly flapping its wings and setting off a tornado in Texas – or so the classic chaos theory meme goes – the impacts are either so diffuse as to be global or so distant as to be easy to ignore. Not so much out of sight, out of mind, this time, as so ubiquitous to be invisible. This is, after all, the practical stuff of our daily lives, from household rubbish to a bedside table, as to be equally unnoticeable. What about, though, items at the other end of the scale, the rare and the irreplaceable?

CHAPTER 15

OLD MASTERS FOR SALE AND SECURITY

In 2002, a Dutchman called Octave Durham, a self-described 'born burglar' known as 'the Monkey' for his uncanny climbing abilities, broke into the Van Gogh Museum in Amsterdam. Three minutes and forty seconds later, he and an accomplice were out, having stolen two works: *Congregation Leaving the Reformed Church in Nuenen* and *View of the Sea at Scheveningen*. The pictures were worth tens of millions each, but ended up being sold for €350,000 (£320,000) to a member of the Neapolitan Camorra organised crime syndicate. In 2016, they were recovered by Italian police when they raided the mobster's home in the seaside town of Castellammare di Stabia. They had been wrapped in cloth and stuffed in a hidden wall space by the kitchen: it seemed they probably had been hidden pretty much as soon as the mobster had bought them. So why bother with them?

As investments, as security. What price beauty? Or, rather, what price exclusivity? A beautiful painting is a beautiful painting, but the signature of a famous painter and a (genuine or carefully forged) provenance elevate its value beyond the merely aesthetic. In fairness, art has never been for art's sake. When the Buddhist Mahāsāṃghika sect began carving an extraordinary and intricate series of shrines in the Karla Caves from the second century BCE, they did so not only to create a place of beauty, but also to attract travellers and demonstrate their skill and status, just as the Medici and other Renaissance princes commissioned art to show off their wealth, cultural standing and confidence. Of course, while cave complexes cannot be stolen, anything portable, from Roman busts and Leonardo da Vinci sketches to Vietnamese temple statuary and Warhol prints, can – and they can also be forged.

In the modern age, one might think that art crime would hardly be worthwhile. As Noah Charney has noted, 'There have been almost no known, real-life art thieves who steal art in order to admire it.'[1] (Although in fairness, he does recognise one exception, when in 1907 Pablo Picasso and an accomplice stole a pair of ancient Iberian statue heads from the Louvre Museum, which he then kept in his sock drawer.) It is a business, and, after all, what is the real value of a stolen masterpiece, given that it will be in Interpol's Stolen Works of Art Database? Or a forgery, considering all the new technical means of detecting a fake? Yet this remains a massive and lucrative illegal market: some $6 billion is the current estimate.[2] In other words, stolen and forged artworks clearly do have sufficient value to some.

From faith to forgery

Many of the earliest forgeries were religious: it was their supposed spiritual power that made them valuable. In ancient Egypt, crocodile mummies were powerful votive offerings, especially to the crocodile god Sobek, a means of averting their attacks and petitioning for fertility. So, of course, a sideline in fake crocodile mummies emerged: an analysis of relics carried out by the University of Manchester found fully a third to be fake, crocodile-shaped but stuffed with mud, sticks, feathers, eggshells and sand.[3] Likewise, medieval Europe was so densely strewn with alleged saints' bones and other holy relics that Protestant theologian John Calvin, in his *Traitté des reliques* (1543), scathingly noted that 'if we were to collect all these pieces of the true cross exhibited in various parts, they would form a whole ship's cargo', in all more 'than three hundred men could carry!'[4] Likewise, judging by the proliferation of sacred bones and other portions held in reliquaries around the continent, 'every apostle had more than four bodies, and each saint at least two or three'.[5]

Originally, this was because there was power – both spiritual and secular – in such relics. In an age when it was not easy to move goods halfway across the globe and away from people who might know from personal experience if an artwork was real or not, better to stick to items which were difficult to identify (one wooden sliver looks much like another, whether from the Cross or the log pile) or else supposedly possessed of a numinous authority that the potential buyer cannot or does not want to question. Churches that were offered saintly relics *wanted* them to be genuine, after all. This gave them spiritual authority. Likewise, although forged land grants were the usual way whereby conmen tried to lay claim to territories in Spanish-conquered areas of South America, fake diadems and other symbols of traditional rule were also used to overawe locals into obedience.[6]

In all these cases, the forgers and dealers in fake artefacts were as often as not working in the same communities as the buyers, possibly even in cahoots with them. They had a common interest in portraying bogus as bona fide. Even today, museums and collectors will often waive necessary checks and display what seem in hindsight obvious forgeries, so eager are they to assemble an impressive collection. The Museum of the Bible in Washington DC had for years made much of 16 shreds of leather that it claimed were fragments of the Dead Sea Scrolls, the oldest copies of the Old Testament, discovered by a shepherd in the Qumran Caves back in 1947. In 2020, though, it had to acknowledge that they were all forgeries, something that ought not to have been that hard to divine, considering that instead of leather they ought to have been written on parchment and that examination under a microscope showed that the ink had, while still wet, bled into cracks that would only have opened over time.[7] Nonetheless, while there is no suggestion the museum was deliberately deceptive, the most charitable explanation is that delight at being able to display such historical artefacts overruled the necessary caution.

Largely, though, the draw of the numinous has since given way to the appeal of the novelty. The thriving trade in forged relics in colonial Latin America, for example, has ranged from supposed Aztec black pottery (widely produced in nineteenth-century Mexico) to the stunning 'pre-Columbian crystal skulls' that inevitably also launched myriad excited theories about ancient spacemen and New Age magic. These were, in fact, triumphs of nineteenth-century multinational forgery, made of Brazilian quartz, carved by Germans, and sold by a French entrepreneur.[8] As travel became more accessible to more people, this generated a mass market in stolen and forged artefacts and artworks of lesser value and exclusivity, but the modern era has instead seen a pivot to different kinds of cultural crime.

Old masters for sale

Technology is making life so much harder for the classic art forgers. Consider that stalwart of the movies, the forged painting. Advanced optics, particularly stereo microscopes, can show how paint was layered on a canvas, to see if a signature was added later, and assess whether the craquelure, the delicate filigree of cracks that appear in older paintings over time, fits the right time frame and even pattern, based on the materials used and the conditions of storage. A forger may have used a canvas of the right age, but X-rays and infrared reflectography will reveal if there was originally another painting below it, or the right preliminary sketching. As for the pigments, mass spectrometry can identify exactly whether they conform to what would have been available at the time.

Much the same is true of the other potential treasures to be forged. Does the ink of the scrawl on that first edition or signed baseball have the right profile under chromatography? The US Secret Service has its own International Ink Library with more than 11,400 specific ink 'fingerprints'. How about a replica sculpture? The notion of artificially ageing work to make it seem antique has been known for centuries. In 1496, right at the start of his career, an impoverished Michelangelo carved *Sleeping Eros* in the Roman style and – depending on whom you believe – either he or the art dealer Baldassare del Milanese had the idea to bury it in a vineyard in order to age it in the acidic soils. It was duly sold as an antiquity to Cardinal Raffaele Riario, who eventually saw through the con, but was sufficiently impressed to commission two statues from Michelangelo, helping him launch his career. Modern techniques and technologies would have made this distinctly trickier, from forensic interrogation of provenances to chemical tests. For more than 40 years, New York's Metropolitan Museum of Modern Art had prided itself on its rare 'Etruscan warrior statues' until it was discovered that their black glaze contained manganese, which Etruscans did not use: they had been cobbled together by the Riccardi family in Italy, and then artfully shattered and reassembled, all in the name of verisimilitude.[9]

Of course, the most talented forgers can get away with their scams for a long time, even today. Sometimes, this is because even when the buyer realises what has happened, he or she wants to avoid the embarrassment of a public admission. Géza von Habsburg, by courtesy Archduke of Austria and Prince of Hungary and Bohemia, is one of the world's leading experts on Fabergé eggs, the exquisite and extravagant jewelled baubles crafted in St Petersburg before the 1917 revolutions. Perhaps 69 were ever made, of which at least 12 have been lost or apparently destroyed which, given that they are worth millions, creates intriguing opportunities for the skilled and subtle criminal. By his account, 'ninety-nine per cent of what is sent to me to authenticate are forgeries', but in one case, an 'unnamed gentleman' from the Middle East dropped $60 million on a Fabergé collection that proved to be entirely bogus. Whoever he was, he opted to take no action, and keep his embarrassment to himself.[10]

Of course, sometimes proving forgery can be not just humiliating but difficult. For more than 30 years, Wolfgang Beltracchi produced a steady stream of fake masterpieces that ended up in the hands of galleries, museums and collectors across the world, including one for which the actor Steve Martin paid $850,000. He was eventually unmasked in 2011, when the pigments in a supposed painting from 1914, *Red Picture with Horses*, by the modernist Heinrich Campendonk, turned out to include titanium white, which did not exist at the time. Ultimately, Beltracchi was convicted of forging 14 works of art, which sold for more than $20 million overall, but while another 33 are suspected of being his handiwork, this turned out to be impossible to prove, so skilled was his craft. Beltracchi was unapologetic: 'I didn't much like the art market or the dealers,' and so 'I really enjoyed doing it. You have to know how the art market functions and where the greediness is greatest.'[11]

The art of the steal

Beltracchi was caught, though, and although it is obviously impossible to know which master forgers may well still have gone unnoticed, in a day of complex checks of provenance, of scientific analysis and scholarly debate, there are far fewer opportunities for the forger. Hence why theft of the real thing still happens. Sometimes, indeed, theft and forgery go hand in hand. It was only when a bemused collector contacted the Contemporary Art Museum of Caracas in 2002, asking them if they still had Henri Matisse's *Odalisque in*

Red Trousers, which he had been offered, that they discovered that it had been stolen a couple of years earlier and replaced by a pretty indifferent replica.[12] Likewise, Xiao Yuan, chief librarian at the Guangzhou China Academy of Fine Arts, spent years stealing more than a hundred paintings from the gallery and replacing them with his own copies. When tried, he claimed that everyone else was doing the same – indeed, he had noticed that one of his *copies* had subsequently been stolen and replaced by an even less accurate replica.[13]

It seems that no more than 10 per cent of all stolen artworks are eventually returned, but even so, the market for stolen old masters is very limited.[14] There are suggestions that they might fetch on the black market perhaps one-tenth to one-twentieth of their legal value. This may not sound much, but the haul in 1990 from the Isabella Stewart Gardner Museum in Boston – the largest such theft in history – was 13 works of art including a Vermeer, two Rembrandts and a Manet, together worth $300 million. Even one-twentieth of that would be a cool $15 million, but only if suitable buyers could be found.

In 1983, more than 200 rare timepieces were stolen from the L.A. Mayer Institute for Islamic Art in Jerusalem, including one made by French-Swiss watchmaker Abraham-Louis Breguet for France's Queen Marie Antoinette, worth an estimated $30 million. Most of the clocks and watches have been recovered, including the 'Marie-Antoinette', but in almost directly inverse correlation with their value.[15] In other words, the more pricy the loot, the more identifiable. The real market in stolen art is not the big-ticket masterpieces that are immediately recognisable and the subject of major investigations. It is in the unremarkable-but-creditable works which may be stolen off the wall when a gang is plundering a wealthy home, the Meissen porcelain figurine, of which a thousand may be in circulation, the cuneiform tablet looted from a site in Iraq that never even got catalogued. These, after all, can easily enough end up in someone's private collection without great risk. Those stolen masterpieces of rather greater jeopardy may very occasionally end up in the hands of a connoisseur of elevated taste and rock-bottom morality to enjoy in secret, but these days they are more often just tradeable commodities.

Blood antiquities

Tomb raiding and the looting of archaeological sites have been cottage industries in many parts of the world for centuries. In Italy, the *tombaroli* who plunder the still-rich pickings of Etruscan and Roman remains are often born into families which have been digging and looting for generations. In western Turkey, 90 per cent of all known Iron Age sites have been ransacked, but even more impressive and depressing is that the majority of the tombs in Egypt's Valley of the Kings, dating back to between the sixteenth and eleventh centuries BCE, had been plundered within a century of their construction. However, this has become an industrial-scale process, one also facilitated by the rise of organised crime with international connections and insurgencies needing to arm themselves through global illicit markets.

In the late twelfth century, one of the Khmer Empire's greatest rulers, Jayavarman VII, founded a temple in north-western Cambodia. Banteay Chhmar – which roughly translates as Citadel of Cats – is a massive grey sandstone complex, its outer gallery and many of its walls carved with intricate bas-reliefs showing everything from battle scenes to daily life at the time. It is now a contender to be granted the status of being a UNESCO World Heritage site, but Cambodia's turbulent recent history has left its mark. In November 1998, a convoy of drab green army trucks rolled into Banteay Chhmar, carrying soldiers from a renegade army unit. Some began rounding up locals at gunpoint, others dragged pneumatic drills and masonry saws from their trucks. There followed two weeks of destructive looting, with villagers pressed into service as labourers while a 30-metre stretch of carved wall was broken down into dozens of sections. Some 500 statues were cut from their pedestals, or their heads carved off when this was impossible, and much of what couldn't be taken was simply destroyed. It turned out that the mercenaries had been engaged by an organised crime gang, and while some of the trucks taking the looted antiquities across the border into Thailand were fortunately intercepted by the police, most were not, the remains ending up being sold off around the world.[16] Then again, Cambodia's 1,200 or so temples had had a rough time of it, having already been looted by Khmer Rouge militants in the 1970s, by the Vietnamese troops who toppled their bloody regime in 1978–9, and now by gangsters.

The trade in looted but genuine antiquities from Africa, Asia, South America and the Middle East, now worth anything from $2–6 billion, was once often not considered criminal at all. Western colonists and explorers, travellers and administrators simply helped themselves to so much of what they found, filling museums and private collections across Europe and North America (the rise of the museum, as we understand it today, was really an eighteenth-century notion). Eventually, this was illegalised. First, relatively antiquities-rich nations, such as China, Greece, Italy and Egypt, outlawed the export of their cultural treasures, even if enforcement was often problematic. In due course, recipient countries also (sometimes reluctantly) joined the fight, with greater import controls. In 2017, for example, the American retail chain Hobby Lobby, whose president Steve Green is behind the aforementioned Museum of the Bible, was fined $3 million for being involved in the illegal import of thousands of ancient clay tablets potentially looted from Iraq. The case turned not so much on the tablets themselves, but on the fact that they were brought into the United States under customs labels

202 | Homo Criminalis

claiming they were ceramic slates or samples from Israel and the United Arab Emirates.[17]

So long as there is a demand, though, there will be a supply, and when more legitimate actors are squeezed out of the market by law, the underworld will step up. Sometimes, these are freelance actors, such as the *tombaroli*, and their Chinese counterparts, whose numbers were recently expanded by newcomers inspired by *Ghost Blows Out the Light* (2006), the bestselling online novel of its year, which kicked off a series of stories glorifying maverick grave robbers braving cursed ancient tombs (and making money out of the adventure). Sometimes, the culprits are organised crime groups, although in practice this seems quite unusual. Of late, though, the most prolific tomb robbers and plunderers of antiquities have been terrorists or insurgents, movements needing money and often with an ideological axe to grind.

The sixth-century Buddhas of Bamiyan were huge statues carved into the cliff-face in the Bamiyan Valley in central Afghanistan, and when fighters from the Taliban movement dynamited them into rubble in 2001, it was because they considered them blasphemous idols. However, the Taliban, and other Islamist militants, have not been averse to profiting from idolatry. Through the 1990s, museums were looted and archaeological sites bulldozed for artefacts that could be sold on the open market. Indeed, according to one account, Mohamed Atta, the Egyptian-born ringleader of the al-Qaeda cell behind the 9/11 terrorist attacks on the United States in 2001, had two years previously tried to sell looted Afghan antiquities to a professor at the University of Göttingen – and according to the BND, Germany's intelligence agency, let slip that he was hoping to buy an airplane.[18]

State collapse sadly tends to lead to looting. As the Iraqi state imploded in April 2003 in the face of Allied invasion, the Museum of Baghdad's priceless collection was subject to a 36-hour orgy of looting that saw 15,000 items taken, including more than 5,000 easy-to-carry and relatively easy-to-sell cylinder seals. However, such incidents are usually just temporary phenomena, exploiting the interregnum between the old order and the new. Civil wars, though – notably in Afghanistan, Iraq, Yemen and Syria – offer opportunities for extremist insurgent movements to strip museums, rob tombs and loot sites as an ongoing venture, without fear of the authorities or because they have become the de facto authorities. These conflicts have thus become the source of a flood of illegal antiquities. For groups that are barred from the legitimate banking sector, that have no concern for international norms, that often despise other communities and their cultural heritage, this is a crucial means to finance their operations.

In Syria, for example, while at its peak, the Islamic State of Iraq and Syria (ISIS) made much of its religious and cultural jihad against sites they deemed impious, from dynamiting the 1,900-year-old Temple of Baalshamin, one of the best-preserved ruins in Palmyra, to tweeting pictures of its men bulldozing the 1,500-year-old Monastery of St Elian. However, this destruction was also cover for systematic looting. Mosaics were dug up, tombs ransacked and shrines dismantled, all to be sold on the black market, netting the organisation tens of millions of dollars in its heyday. They even encouraged and then taxed freelance thieves, with one admitting that 'If you find an artefact, you take 80 per cent and ISIS takes 20 per cent,' with the militants' cut rising to 40–50 per cent if ISIS supplied the equipment used to unearth the loot.[19] The money went to paying ISIS fighters (who were often more mercenaries than convinced militants) and arm their war. Detailed financial records captured during a raid in Mosul in Iraq in 2014, for example, revealed a $2 billion operation, in which antiquities theft featured prominently. Simply plundering the al-Nabuk region west of the Syrian capital Damascus, including 8,000-year-old artefacts, had netted them $36 million, for example.[20]

This has become a wider pattern. An investigation by the Italian newspaper *La Stampa* in 2016, for example, revealed that the Calabrian 'Ndrangheta organised crime gangs were buying Kalashnikov rifles and rocket-propelled grenade launchers from underworld markets in Moldova and Ukraine, then trading them to Islamic State in Libya, in return for Greek and Roman antiquities looted there. These, in turn, were auctioned as legitimately acquired finds to collectors, especially from China, the Gulf States, Japan and Russia. The provenances provided for the relics may have been flimsy, but they were not so much drawn up to fool the buyers so much as to give them deniability if ever challenged. As for the Libyan archaeologists who were trying to protect their digs and who could blow the whistle on the deals, they were subject to death threats to silence or scare them off.[21]

The problem is not simply that where insurgents have territorial control of a region they can exploit its archaeological resources just as easily as its natural assets. It is that there is a market for their loot, and in particular the less immediately identifiable items. Statuettes, cylinder seals, pottery shards and tablets may not have the same cachet, but they are relatively portable and relatively anonymous – or at least it is harder to prove that they were looted. One British police officer who had worked with Interpol on trying to track stolen relics from Afghanistan admitted, 'Amateurs go for big-ticket artefacts that no one can really sell; the professionals go for the little things that don't need to go to a museum, and an unscrupulous buyer can plausibly say it was a lucky find in a market somewhere.' He added, though, that while the insurgents sell whatever they can, in his opinion a fair number never made it into the hands of collectors but instead were snapped up by the criminals who acted as their brokers. Why? 'It's an investment. Or rather, it's a different kind of currency.'

Commodifying culture

Where some swear by diamonds or Rolex watches, and others bearer bonds or a pocket full of diamonds, art can be used by criminals as portable currency or collateral. The Camorrista who had walled up his purchases from 'the Monkey' presumably considered them part of his pension plan or rainy-day fund, while the balaclava-masked Norwegian gunmen who stole Munch's *The Scream* and *Madonna* in 2004 may have been looking to finance a drug deal. Artworks can even be used as means of settling debts or moving money across borders that don't show up on bank statements. But this should hardly surprise us, in an age when fine wines and whiskies are recommended not for drinking but as investments to store in vaults. As one *carabiniere* from the Italian police's elite Command for the Protection of Cultural Heritage put it to me, 'This doesn't tell us that the criminals appreciate art – it is that even art, great art, has become a commodity. That everything these days is a commodity.'

This is just another example of the 'financialisation' of every aspect of modern society. This is, after all, also an age in which our private pensions are heavily invested in foreign currencies and equities, in which traders on futures markets buy still-unharvested crops and still-unmined minerals, and in which Russians in the 2000s took out mortgages denominated in dollars and euros to take advantage of lower interest rates abroad (and then regretted it when the ruble collapsed and the cost of repaying them went through the roof). Like it or not, we are all more intimately connected than ever with the global financial system, often without even realising it.

Criminality has become equally globalised, and terrorists and drug dealers are just as likely to require loans, be looking for investment capital, and need easy ways to move their funds across borders. As will be discussed in the next chapter, they have various options, from relying on dodgy upperworld financiers to informal transfer systems such as the brokers of the *hawala* network of the Middle East and South Asia. However, they also manage matters between themselves; many criminal organisations may at some point be embarrassingly (and dangerously) cash-rich and keen to turn that into investment and obligation by making a loan to some counterpart experiencing temporary cash-flow problems or looking to exploit some new opportunity. However, especially among people with traditionally poor impulse control and a propensity to turn to violence, mechanisms emerge to try and avoid the kind of disputes which can lead to conflict. Securing a loan with collateral is much safer for both parties, avoiding putting too much weight on a handshake and an implicit threat.

Besides, these artefacts offer a perfect way to move value almost invisibly. Often, a stolen (or even legal) artwork is safely and anonymously secured in a high-security vault in a bank or, better yet, a free port, a virtually extraterritorial tax-free and regulation-light special economic zone. Back in 2013, for example, the Geneva free port reportedly held perhaps 1.2 million artefacts and artworks (to say nothing of several tonnes of gold and 3 million bottles of vintage wine).[22] With a single piece of paper, ownership of the asset can be transferred, and until the new owner wants to sell, this need not even be disclosed. No annoying paper trail, no irksome publicity, no need for the trophy in question even to be moved. Most of the time, though, criminal transactions do leave paper trails – and you'll need a specialist to prevent them from being followed by the police right to your door.

CHAPTER 16

WHITE-COLLAR MOBSTERS AND THE GLOBAL ECONOMY

When I used to live in Brooklyn, from time to time I would take the rather dilapidated Q line, rattling along its elevated tracks to the heavily Russian-speaking Brighton Beach neighbourhood. There, my favourite place just to sit and take the air was a particular bench facing the sea. It was not just for the crash of the waves and screech of the seagulls, it was that this bench, in this singular neighbourhood – which always felt like a slice of a Soviet Union that never was – sat suitably far from any others, faced away from buildings from which a shotgun microphone or a lipreader with binoculars may have been ensconced, and enjoyed the constant white-noise background of the Atlantic. This made it an ideal spot when representatives of the Mafia's Colombo crime family and the ethnic Russian *Organizatsiya* wanted to sit down to thrash out the terms of a deal in 1982. Neither drugs nor contract killing were involved, but something far more prosaic, and far more lucrative: fuel excise tax scams. Through forged tax forms, relabelling consignments, and above all 'daisy chains' (feeding transactions through a series of fake 'burn' companies that soon disappeared without trace), Russian and Armenian gangs were pocketing from 40–50 cents per gallon. Pocket money? This was America, with its love of gas-guzzling cars: the total take was conservatively estimated at around a billion dollars a year (back when a billion meant something . . .).[1] No wonder the Colombos, and later the other Cosa Nostra families, wanted to get in on the action.[2]

Then the Russians – well schooled, after all, in how to dodge and weave round clumsy and sprawling bureaucracies – also taught them how to make a killing in Medicare and Medicaid fraud, which netted them another billion a year. Making the money was in some ways the easy part, though. As one Mafioso involved at the time lamented – on, he would later discover to his cost, a tapped phone line – 'We've so much dough that we don't know what to do with it. It's crazy! I'd never thought I'd be complaining about something like this! The trouble is that if I start spending even a buck in every hundred, even stashing it in the bank, it'd be just too obvious. And there's only so much cash I can fit in my house.'[3] They needed to up their game moving and laundering their money. And here, once again, the Russians could help. By the mid-1980s, they were already finding their feet in the realms of global illicit finance, something that would be crucial when the USSR collapsed at the end of 1991, and its fledgling capitalist banking system was open for (dodgy) business.

Making the world go round

Hiding the source of ill-gotten gains, or at least obscuring its origins enough that it is hard to prove in court that it is the profit of crime, is hardly anything new. Films notwithstanding, pirates never really buried their treasure (although the Scottish captain William Kidd, who managed to fall foul of both England and France, apparently did bury some of his loot before sailing into New York, hoping to use it as a bargaining chip with the authorities: he was hanged as a pirate, so we can safely say that didn't work out). Much of what they made was spent on resupply, maintaining their ships, and the appropriate hedonism when they made it back to a pirate haven. On the whole it may be true that, as Angus Konstam put it, 'From the pirates' perspective, if you couldn't eat it, drink it, smoke it or spend it, plunder was of absolutely no value to them.'[4] Nonetheless, pirates who struck it lucky could do very well for themselves from their shares in the loot.

The Indian Mughal emperor's ship *Ganij-i-Sawai* was aptly named, as it meant 'Exceeding Treasure'. When it was taken in 1695 by a small pirate flotilla led by Henry Every in his frigate *Fancy*, the loot included half a million gold and silver coins, jewels, silks, even a saddle encrusted with diamonds. Together, it was worth up to £600,000 at the time, equivalent to over £95 million today, enough for every member of the crew to retire if they wanted. Every himself wisely disappeared from view, the subject of what was in effect the first worldwide manhunt, with the East India Company – which was facing serious pressure from Emperor Aurangzeb – offering the then-unheard-of bounty of £1,000 on his head. So what could you do with your earnings, if you struck it that rich? For the lucky few, if they did not want to set themselves up as investors from the safety of Tortuga, Fort-Dauphin or another pirate haven, the answer was often to find a merchant, likely one they had dealt with in the past selling on their plunder, to help manufacture a backstory for themselves and an excuse for their wealth, admittedly at a price. A distant cousin who had made his fortune in the Indies, a prince from a distant land, the beneficiary of an unexpected inheritance, anything goes as long as it provides some cover for the suddenly arrived and wealthy newcomer. Even in ages before specific money-laundering laws, it was prudent for criminals not to make the source of their wealth too obvious.

Indeed, according to Sterling Seagrave, in ancient China, merchants who were engaged in banned forms of commercial trading – and eager also to pay as little tax as possible – found all kinds of ways to hide and launder their profits, converting it into portable (and in a pinch saleable) assets, moving their money from jurisdiction to jurisdiction through informal deals, swapping debts, and generally making their accounts as opaque as possible.[5] Likewise, medieval laws against usury – charging interest on loans – forced early bankers like the Lombards of Italy, and even the crusading orders of the Templars and Hospitallers, to find artful ways of disguising such activity. They would flip accounts from one currency to another to conceal any gains, or require lenders to accept the *contractum trinius*, three separate contracts that together in effect replicated the effects of an interest-bearing loan while side-stepping the letter of church law.[6] Although the actual term 'money laundering' is a product of 1920s America, as its courts and cops tried to stem the sudden tidal wave of cash generated by bootlegging during the Prohibition, and the practice has become much more common in this age of forensic accounting and expansive laws, the concept clearly is an historically familiar one.

Of course, the modern global financial system is a particular playground for criminals, but at the same time states have acquired vastly greater capabilities to track money back to its question-able source. The worlds of financial fraud and money laundering have become inextricably intertwined, and the province of every-one from individuals looking to evade taxes by doing jobs off the books in return for cash, through syndicates of financiers rigging the exchange markets, all the way to transnational organised crime. The Japanese Yakuza became deeply involved in domestic stocks and finance, but then spread away from their home shores to diver-sify their portfolios and minimise their risks, including buying up companies along Russia's eastern coastline. The Chinese 14K Triad has used front organisations to build a financial empire in Myanmar and Cambodia, whether dealing in real estate or mining cryptocur-rencies. Every modern organised criminal combine in one way or another is a transnational corporation. (And some would say that every transnational corporation is an organised criminal combine, but let's not go there.)

Flying the money away

This is in many ways an inevitable result of the need to both move and launder the proceeds of crimes, which are often, but not always, the same thing. As already discussed, sometimes this is simply done by transferring ownership of a high-value item whose provenance is unclear, such as an artwork. The trouble is that these days it is not so easy simply to conjure such items from nowhere, or indeed to hand them over without notice. An alternative is to come up with a suitable excuse to explain away any ill-gotten gains. If you have a winning lottery ticket and know the right people, you may well be able to sell it for substantially more than the prize, as for the criminal it is considered something of a 'Get Out of Jail Free' card, evidence which can explain away a certain amount of otherwise suspicious money. In 1991, for example, the notorious Boston gangster James 'Whitey' Bulger allegedly paid $2 million in cash up front to buy a one-sixth share of a winning lottery ticket. The police claimed he planned to use the annual pay-outs of $119,000 he would thus be due to legitimise his drug and extortion earnings.[7]

However, it is usually better to try and just move the money. There are pre-modern practices that have acquired a new relevance in an age of forensic accounting precisely because they do not leave the same paper trail. The *hawala* system has its roots in Islamic tradition and the way eighth-century Indian, Arab and Muslim traders along the Silk Road handled transactions and avoided the risk of theft. It has become popular among migrants sending money back home to their families. Essentially it rests on trust and a network of *hawaladars*, money brokers. You go to one, pay them and tell them to whom you want the money sent. No actual funds will at that time be moved; instead, the *hawaladar* will contact a broker at the other end of the process and arrange for the recipients to be able to pick up the money, less the *hawaladars'* fees, on receipt of some kind of password or similar recognition signal which you will have given them.

The key thing is that no contracts are lodged, no promissory notes exchanged. Both brokers keep their own records, but everything is based on the honour system: *hawaladars* often are dealing with people from their own clan or family, and also depend on their reputation for honesty. The two brokers keep a tally of their respective credits and debits, and then at some time settle the account, which may mean a payment of money, but could as easily be through the transfer of goods or the provision of services. It is quick, it tends to be much cheaper than banks and similar regular money transfer systems, and it is off the books. This last is especially appealing for illegal migrants sending money to their families, or payments to people living under corrupt or authoritarian regimes where no one wants to attract official attention. Even aid organisations sometimes use it for that last reason.

Of course, though, that also makes it appealing to criminals. *Hawala* and similar, albeit less global informal, value-transfer systems such as the Chinese Fei Qian ('flying money') equivalent offer obvious advantages. Although the authorities seek to police it, this usually requires intensive investigation and close cooperation with other countries. To be blunt, often the decision is made that it is not worth the necessary commitment of always-scarce resources. Even the FBI, arguably the best-resourced law-enforcement agency around, suffers from, in the words of one special agent, 'too many cases, too few accountants, too much pressure from above for quick results and slam-dunk prosecutions', such that 'often, we just have to file the case and move on', as soon as it becomes clear that such unofficial financial systems are involved. The exceptions tend to be terrorism-related cases, and certainly many *hawaladars* opted to no longer work with al-Qaeda after the 9/11 attacks precisely because of the potential attention this might garner.[8] (In part as a result, al-Qaeda took for a while to moving their money by couriers carrying gemstones until, reportedly, one too many decided instead to disappear and start well-funded new lives for themselves.)

Send in the smurfs

However, most money is laundered through the (kinda) legitimate financial sector. Essentially, there are three stages: placement, layering and integration. This is frequently a complex and geographically diverse process: after all, the aim is to make it hard for the authorities to unpick all the different stages. Placement entails feeding the dirty money into the financial system. This may be through a compromised bank or perhaps by adding criminal proceeds to a business's legitimate earnings, or by breaking large sums into smaller amounts that various companies or individuals can pay in separately. These agents are known as 'smurfs' after the faintly creepy blue Belgian cartoon characters, and the point of using them is to ensure that each transaction remains under the usual threshold for anti-money-laundering reporting. This is often easiest where the rules are lax and the opportunities considerable, which means jurisdictions which are under-controlled enough to be negligent, yet legitimate enough to be connected to the global economy. For example, the Lebanese Hezbollah militia reportedly launders and invests up to half a billion dollars generated by drug and cigarette smuggling through the Tri-Border Area where three cities in three different countries meet: Argentina's Puerto Iguazú, Paraguay's Ciudad del Este, and Brazil's Foz do Iguaçu. Overall, more than $6 billion is reckoned to be laundered each year there.[9]

However, such jurisdictions are also inevitably notorious, and so once the money is in the system, it is moved and metamorphosed, transferred around the globe and often into different types of asset, to make it hard to trace: this is the stage known as layering (sometimes called structuring). On and up the pecking order of jurisdictions it will go, through others with something of a reputation for being less than especially picky, such as Cyprus, Delaware, Dubai, Hong Kong and Panama, until the funds are ideally lodged in one of the A-list financial rookeries, such as London, Frankfurt or New York, after sufficient 'pre-washing' elsewhere. It may move from bank to bank, currency to currency, form to form, perhaps used to buy property here that is then exchanged for shares there, which in turn can be cashed out and then moved on. The final stage, integration, is precisely when the funds have been so extensively washed, their origins obscured, that they can be used safely. At last, those crimes pay, even if at the cost of 'shrinkage' from launderers' fees, transaction charges, deliberate losses, tax payments and the like, all of which could easily account for half the original sum. Nonetheless, it is deemed worth it.

As economies evolve, there are always more ways to launder money. Indeed, as online games such as Fortnite or World of Warcraft began to allow people to use real cash to buy in-game currency, or magic items and other goods, they too have been thrown into the mix. A cunning launderer can convert dirty money into in-game assets through lots of small-scale transactions unlikely to get onto an official radar, then sell them to gamers for (presumably) clean real money that can then be cashed out. This is just an extreme example of how laundering money has become so much easier thanks the virtualisation and globalisation of finance; money is no longer a physical good and rather a virtual commodity. (Not least because strings of digits are a great deal lighter than actual cash: a million dollars, for example, weighs more than 110kg if in high-denomination notes, and a lot more in smaller ones.) Laws are still geographically defined, and launderers take fullest advantage of this, especially when they can leverage poor cooperation between states. China, for example, is often unwilling to cooperate with Western law enforcement, and thus some launderers make a point of trying to wash their funds through its banks and businesses precisely to introduce a roadblock to any investigations. Conversely, when the US government introduced the Patriot Act in 2001, in response to the 9/11 terror attacks, it suddenly increased the cost and risk of laundering through American banks. This hardly stopped the criminals, though. Their dirty money simply shopped around for new jurisdictions to use, especially in Europe. Italy, for instance, witnessed a 70 per cent rise in money laundering through its banks between 2001 and 2004.[10] Where there is a demand, there will be a supply, somewhere in the global economy.

How much for cash?

Money laundering is, of course, a fraudulent transnational enterprise, and one carried out to a large extent by financial professionals. The notorious Bank of New York case, for example, saw two Russian émigrés, one of whom was a vice president of the bank, establish a money-laundering ring that was originally intended for Russian clients (mostly businesspeople looking to avoid taxes and currency controls, but also a smattering of gangsters) and opened it up for other customers of choice, an offer the Italian Mafia could not refuse. Between 1996 and 1998, they ended up laundering $7 billion.[11] Still, this was peanuts compared to the activities of the Estonian branch of Denmark's Danske Bank. Between 2007 and 2015, it laundered an estimated €200 billion, much though by no means all Russian, and possibly including funds held by Vladimir Putin's own family.[12] Money laundering is big business: according to the UN's estimate it accounts for 2.5 per cent of global GDP, which would amount to $2.6 trillion.

Speaking of big business, a survey of major global organisations in 2018 suggested a total loss to financial crime of $1.45 trillion (equivalent to the GDP of Spain).[13] This is just the tip of the iceberg, though. Losses from fraud and other economic crimes accrue to everyone from the individual citizen (whether directly or indirectly, as suppliers increase prices to cover their losses) up to the state, losing money to tax evasion and corrupt procurement deals. And, of course, what is lost to the state ultimately ends up costing the citizen again, in higher taxes or poorer services. When the Russian government was building the facilities for the 2014 Sochi Winter Olympics, sweetheart deals with contractors close to Putin were commonplace, and the costs skyrocketed as a result: the road to the resort town of Krasnaya Polyana cost almost $7 billion, and it was later estimated that it would have been cheaper to cover it with caviar than the tarmac they used.[14] This money certainly doesn't get clawed back from the construction companies, just poured out of the public purse.

The truth of the matter is that the biggest criminals, if measured in terms of turnover, are crooked politicians and businesspeople. We honestly don't know how much corruption as an industry is worth, although inevitably rough estimates put it at over a trillion dollars. Nonetheless, it helps give a scale of the sums involved, and the degree to which it has knock-on effects around the world. Corruption diverts sums meant for social goods, empowers the crooked, undermines public trust in institutions and distorts the legal process. For richer countries, this simply means, in effect, an extra, invisible tax; in the poorer ones, it can literally be a matter of life and death. A World Bank report, for example, found that 7.5 per cent of all aid sent to the poorest countries ended up diverted to banking havens.[15] Money meant for impoverished Lesotho and fragmented Somalia ends up in places like Liechtenstein and Switzerland.

Hooked on the dirty green

However, we probably ought to recognise how far the world's economy is hooked on dirty money. At the end of 2009, Antonio Maria

Costa, the head of the UN Office on Drugs and Crime, caused something of a storm when he claimed that it was criminal funds that stopped the global financial system from grinding to a halt during the 2008 financial crash. Years of rock-bottom interest rates and lax lending standards had fuelled a housing price bubble, above all in the United States. People took advantage of this to buy into and up the property ladder, and deregulated banks that seemed to think the good times were never going to end were extending mortgage loans even to so-called 'subprime borrowers', those with bad or no credit history. Lenders sold packages of their loans on to other financial institutions, until everyone was resting on a foundation of questionable credit. For a while, everyone was happy. But the boom in house prices could not last forever, and when they started to fall, many borrowers found the value in their houses tumbling even as their mortgage costs grew. Banks were left holding billions of dollars in worthless investments, loans that could not be repaid on homes that were now worth less than the debt. The financial system is global, and many of these debts had been sold abroad. As lenders began to go bankrupt, the shockwave blew around the world. The 2008 Crash and the ensuing Great Recession was marked by a worldwide liquidity crisis: there simply wasn't enough cash and credit moving around, lubricating the global financial markets. Banks were running out of money.

Enter the criminals. According to Costa, their dirty money was 'the only liquid investment capital' available to many financial institutions tottering on the edge of collapse. 'The system was basically paralysed because of the unwillingness of banks to lend money to one another,' but a number of institutions were rescued by 'interbank loans . . . funded by money that originated from the drugs trade and other illegal activities'. In the process, most of some $352 billion in profits from the narcotics trade alone was absorbed into the legal economic system. The underworld laundered its cash on a gargantuan scale; the upperworld got through the crisis.[16]

Many question Costa's take, not least because the sums he mentioned were dwarfed by the amount of credit extended to unfreeze the financial system by the US Federal Reserve (over $1.3 trillion) and other institutions. However, there needs not be a contradiction here. In the main, it was eye-wateringly expensive action by governments that prevented total economic meltdown. However, in the words of a British National Crime Agency officer who works on financial shenanigans, 'that criminal money was there quickly, and flowed especially into the kinds of banks that weren't at the top of the list for government bailouts. Don't let anyone tell you it didn't make a difference.'

So this is the modern world. Largely legal, orderly, regulated and stable, but behind the scenes awash in dirty money, riddled with compromise, fraud and financial crime, plundering its own habitat to ruin, and as globalised in the criminal as the legal economy. And yet it works, more or less and in its own way, especially for the richer countries. Facing new pressures and crises, though, many associated with the new worlds of the virtual and the e-everything, can it manage to maintain this equilibrium?

PART FOUR
BRAVE NEW WORLD

CHAPTER 17

WANKERS, VISHERS, CYBERCRIME AND SEMANTICS

Cybercrime is the present Big Thing, especially given that it seems to blend seamlessly with espionage and great power politics, as Russia hires hackers to work as government agents, China seeks to plunder the West's latest technology, and North Korea carries out insurance fraud to earn hundreds of millions. Just what is cybercrime, though? Are we ironically enough dating ourselves by using the term? The first case of a kind of hacking, after all, dates back to June 1903. Guglielmo Marconi, pioneer of the wireless telegraph – radio – was remotely demonstrating his leading-edge technology to an expectant audience in the Royal Institution's lecture theatre. He was at a clifftop station in Cornwall, almost 500 kilometres away, and preparing to transmit a message in Morse code to London. Suddenly, the receiver began to tap out a word, again and again: 'rats'. Then, it moved on to a scurrilous poem, pecked out in dots and dashes, beginning 'There was a young fellow of Italy, who diddled the public quite prettily.' Although Marconi had claimed that he could tune receivers to a precise wavelength to prevent anyone being able to interfere with the signal, the ingenious music-hall magician Nevil Maskelyne had found a way. A dabbler in wireless communications himself, Maskelyne was embittered by the way Marconi's patents frustrated his own ambitions. Hired to make some mischief by the Eastern Telegraph Company, to whose expensive industry this new-fangled technology represented a serious threat, he first built a 50-metre radio mast to eavesdrop on Marconi's communications, then set up a transmitter at a nearby West End music hall to steal his nemesis's thunder.[1] Nothing, it seems, is wholly new.

Nonetheless, it's easy to see cybercrime as some qualitative and quantitatively new challenge, not least as it has acquired its own lexicon, such as phishing, vishing and smishing, getting a victim's personal information such as passwords and card numbers respectively through emails, phone calls and text messages purporting to be from reputable companies. Official definitions of cybercrime as such tend to revolve around crimes committed using computers or the internet, which seems straightforward enough, but what if the criminals agreed to commit an entirely physical offence by an exchange of online messages? Is it a cybercrime if someone breaks into your car with a crowbar and steals your laptop? Or if the loot is fenced illicitly on eBay? Or if ill-gotten gains are moved by online banking? As the virtual, the connected, become increasingly ubiquitous, as we enter a world of the Internet of Things, in which our fridges will restock themselves by automatic online ordering, and our retina, fingerprint or face is our bank PIN, at what point will all crimes be 'cyber' in some form or another?

Beyond the lack of gelignite and stocking masks, what is the real difference between the classic bank heist and the modern, digital one? At one remove, we are all already cyborgs – machine-human hybrids – thanks to our phones, pacemakers, smartwatches, and smart-everything-elses. So too are our crimes; even the meanest hustler selling drugs on a street corner is part of a global economy that depends on mobile phones, emails, messaging apps and internet bank transfers.

Hacking for fun and profit

Classic cybercrimes involve either breaking into systems to get them to do something, such as transferring money remotely to a different bank account, or else persuading their users to do something instead. This could be anything from romance scams in which the criminals con their victims into thinking they are a potential bride so as to manipulate and steal from them, to brute-force hacks of someone's bank account. The range of different forms cybercrime can take is myriad, and beyond the capacity of a single chapter to chronicle. Sometimes, at least, this is fortunately just harmless fun, such as when hackers reprogrammed a computerised roadworks sign in San Francisco in 2014, to warn 'GODZILLA ATTACK – TURN BACK!' just as the rebooted film (in which the city becomes a monster battleground) was released. Or the unknown hacker who, in 1987, interrupted TV broadcasts in the Chicago area with brief and anarchic sketches in which a man masked as Max Headroom – an artificial intelligence from an eponymous cyberpunk series – insulted broadcasters, gibbered and, as the *pièce de résistance*, was spanked with a flyswatter.[2]

It can also be deeply personal. Given that phones can be hijacked to become eavesdropping bugs or tracked across a city, that wireless security cameras can open eyes onto someone's home, and that smart electricity meters give a pretty good indication of whether anyone is in or not, no wonder that the opportunities for peeping toms, stalkers and anyone with a grudge are frighteningly expansive. Indeed, go on the darkweb and you can find people who will hack someone's email account for you for $500–800 or locate them by their phone for $120–160.[3]

Other times, it is political activism. Arguably the first ever case of 'hacktivism' was the infamous 1989 WANK case. WANK (Worms Against Nuclear Killers – one has to assume they came up with the acronym first) are believed to have been two Australian hackers who, in protest at the use of plutonium modules in the Jupiter-bound Galileo probe, infected NASA computer systems with a worm (a program that replicates itself across connected machines) so that their screens displayed an anti-nuclear message ending 'You talk of times of peace for all, and then prepare for war,' yet not before warning that 'Your System Has Been Officially WANKed.' I'm sure everyone was very amused.

However, most cybercrime is all about the money. Of course, no one really knows how much the global haul may be. There are expansive estimates that it cost the world $6 trillion in 2021,[4] and that this will soar to $10.5 trillion by 2025 – equivalent to more than half the EU's combined GDP.[5] This can range from individual identity theft, stealing someone's money by mimicking them, all the way to industrial espionage. The Greek hacker known as ASTRA, who has never been definitively identified, spent years breaking into the systems of the French aerospace giant Dassault, ransacking their technologies for secrets that he could sell on, reportedly costing the company some $360 million.[6] Many of these attacks are small, others massive, with 'ransomware' becoming a particular large-scale problem. The criminals secrete their malware (malicious software) into a target's system, and then threaten permanently to block access to it, or else publish sensitive data, unless a ransom is paid. Typically, this is paid in the form of some hard-to-track digital currency. The largest such ransom paid to date appears to be $75 million, paid in 2024 by a *Fortune* 50 company to a group of hackers calling themselves the Dark Angels – the previous record had been a mere $37.8 million.[7]

By definition, the bigger the target and the more crucial the information, potentially the more lucrative the extortion. Thus, critical infrastructure providers – the people and services on which we all depend – are the victims of choice. The FBI's 2023 Internet Crime Report showed that healthcare providers and companies were the largest individual target, for example.[8] Likewise, there was something of a furore at the end of 2022, when it emerged that a majority of the British government's recent 'Cobra' cross-departmental crisis management meetings had been convened to respond to ransomware incidents rather than any other kind of emergency – again because they were likely to involve the National Health Service or other key public institutions.[9]

But is it something new – and even something?

Is ransomware different from older kinds of extortion, though? In 1996, extortionists began threatening European food companies that they would inject lethal cobra and mamba venom into food products, unless they were paid 400 million Deutschmarks (equivalent to $266 million) in diamonds. Indeed, the 1980s and 1990s were rife with similar cases of product tampering for fun and profit. These ranged from lacing Tylenol painkillers with potassium cyanide in Chicago in 1982 (seven people died, but no demands were ever made) to the threat to Australia's Arnott's biscuit company in 1997 to put poisoned packs on supermarket shelves unless four police officers who had given evidence at a murder trial in 1993 were given lie-detector tests (a suspect was eventually arrested, although charges were later dropped).

What is different between 'old' crimes and their 'new' digital versions? One distinction is the speed and scope of the crime. Where physical attacks would generally need to be carried out against one target or industry at a time, computer crimes can simultaneously strike thousands, at the speed of information. In May 2017, for example, a fast-spreading worm known as WannaCry suddenly began attacking systems across the world. Within a few hours, it had infected more than 300,000 computers in some 150 countries, from Aristotle University in Greece to the Vivo telecommunications company in Brazil. It left data in the systems unharmed but inaccessible, accompanied with the message 'Oops, your files have been encrypted!' and a demand for ransom: $300 payable in bitcoin within three days, or $600 within seven. It only took a few hours for a counter to be identified and applied, but even so, more than $130,000 had already been paid by frantic victims to the criminals, thought to be connected to the North Korean government.[10] Likewise, consider all those implausible spam emails offering everything from chemical expansions of an intimate nature to the chance to earn a share of a multimillion-pound legacy or lottery win. No one is so stupid as to take them at face value, right? Almost no one, true, but that is enough. One study of a spam network offering bogus 'herbal aphrodisiacs' found only one in 12.5 million emails led to a sale. However, because they were blasting out so many hundreds of millions of emails through a botnet (a network of hijacked computers), even this 0.00001 per cent strike rate was enough to net them more than $2.5 million a year, for minimal outlay, testament to economies of scale.[11]

Whether it is a case of an individual being blackmailed over hacked webcam footage or a corporation threatened with the leak of proprietary or embarrassing files, there is also a physical distance embodied within cybercrimes that becomes a distinguishing factor in its own right. Does it change anything when the criminal never needs have any contact with the victim or any proceeds of the crime? Or when the criminal need not even know the identity of the victim, as malware copies itself from machine to machine? After all, this applies to other kinds of cybercrimes beyond extortion: a vandal can cause damage by triggering fire sprinklers without venturing into the target building, and a thief can steal money with keystrokes rather than picking a pocket. Cybercrime can also be not just remote but fully automated, viruses and worms unleashed to find their own targets for themselves.[12]

So this is why the term cybercrime is not wholly redundant. When most ambulances were horse-drawn, it made sense to call the few horseless ones 'motor ambulances', just as 'mobile phones' have now generally become just plain phones. Technological prefixes disappear when the novelty becomes the norm. When an assassin moves from the knife to the gun, he can do his grisly work at more of a remove, but the essence of the act is still very much the same, not least in its physicality. However, the new online world does create genuinely new crimes, and give old ones distinctive new characteristics. At the same time, the criminality embedded within this new world shapes it.

New communities, new criminals

The importance of criminals' environment matters just as much when talking about the virtual world as the rookery or the pirate haven. The internet is truly revolutionary in the way it has generated so many ways for new communities not just to form, but to act, spawning a different kind of criminal. However much the media may enjoy shorthands like 'cyberpunk meets *The Godfather*', these types of criminal groupings are typically very different from their 'meatspace' – physical world – counterparts.[13] They emerge from very different social environments. Gaming clans play together and generate endless threads on discussion sites such as Reddit as fans dissect their latest streamed matches and future prospects. Dispersed teams work on projects through Slack and other online collaboration tools. Students log into virtual lectures and chat with each other in the margins. The Covid-19 pandemic only accelerated this process, and one survey found that in 11 out of 15 countries, the largest share of respondents said that the most important community in which they were involved was primarily online. Lest this be assumed to be just a high-income nation trend, the three where the all-online community proportion was highest were Mexico, Morocco and Brazil.[14] This environment creates its own distinctive criminal, one whose roots, culture, power and opportunities are in the virtual world, who may never meet or even be in the same country as their victims and their colleagues alike. The LulzSec gang that hacked the Fox website and released the personal data of 73,000 *X Factor US* contestants with the message 'We don't like you very much. As such, we cordially invite you to kiss our hand-crafted crescent fresh asses,' not only had never met IRL – 'In Real Life' – they were not even aware of each other's identities, knowing each other simply through 'handles', nicknames, such as Viral, Tflow and the disarmingly twee Topiary.[15]

This criminal milieu is constrained to its medium, to be sure: to what can be influenced through the computer. However, the horizons of that medium are daily pushed further back, as everything from supertanker control systems to implanted heartbeat monitors are hooked up to the internet. In the port of Antwerp, for example – a key entry point for cocaine into Europe – criminals hacked into the internal security grid in 2015, so they could track the containers within which their drugs had been hidden. More to the point, this milieu is liberated by its anonymity, fluidity and transnationality. Muscle is less important than wits (although many cybercriminals are using off-the-shelf tools and malware rather than developing their own on the fly, as in the films), and age, gender, ethnicity and location need not be limiting factors. While picture editors appear to assume that all cybercriminals are hackers, and that all hackers are socially maladroit, teenage white boys in black hoodies, their actual profile is rather more complex (even if there is more than a little truth in the cliché). One study found them to be typically between 29 and 49 and male, but most worked in groups, usually of a truly international character. Tropes about 'Russian hackers' notwithstanding, nearly half of all cybercriminal attacks are from the Asia–Pacific region, and in particular Indonesia and China.[16]

A study of convictions of foreign citizens in the United States between 2009 and 2017 also helps flesh out this picture. It found offenders' ages ranged from 19 to 73, with an average of just under

35. The overwhelming majority (94 per cent) were male, and their nationalities – and remember that this is of non-US citizens – were Chinese (27 per cent), Romanian (12 per cent), Russian (7 per cent), Estonian (5 per cent) and so on. Just over two-thirds were part of organised groups.[17] Of course, one cannot generalise from one sample set, but it already hints at a greater diversity than may have been assumed. Furthermore, as computer technology and expertise spreads, anecdotal evidence cited by a US law-enforcement analyst to me in 2018 suggests that 'It's the Global South that is seeing the greatest increase in their [cybercriminal] populations – and we in the Global North who are the targets.' Of course, the reason is because that's where the money is to be made, but it is possible it is also regarded as just deserts, the tax the Global North pays for being relatively rich and secure.

Whether or not they can be considered Robin Hoods with keyboards, there is also the particular phenomenon of the 'ethical hacker', who actively tries to break into systems, but only to uncover security vulnerabilities that can then be fixed. Often, these 'white hats' are hired by companies to stress-test their information security. Sometimes, though, they are 'grey hats', virtual vigilantes of sorts, acting without permission but in a self-appointed quest to cause a bit of trouble and have a bit of fun, all in the name of highlighting serious security flaws and making cyberspace a safer place. Sadly, there is a distinct dearth of 'meatspace' burglars who simply leave behind a note warning the householder of the foolishness in leaving a spare key under the doormat, for example, or fraudsters who return their loot with an acerbic warning as to the foolishness of believing that the beauteous Olga from Omsk or Mahalina from Manila really wants to marry you, as soon as she gets money for the visa application. This is another way, then, that the cybercriminal community really is different from the physical underworld.

Cryptocurrencies and the cybercriminal service sector

In contrast to the lone wolf image, not only do most cybercriminals work in teams or communities of some kind, they also connect to and rely on a whole infrastructure of suppliers and specialists. Just like the pirates of the briny rather than digital vasts, their freebooting myth must give way to practical necessities. They may well need secure servers, the actual computer on which their data is stored and through which it can be moved. Perhaps the most notorious, for example, was the Russian Business Network, which began as a legitimate internet service provider yet whose owners quickly realised where the real money was to be made, and began offering so-called 'bullet-proof hosting' for everyone from identity thieves to child pornography dealers. When internet security company VeriSign called it 'the baddest of the bad', this actually did its underworld reputation a world of good.[18] In its day, it was connected with up to 60 per cent of all internet crime, and became so notorious that even the relatively lax Russian government – which tends to turn a blind eye to cybercrime that isn't targeting its own citizens – began to consider it an embarrassment.[19] In November 2007, it disappeared overnight from its base in St Petersburg, only to pop up again a week later in China in the guise of a hastily created Italian-registered front company. Almost immediately, it disappeared again, but industry professionals suspected it had instead gone to ground, deliberately fractured into a number of other, smaller entities. In any case, there are always new providers, new havens ready to offer this service.

The cybercriminals may also need to pick up tools of the trade. Instead of a dodgy pub where a sawn-off shotgun may be for sale, they can go to the many underground hacker marketplaces on the darkweb to look for malware, stolen credit card details or even partners for their next crime. In 2004, for example, hacker Max Butler, going

by the online name Iceman, set up CardersMarket, a forum for criminals to buy and sell credit card details. With cannibalistic ingenuity, he
largely established it by hacking into a number of rival criminal markets and stealing more than 2 million sets of records, at once building
up his own stock and tearing down his rivals.[20] Butler was arrested in
2007 and convicted, but similar markets still proliferate in the depth of
the darkweb, many professionally managed and, in their own terms,
honest: 'More Amazon than Mafia' as one article put it.[21]

Of course, so long as crime is being conducted for profit (rather
than ego, kicks, politics or personal malice), then there is the usual challenge of moving and laundering it, so that it can safely be used. In this
context, the parallel rise of the aforementioned cryptocurrencies such
as bitcoin or ethereum has been especially fortuitous. Arguably, these
days almost every currency is essentially a consensual shared halluci-
nation, not backed by gold or the like but by our belief that it is worth
something beyond the value of a piece of paper or disk of metal. However, they are at least backed by governments and mediated through
myriad exchanges. Cryptocurrencies, by contrast, are purely digital
constructs, generated by intensive computer number-crunching, held
in digital wallets, unregulated by any state or bank. To some, they are
the future of finance; to others, another bubble waiting to burst. There
are, to be sure, different varieties, but in the main they are volatile and
can be troublesome to convert into 'hard currency', something of a
necessity as still today, years after bitcoin was first launched in 2009,
relatively few places and people will accept them.

They are also subject to the same risks as anything else in cyberspace. In August 2016, the Hong Kong-based Bitfinex cryptocurrency
exchange was hacked and 119,756 bitcoins, then worth about $72
million, were stolen. The hackers had lurked in the system for weeks,
watching data traffic the same way bank robbers might case the joint,
before moving funds from more than 2,000 users' digital wallets into
a single one. With no regulators in this virtual domain, no one could

close, freeze or seize that wallet, and next year, funds began to be withdrawn in relatively small amounts to be laundered. First, they went through a darknet market called AlphaBay, but when that was closed down later that year by a combined US, Canadian and Thai operation, the hackers turned to the Russian marketplace Hydra. In 2022, the US authorities charged a couple living in New York with trying to launder these funds, the value of which had skyrocketed to $3.6 billion thanks to the vagaries of the market.[22] It says much, though, that while most of the bitcoin had not yet been laundered, that which had, had largely gone into those most old-fashioned of assets: gold and conventional currencies. The cybercriminals also know how vulnerable their cryptocurrency holdings can be.

Given their intangible and unregulated nature, states have begun stepping up their measures to bring some control to cryptocurrencies, and this represents one of the front lines between the old, territorial forms of power in the world, and the anarchic new ones.[23] Some countries have tried to ban their use, or to impose regulations. However, this has largely worked only with those currencies, markets or individuals who want the security and respectability of going legitimate; there are still many, for financial or ideological reasons, happy to ignore and subvert these new controls, and these are the ones to which the criminals turn most readily. The anonymity of most cryptocurrencies is hard to break. This is why Russia, which in 2022 was toying with banning cryptocurrencies, has since made a dramatic U-turn. Facing Western sanctions intended to isolate its banking system after the 2022 invasion of Ukraine, it instead has moved to legalise and even encourage them, with a law passed in 2024 calling for them to be used for international payments.

The blockchain data company Chainalysis concluded that some $8.6 billion in criminal assets, from tax evasion to drug profits, was laundered through cryptocurrencies in 2021, up 30 per cent on the previous year.[24] Increasingly, this is flowing through a handful of dedicated criminal cryptocurrency exchanges, many operating out of Russia, and this also generates new markets. Many Russian oligarchs, minigarchs, mobsters and merely well-to-do found themselves hemmed in by sanctions. Even their cryptocurrency wallets are often inaccessible. Therefore, a number of darknet exchanges are now offering their services to unlock their funds, in effect hacking them free – although certainly not for free, but a 35–85 per cent commission.[25] Even the virtual world is under the shadow of the old states, and while their authority can be questioned, bypassed or ignored, it is still neither easy nor cheap to do so.

The cyborg era

In short, criminals are among those blazing the trail into a new era. Just as cyborgs are hybrids of human and machine, so too we are in a cyborg era, our societies fusing humanity and technologies. Criminals are often early adopters. Not all of them, of course. Most criminals are no smarter, imaginative or foresighted than the rest of us, or if anything rather more stupid, conservative and blinkered. However, such is the social Darwinism of the underworld that those criminals who fail to adapt are more likely to get caught, devoured by their rivals, or forced dispiritedly to accept a life flipping burgers or on benefits. We tend, after all, to hear about the successes (and, to be fair, the more catastrophic or comic failures, like Arthur Bailey, who decided to rob a bank in Fairfield, Connecticut, but to save time called in advance to let them know that they should have the money ready for him; needless to say, the police were ready for him, instead). However, whereas states have more resources, the criminals often are nimbler, and have good reason to be first into a new marketplace, from seeking to create a monopoly to seizing the opportunity before the government follows with its pesky laws and regulations. Sometimes, this is on a grand scale, such as the use of cryptocurrency to move and launder billions, at others it's on a very granular one. Burglars, for example, soon learned that social media is a great place to identify who locally has just made a major purchase, where they live, and when they conveniently will be on holiday. In some cases, they have even made duplicate house keys from high-quality pictures shared with #NewHome or some similar hashtag.[26]

But all the same, where criminals go, states do eventually follow, with all the massive resources at their disposal. The Americans, for example, are at the forefront of finding ways to crack criminal users of cryptocurrencies, suggesting that the early hype about how they would be invisible and anonymous to the state may have been just that. The tide really began to turn in 2015, when Ross Ulbricht, creator of the darkweb market Silk Road, which had facilitated some $1 billion in narcotics deals, was sentenced to life in prison. (Until, it turned out, January 2025, when he received a full and unconditional pardon from new US president Donald Trump.) Later that year, the assets of a Czech man suspected of laundering $40 million in stolen bitcoins were seized, the mastermind behind a $150 million bitcoin fraud was convicted, and a Frenchman was arrested on charges of having embezzled $390 million from a bitcoin exchange.[27]

As the pace of technological change only accelerates so too does the evolution of the underworld, and with it the ways in which it influences the upperworld. Artificial intelligence (AI), for example, is already being pressed into service to replicate people's voices: in 2019, in apparently the first case of vishing ('voice phishing'), the distinctive speech patterns and slight German accent of a company executive were used to trick a UK-based energy firm to transfer €220,000 ($240,000) into a dummy account.[28] In an age when AI is also being used to generate increasingly credible 'deep fake' videos of people, seeing is no longer believing. There are real questions as to who is winning in the constant struggle between underworld and upperworld.

CHAPTER 18

IMAGINATION RACES AND THE CRIMES OF THE FUTURE

The unofficial internet maxim 'Rule 34' states that if something exists, then it features in online pornography in some way. Equally inescapable is that anything that exists, or may come to exist, will in some way be criminalised. Coinage begat counterfeiting; the letter of credit, new kinds of fraud; medical drugs become recreational. The famous 'Tommy gun', more properly known as the Thompson submachine gun, was originally intended for military use, but its lacklustre sales were dramatically boosted when it became a firm favourite of gangsters in the age of Prohibition. The so-called 'gun that made the Twenties roar', the 'Chicago Typewriter', became, to pick an overused modern term, iconic, not least for its use in the 1929 St Valentine's Day Massacre.[1] Law enforcers adopted it in turn, but the degree to which a gun intended to clear trenches gave criminals a hitherto-impossible degree of mobile firepower revolutionised their activities, not least their bloody internecine battles over businesses and turf.

Later, hydroponics meant that marijuana could be grown in suburban bedrooms, and basic chemistry could turn pseudoephedrine-based cold medicines into crystal meth. Online banking and selling meant a new bonanza for money launderers and fraudsters. Now, three-dimensional printers which may have started as tools to create spare parts or prototype models can be used to create plastic guns that don't show up on metal detectors, or sex dolls whose features are modelled on a real person's. Drones were originally aerial targets and military surveillance devices, but they are now being used to fly drugs or mobile phones into prison yards, and reconnoitre before truck heists. In 2016, one was hovering over an ATM at Templepatrick in Northern Ireland, apparently filming people entering their PINs.[2] When it was spotted, though, it flew away but into the path of a car, and from the wreckage it proved impossible to prove that it was being used for criminal intent. A trio of Swiss artists coded an automated online shopping bot to blow $100 a week on an extensive darknet market and it ended up buying some counterfeit Diesel jeans, ecstasy, cigarettes and a range of other illegal, semi-legal and perfectly legitimate goods. This was to prove a point – can a robot be guilty of a crime? – but it does open up a world of arm's-length and automated illegal shopping.[3] What's next?

Major problem or moral panic?

What was once seen as an essentially domestic problem, and a law-enforcement one at that, is now a global concern, a threat to national and international security. The US government classified drug trafficking as a national security threat back in 1986, but in 1996 this was expanded to cover transnational organised crime as a whole. Nor is this a purely national perspective: former UN Secretary General Boutros-Ghali warned that 'transnational crime undermines the very foundations of the international democratic order'[4] and in its 1999 Strategic Concept, the Western defence alliance NATO acknowledged that the national security of its member states is at risk not just from the old threats of guns and bombs but organised crime, too.[5]

Admittedly, to an extent this last development reflects the end of the Cold War: before 9/11 put terrorism at the centre of so many agendas, security agencies were desperately casting about for new threats and enemies to justify their powers and budgets. Organised crime seemed to fit the bill. The Royal Navy and its US counterparts, for example, threw themselves into a new mission interdicting drug smugglers' boats in the Caribbean. Yet, this was not just a bid to find a new role for Cold War services, it also reflected a genuine growing awareness of the power, wealth, sophistication and dynamism of transnational criminality and the extent to which it challenges and exploits our assumptions about the processes of globalisation and modernisation. The very concept of state sovereignty, essentially a child of the eighteenth century, is coming increasingly under question at the beginning of the twenty-first, and while organised and transnational crime is only one of the challenges it faces, there were concerns it may prove its most ruthless.[6]

The state–crime nexus

This growing concern also reflects the blurring of the boundaries between criminal groupings and those using violence and conspiracy for political ends. Many terrorist movements, after all, turn to criminal activity to raise funds, and among them more than a few, seduced by the profits to be made, effectively lost their ideological commitment and like Peru's Sendero Luminoso Maoist rebels, Nigeria's Black Axe student movement,[7] or some white supremacist groups in the USA, became little more than organised crime groupings wrapped in red flags, pan-Africanism, or race-war rhetoric, respectively. Examples of the reverse process, or organised crime gangs becoming terrorists – as opposed to using terroristic methods against the government or their enemies – are rather less common. There are some cases, such as Dawood Ibrahim's D-Company, which began as criminal gang in India, but became increasingly committed to a political agenda, being behind the 1993 Mumbai bombings which left 257 dead and 1,400 injured, and spreading into Pakistan and beyond.[8] On the whole, though, it seems that money is more attractive than politics.

But what about the blurring of boundaries between the state and the underworld? Consider, for example, what happened on the night of 3 November 1996 at Susurluk in western Anatolia. A truck hit a car, killing three of its passengers and wounding the fourth. To anyone who knows Turkish driving, so far so unremarkable, even if tragic. However, one of the dead turned out to be a local police chief and the other a gangster by the name of Abdullah Çatlı, who at the time was on Interpol's wanted list and who had officially been on the run from the very same Turkish police since 1978. Not only had he been enjoying a jaunt with a police chief (and his girlfriend, the beauty queen Gonca Us), but the mobster had also been carrying no fewer than six different sets of identity documents, all issued by the Turkish authorities (including a diplomatic passport), and the trunk of the car contained an arsenal of pistols and machine guns. As if all that were not enough, the wounded man was parliamentarian Sedat Bucak, a representative of the governing True Path Party and a key figure behind the Village Guards, a rural militia force the government raised in its war against the Kurdish separatists and revolutionaries, the PKK. Nor was this just a case of some 'bad apple' officials having some personal shady connections. Interior Minister Mehmet Ağar was forced to resign when it emerged that he had met the three men just before the accident, and Tansu Çiller, leader of the True Path Party and prime minister in the years 1993–6, publicly eulogised Çatlı for his role in a secret death squad established by Ağar to target suspected terrorists.[9]

The Susurluk incident dramatised the way the Turkish 'deep state' covertly used organised crime as a weapon against insurgents from the late 1970s into the 1990s, even at the cost of empowering the massive heroin trade through the country.[10] This was not

unique, though. The Mafia murdered leftists and trades union workers with the apparent sanction of the dominant Christian Democrat
party during the post-Second World War creation of the Italian
Republic.[11] The Japanese Yakuza likewise enthusiastically suppressed
the left in the interests of the comparable Liberal Democrats.[12] When
Hong Kong was about to be handed back to China in 1997, Beijing
encouraged 'patriotic Triads' to stay and work with the Communist
administration – and they later repaid the favour by beating up pro-
democracy protesters.[13] Indeed, criminals can also be especially useful
as agents abroad. Foreign policy tends to be marked by a degree of
pragmatism, to the point of amorality, that means that even a country
such as the United States, which has a clear and passionate commitment to fighting organised crime at home, has in its time been willing
to work with criminals abroad. In the Second World War, it co-opted
the Mafia to assist the Allied invasion of Sicily.[14] Then the Cold
War provided another excuse for such collaboration: in 1960, for
example, the CIA offered the Mafia $150,000 to assassinate Cuban
leader Fidel Castro.[15] Later, it was willing to work with figures such
as Afghan warlord Gulbuddin Hekmatyar (sanctioned in 2003 by the
US as a 'Specially Designated Global Terrorist' after having received
millions in US support while he was fighting the Soviets 1979–88)
and Panama's General Manuel Noriega (who made millions off the
cocaine trade, even as he funnelled CIA aid to rebels in Nicaragua).[16]
Arguably, this is just the modern-day answer to the privateers, the
pirates encouraged and empowered to target enemies as auxiliaries
in wars declared and undeclared. It just takes new forms, including
the hiring of hackers and buying zero-days – hitherto unknown and
unexploited software vulnerabilities – they may have discovered. In
2013 alone, for example, the US National Security Agency had a
budget of more than $25 million to purchase them, and although
most were not from criminal hackers, it appears some were.[17]

Criminal warfare

What is different, though, is the growing fusion of some states and regimes with organised crime. On one level, this seems nothing new; from the *razzia* to the privateer, states have used crime as an instrument. However, two things have changed in the twenty-first century. First of all, we are going through what could be described as a 'post-Westphalian' moment. The 1648 Peace of Westphalia ended the ravages of the Thirty Years' War in Europe and in many ways marked the beginning of the era of true national sovereignty as we understand it, and the basis for international law. With it came a growing binary clarity between war and peace. In the ancient, medieval and even Renaissance eras, the dividing lines between them, and indeed between public and private, were often hazy. This was exported beyond Europe and, with all kinds of exceptions and ambiguities, largely prevailed until the end of the Cold War. Today, as a Western-crafted global order creaks at the seams, increasingly 'war is outsourced and sublimated, fought as often through culture and credit, faith and famine, as direct force of arms'.[18]

Meanwhile, organised crime has also changed. Its internationalisation, whether in terms of its direct operations or its connections, makes it all the more appealing to states looking for traction on events and processes beyond their borders. At one extreme is the impoverished, isolated tyranny of North Korea where, as already discussed, Bureau 39 of the Workers' Party of Korea is where civil servants become gangsters (or vice versa), responsible for everything from illegal coal exports and insurance fraud to counterfeit clothing and very real methamphetamines, the last brewed not in hidden meth labs but government chemical works. In the process, it earns the regime perhaps up to a billion dollars annually, spent not just on keeping Supreme Leader Kim Jong-Un's 80-metre superyacht with

Olympic-sized swimming pool and two waterslides in trim, but above all subsidising North Korea's nuclear programme, even as its population continues to suffer from endemic malnutrition. Such initiatives are generally about preserving a regime, though, and echo the way Iran's Revolutionary Guard Corps generates funds for its operations at home and abroad by smuggling Afghan heroin (or at least taxing the gangs smuggling it across the country's borders). Indeed, in 2012, the US government labelled General Gholamreza Baghbani, one of its senior officers, as a 'Specially Designated Narcotics Trafficker'.[19]

However, in the interconnected modern world, it is Vladimir Putin's Russia which seems to have most clearly identified the way a state can use crime not simply as a means of support, but as a weapon.[20] Drawing on pervasive traditions of co-opting criminals as instruments, including keeping Gulag prison labourers in line during Stalin's Terror, at first the Kremlin simply proscribed certain activities and targets.[21] The rampant gang crime of the 1990s quickly subsided in the 2000s for a range of reasons, but one was undoubtedly the quiet social contract that offered the criminals a degree of tolerance, so long as they did nothing that offered any direct challenges to the state. It soon became clear that so long as hackers were targeting foreign systems, it was unlikely that the authorities would go after them, for example. Most Russian-designed ransomware simply will not load on computers with Cyrillic virtual keyboards installed – in other words, which are geared to writing in Russian – so as to avoid accidental infection of the 'wrong' systems.[22]

As Putin's relationship with the West became increasingly antagonistic, though, the Kremlin began to look for asymmetric advantages. The West was richer and stronger, but it had also become interpenetrated by Russian-based criminals who both operated directly on its streets and, more often, had become strategic allies with local gangs, wholesale suppliers of everything from drugs to money-laundering services. Proscription became prescription, as the Russian intelligence services began recruiting the criminals for specific operations across the whole spectrum of covert operations. They could be engaged as assassins, like the contract killer who put three bullets into Georgian Chechen anti-Russian organiser Zelimkhan Khangoshvili in the middle of a park in Berlin in August 2019.[23] They could be saboteurs, like the English criminals who burnt down Ukrainian-owned warehouses in north-east London in March 2024.[24] They could be low-level intelligence collectors, like the smugglers Estonian Kapo security police officer Eston Kohver was investigating when a Russian commando team snatched him across the border in September 2014.[25] They could be buying up embargoed microelectronic components that Russia needs for weapons systems, like the US-based network which was put in the dock in 2022,[26] although an easier approach has apparently been to smuggle in fridges for their microchips[27] or, reportedly, stolen Swedish traffic speed cameras for their optics.[28] Or they could simply be, in effect, taxed: told to deposit a portion of their profits into some Western bank account, if they know what's good for them. The last became especially significant following the imposition of sweeping controls on monetary transfers to and from Russia in the wake of its invasion of Ukraine. Its intelligence agencies turned to this to accumulate *chyornaya kassa*, 'black account' funds with no provable Kremlin connection, to bankroll operations abroad. In short, what Putin's Russia came to understand was that in an age of global interconnectivity, the old model of privateering could be expanded massively, such that a state ruthless enough and sufficiently uncaring about its reputation could weaponise crime to undermine its enemies, bypass their sanctions, and fund its covert activities.[29] It is a lesson that other states are likely to be learning.

New crimes

Resisting such crime–state alliances will be hard enough but, as one British National Crime Agency analyst put it to me over a beer, 'Everything is changing so fast, technology driving society, that we're faced with a terrible choice: push hard on yesterday's crimes, or guess at what tomorrow's may be.' This is, after all, an era in which the best futurists may well be science fiction writers, and it is hard to know where imagination ends, and real threats begin.[30]

The rise of synthetic drugs and hydroponic cultivation has been challenging enough, but given that a drug's high is really just the feeling experienced when it triggers a surge of neurotransmitters in the brain, what happens when the chemical middleman is cut out and the same effects are generated by direct electrical, sonic or visual stimulation? There have already been cases of home security cameras being hacked for the purposes of voyeurism, but what about when they are used to watch someone type in their bank code? So much of our personal data is already available to governments, tech giants and financial industries and thus inevitably sold, stolen or leaked. In 2013, for example, a data broker mistakenly sold a Vietnamese organised crime group the personal data of nearly two-thirds of all US citizens, assembled by the Experian credit bureau.[31]

What happens when artificial intelligence is able not only to process data at astonishing speed but also to make conceptual jumps that echo human intuition, impersonate people for fraudulent purposes, uniting a comprehensive knowledge of their details – including mother's maiden name and the street they grew up in – with the capacity to imitate a phone or even video call?[32] Modern cars are complex computers on wheels, and although it is not easy, there have already been successful wireless hacks to control their systems,[33] but the prospect of driverless cars offers even more outré possibilities, from assassination and terrorism by remotely guided crash to out-right kidnap. On a much grander scale, while at present it would be difficult to take control of a ship without being physically on the vessel, it may be that future pirates will simply need internet access and a laptop rather than a fast boat and an AK-47.

The panopticon age

More broadly, the struggles to control cryptocurrencies and police the virtual world hint at the wider political and social dilemmas poten-tially raised or exacerbated by the crimes of the future. It is as easy to posit a dystopian future of total surveillance, where there is as little room for crime as dissent, as to imagine a techno-anarchic free-for-all. Both are over-extreme positions. We are certainly entering the pan-opticon age, one of ubiquitous cameras – not just CCTV on buildings, but everywhere from dashcams on passing cars, to video entryphones on homes – and so many other ways of locating and identifying us. Our mobile phones constantly report our locations and movements, and our smartwatches track our physical activity; and some day, our internet-connected refrigerators, programmed to order restocks when supplies run low, will implicitly also register when we are home, when we are entertaining, and when we are raiding the comfort food.

Higher definition cameras, more powerful computers, auto-matic car numberplate readers, and facial recognition software mean that we can be identified and followed on the street or in the train, even if we are wearing hat, sunglasses and mask. Newer techniques pin us down by how we walk (which reflects our unique physiognomy) or hand vein patterns. The US drone-mounted Gorgon Stare system can capture imagery of an entire city, which can then be analysed by artificial intelligence, while at the other extreme, insect-sized drones with microscopic cameras are already being developed.

Technology has always been used by the state and law enforcement to give them whatever edge it can. In 1845, Englishman John Tawell became the first person to be arrested thanks to the electric telegraph. He poisoned his mistress and then fled the crime scene by train, but the new-fangled device was used by the police to circulate his description, so he was identified leaving Paddington station in London. In 1910, another poisoner, Dr Hawley Crippen, fled London ahead of a manhunt, heading first for Antwerp, and thence boarding the ocean liner SS *Montrose*, bound for Quebec. The captain of the *Montrose* soon became suspicious, and took advantage of the fact that his ship was equipped with a wireless telegraph, which he used to alert the police. While the *Montrose* plodded its way across the Atlantic, Inspector Walter Dew of Scotland Yard boarded a faster ship to Canada, and was able to arrest Crippen as his ship approached Quebec.[34] Nowadays, it's not just that everyone is in contact with everyone else, 24/7. Drones can monitor crowds and safely tackle armed suspects. Advanced data analytics should help the police concentrate their resources where the next crimes are likely to be. Information is abundant, and it is the state that is acquiring the computing capacity to marshal it.

It is certainly possible that fears of astonishingly dangerous future crimes will be exploited to harness the equally astonishing capabilities of future technologies, to justify oppressive regimes. After all, while we may fear totalitarian statism, it often creeps up on us by promising in the first instance to guarantee our comfort and safety. For example, China is developing a model of 'techno-authoritarianism' based on mass digital surveillance and a 'social credit' model that rates citizens for their loyalty and law-abidingness and punishes those who fail to do well with travel bans, pricier credit and even slower internet. It is already beginning to be adopted in other undemocratic countries, from Belarus to Zimbabwe, often in the name of 'safe cities' and 'fighting crime' (even if the crimes in question tend to be political ones).[35]

So far, so *1984*. However, there are more positive, more human examples of progress being made in combating crime that do not seek to pry, punish and police crime out of existence – as if that has ever worked – but instead to tackle the root causes and to build solutions that go with the grain of human nature. Of course, there are the programmes to address the reasons why people take drugs or shoplift, even if they never seem as appealing to the politicians as 'tough on crime' rhetoric. However, there are also other initiatives which increasingly stress partnerships between police and policed, and which develop community-based solutions. A classic example is in addressing environmental crime. Giving local communities reasons to save endangered species and encouraging them to find ways to manage stocks through local initiatives rather than just at the behest of a distant government bureaucracy, for example, has helped tackle the poaching of elephants in Mali and rhinos in Namibia and Nepal.[36] More broadly, non-government ventures like the Global Initiative against Transnational Organized Crime ('a network to counter networks') move beyond simply uniting scholars and practitioners, and sharing research and best practice, and have even begun conducting activities intended to disrupt criminal activities. Nonetheless, this is all trying to hit a moving target: the criminals are evolving, too.

CHAPTER 19

GANGSTERS WITH FIVE-STAR REVIEWS: THE POWER OF THE NETWORK

Never mind judging a book by its cover: never try to assess a gangster by his mugshot. He certainly looked as unpromising as unappealing, a Russian mobster straight out of Central Casting, flat face glowering out at the camera, the light glinting on his cropped head, an old tattoo just about visible above the neck of his Lokomotiv Moscow football shirt. This walking cliché was, however, no mindless thug but instead a sophisticated criminal entrepreneur who had the good fortune to be holidaying in Europe in February 2022, when Putin invaded Ukraine. The West quickly imposed a series of sanctions, not least closing down direct air routes in and out of Europe and excluding certain Russian banks from the SWIFT international financial transaction processing system. A disaster for many, but not for him. After a couple of days' phone calls and hurried back-and-forth on the Telegram messaging service back to Russia, he had set up a new business venture, whereby African gold and diamonds that previously would have been flown to Antwerp and paid for by direct wire transfers, would instead be moved to the Netherlands via Istanbul (which still had direct flights to Russia), with the buyers sending funds to a bank in Belgrade, where it would be used to buy real estate.

He still had a few days to enjoy wine tasting in the Rhône before making his own way home (again, via Belgrade, which also retained a direct air link). Just with his tablet computer and mobile phone, he had restructured a criminal enterprise worth millions, finding reliable new partners by leveraging existing contacts, and shifted the flow from Russia (which he recognised would become increasingly financially isolated) and into Serbia, a relatively friendly country, bypassing the sanctions regime.[1]

The traditional model of the organised crime gang – a hierarchy of thuggish opportunists, bound by a common code of honour, rooted in a particular impoverished neighbourhood or ethnic community – was always something of a caricature, but in many ways is becoming even less useful as the processes reshaping the upperworld are mirrored below. Globalisation encourages the transnationalisation of crime, as does the increased capacity of law enforcement. This tends to push the more sophisticated organised crime groups out of their old comfort zones, recruiting from different communities and even – the gangsters may have proven early adopters of much technology and eager internationalists, but old macho habits seem to die hardest – women. In the process, they are changing in structure, as well as culture.

Information, we want information

'Our bosses still expect to find pyramids, military-style hierarchies,' one young Russian police analyst complained to me, 'but in fact what we're seeing are more like spiderwebs,' or arrays of interconnected small crews and criminal entrepreneurs. Why that really stuck with me was that I had heard almost the same words from a FBI analyst in Los Angeles only a year before. The old top-down model had always been an oversimplification, but it has come to resemble reality less and less, and kinship and force matter less than information.

Where do you go, if you need to find a money launderer in Montreal or a crooked customs officer in Cork? More to the point, how can you be sure to get a competent and, for want of a better word, trustworthy criminal? You can hardly see how many stars they have on Yelp and there is no 'CrookAdviser' on which you can read reviews. (Although Diego Gambetta does recount the tale of a woman who found a firm called Guns For Hire in the *Yellow Pages* and got in touch to solicit a hit on her husband, failing to realise that they specialised in theatrical Wild West shows.[2]) For that matter, when does the armoured cash truck call at the bank, what's the best way to break the lock on the newest luxury cars, where is your rival gang's marijuana grow house, and how can you best cover up your traces to befuddle those pesky forensic scientists? This last, incidentally, is one of the reasons why law-enforcement professionals often have such mixed feelings about series such as the popular TV *CSI* franchise: it's nice to be recognised as the heroes, but they also worry – probably needlessly[3] – that the spread of tradecraft tricks such as using bleach to cover up DNA evidence comes from the programme.

Information – getting it, trading it, keeping it – has always been central to criminality. Bandits would send members posing as travellers or mercenaries to spy out their next target. Highwaymen would have their informants at coach houses and country fairs or among the ostlers (grooms) at the inns along London's Bishopsgate Street and Smithfield to find out in advance who would be travelling, when and with how much money. A skilled bunco artist (confidence trickster) in interwar America would first have made sure he or she got the straight wire (information) on a prospective mark. What once flowed first at the speed of a fast horse, then the telegraph, now moves not just at the speed of the internet and the mobile phone, but also the density of modern communications. The result is a networking of global crime. That classic old organisational model of the pyramid, with a godfather at the top, captains and lieutenants below, and foot soldiers at the bottom, orders flowing downwards and tribute flowing up, has definite strengths. Yet while it is effective in focusing effort and marshalling muscle, it also has vulnerabilities. The authorities will identify its leaders and concentrate on bringing them down, just as rivals may see decapitation – metaphorical or literal – as a good way to win a turf war. The attempt to kill Don Corleone in *The God-father*, after all, was likely inspired by 'Lucky' Luciano's betrayal of Joe Masseria in 1931 during the 'Castellammarese War' for dominance within the US underworld. The criminals may make efforts to have succession plans in such a situation, but the death or arrest of a leader can all too easily precipitate internecine power struggles and even the fragmentation of the organisation. When the Mexican government adopted a strategy of targeting kingpins in the 2000s, the result was actually to increase violence without diminishing the drug flows, for this very reason.[4] In fast-moving times, the hierarchy is also typically more hidebound, with new initiatives requiring a sign-off from distant, busy and often conservative senior figures. Finally, it is harder for it to integrate with business and political structures, let along operate transnationally. For all these reasons, even many traditional organised crime groups are bit by bit becoming flatter in their structures, less top-down in their management styles – just like their upperworld corporate counterparts.[5] Furthermore, these networks, more secure thanks to their compartmentalisation and ability to reform when one or more component node is taken down,[6] are more likely to connect and intersect, trading information as readily as illicit goods.

Networks of networks

In effect, what emerges is an underworld characterised by fluid networks of interconnected gangs and individual criminal entrepreneurs. Their role is in a way to provide mechanisms that either generate or replicate trust, as well as become the search engines of the criminal world. While most criminals may ideally want to operate on a regular, routine level, there are also numerous crimes which are one-offs or take place in very different conditions. In these cases, it is a little bit of a stretch but not wholly misleading to think of the first half of the classic heist or caper film like *The Sting* (1973) or *Ocean's Eleven* (2001), which show the principal criminal getting his (or her) team together, each with their specific strengths and skills. In their own way, these real-world networks allow criminals to assemble their own constellation of admittedly usually less photogenic allies and conspirators. Like the gig economy in the upperworld, individuals can recruit and be recruited on a job-by-job basis, directly or via a broker, without the need to have sworn oaths, been brought up in the 'right' culture or neighbourhood or even, in extreme cases, to have even actually met any of their collaborators in the real world. Instead, the network provides a way to find them and make sure someone else is willing to vouch for their competence and trustworthiness. In Mozambique, where the effective absence of a functioning navy or coastguard has encouraged an upsurge in heroin trafficking, much of this is handled piecemeal by smartphone: a courier will receive a message to collect a package from here and drop it off there, to be paid likewise through his phone.[7] Nor is this a one-off case. In 2017, two baggage handlers from Heathrow airport and a taxi driver were convicted for their part in the attempted smuggling of three kilos of cocaine. The drugs had originally been sent from Brazil; the London-based trafficker for whom they were intended sent a photo of the suitcase in which they had been packed to the handlers by WhatsApp so they could retrieve it from the luggage carousel. They handed it to a taxi driver who likewise had been simply instructed to take it to an address in Birmingham. The idea had been for the whole operation to be handled by individuals with no sense of the overall plan, each just commissioned remotely for a small part of the whole.[8]

At other times, the network can connect with independent underworld brokers able directly or indirectly to provide vital services.[9] For example, the Colombian brokers called, with depressing unoriginality, Los Brokers, brought their criminal customers together with business operators willing and able to launder their money (an estimated $100 million over a two-year period), while the Turkish-American broker Hakan Ayik organised deals between customers as varied as the Triads, Latin American drug cartels and Australia's Comanchero biker gang.[10]

Information is not just a means of facilitating other criminal activities, though, it is also a more valuable and above all usable commodity in itself than ever. Between 2010 and 2015, for example, a group of Russian and Ukrainian cybercriminals (again demonstrating the transnationality of so many underworld enterprises these days) stole 9,000 embargoed news releases relating to publicly traded companies, which were passed on to select clients in the US who had supplied their own wish list of target companies. Thanks to their advance notice, the traders collectively earned more than $100 million before the authorities broke the scheme.[11] In this case, different kinds of criminals – individual traders eager for an insider-dealing edge and hackers halfway around the world – could come together for mutual profit. There are underground markets for everything from credit card numbers (a US credit card number and the software-generated verification number is worth perhaps $5 to $8, while the 'Fullzinfo' version with everything from the cardholder's full name, address, and mother's maiden name can sell for eight to ten times as much) to so-called exploits, loopholes which allow hackers access into commercial or government systems.

The modern world is fuelled by accelerating and deepening flows of information, locking together economies and societies as never before, and this is transforming the underworld in the process. Increasingly, criminals do not just work together, they pool their contacts, experiences, ideas and expertise. Italian-Americans were schooled in fraud by Russians and Armenians. Chinese criminals launder money for Latin American drug cartels. Scottish gangsters sell cigarettes counterfeited in the Balkans with the advantage of tricks learned by Baltic smugglers. Scandinavians buy cocaine from African smugglers, and Israeli gangsters traffic women to the Arab states. Even while their respective countries were in an undeclared war before 2022, Russian and Ukrainian criminals freely collaborated across the contested border.[12] Criminals: the true internationalists. They certainly appreciate globalisation even if they don't care about the globe itself.

Changing times, changing criminals

As their structures change, so too do their organisational cultures. The tattooed hard men from the Gulags, the *vory v zakone*, still dominated the Soviet underworld up to the later 1980s. However, as the USSR liberalised and then collapsed, giving way to a new constellation of wide open and largely uncontrolled and weak market economies, they were rapidly supplanted by a new breed of criminal leader, the *avtoritety* (authorities). Unlike the *vory*, they did not flaunt their tattoos or confine themselves to criminal activity. Instead, they were entrepreneurs, as happy to operate within as outside the law, doing legitimate business when that struck the right balance between risk and reward, but comfortable using threat, corruption and murder when necessary. One such whom I spoke to in the 1990s scarcely even saw a difference between legal and illegal activity: 'It's all business,' he shrugged, 'I don't make a fetish of being a gangster like the *vory*, but I don't mind breaking the law. That's capitalism, isn't it? Making money, however you can.' He would probably have appreciated the description of the new generation of Golden Triangle meth dealers: 'These people are interested in business, and their sons and daughters go to nice private schools, and they live in normal neigh-bourhoods. They're just really good at moving things from A to B.'[13]

Admittedly, Russia's underworld went through an especially rapid transition – the last of the true old-school *vory v zakone*, Vyache-slav 'Yaponchik' Ivankov, was gunned down in the outskirts of Moscow in 2009, and his funeral was a pageant of gangsters, molls and competitively over-the-top wreaths[14] – but this 'commercialisa-tion' of criminal elites is a common trend. Consider the world of the motorcycle gangs: while many members are still drawn to it simply for the biker lifestyle, within the self-declared 'one-percenters', who pride themselves on being members of outlaw motorcycle gangs such as the Hells Angels and Bandidos, are violent but sophisticated organised crime elements.[15] Bushy beards, leather waistcoats and Harley-Davidsons notwithstanding, these days they are looking for a different kind of recruit, according to a Canadian source: 'a person that not necessarily is willing to kill . . . [but] has an extensive net-work of people that can help bring in money. They're an enterprise. Their focus is not so much on the violence and lifestyle – it's more on the income.'[16]

Italian gangs certainly have a pedigree of involvement in busi-ness. The Mafia played a key role in the so-called 'Sack of Palermo', the rapid expansion of Sicily's capital in the post-war era, as the orchards, fields and traditional villas of the Conca d'Oro green belt was bulldozed, asphalted and packed with ugly and shoddily built high-rises. The gangsters helped push through the plans (in five years, 2,500 of 4,000 building licences were issued to just three Mafia proxies, pensioners with no connection to the industry), drove out existing residents, underwrote the construction and made a for-tune out of an eyesore.[17] However, this was in their backyard and a kind of industry they understood. Ernesto Savona found that in the period 1983–2011, Italian gangs were quite conservative in their investment strategies, putting their money largely into real estate

(52.3 per cent), with companies and corporate bonds very much as an afterthought (8.7 per cent).[18] According to a *carabiniere* police officer specialising in financial crime, though, 'After the 2008 financial crisis, they became more and more adventurous, and international. Within a few years, some of the *capi* [bosses] were reading the financial pages and tracking stocks like any investor. The smart ones, though, were contracting that out to professionals, who were pulling together global portfolios of everything from Eurobonds to futures. The really smart ones were sending their kids to business school and encouraging them to go work in the financial sector for a few years, to learn the ropes.'

As they become more commercial and professional, the larger organised crime groups have also successfully adopted practices from upperworld business. The franchise, for example, has become a widespread model, whereby a criminal organisation with a powerful brand name and a successful formula allows others to use them, for a price. The Chechens had an especially intimidating reputation in Russia, for example, and gangs in Siberia wanting to draw on this in the 2000s and 2010s would pay in order to be allowed to say they 'work with the Chechens' – to have the temerity to do this without approval would ensure that the originals would take measures to protect their brand.[19] This was a relatively simple transaction; in other cases, the deal also includes training, access to specialised services, and weapons. After all, the franchise owner has every incentive to see the franchise prosper, both because the more they earn the more they pay, and because it enhances the brand further. Los Zetas of Mexico, for example, have used this model to particular effect.[20] Originally a squad of enforcers for the Gulf Cartel recruited heavily from veterans of the elite Grupo Aeromóvil de Fuerzas Especiales commando unit, in 2010 they split from the Gulf Cartel – violently and acrimoniously – and for a while were the country's largest drug organisation. A series of reversals and divisions have cut them somewhat down to size since, but their rapid expansion at first – even internationally – was to a considerable extent due to their franchise model, backed up with not just their reputation for mayhem but even 'merch', from baseball caps to pen-knives emblazoned with their tripartite shield logo. Above all, they protected and projected their brand through making a point of photographing and videoing their numerous killings and putting them out on social media, to reinforce their image as the toughest so-and-sos around.

Part of this 'businessification' process has been the way many ethnically based organised crime cultures have begun to recruit more widely. The importance of bringing new skills in-house and having interlocutors able to engage with foreign gangs on their own terms, and the need for new blood at a time when second- or third-generation migrant or minority communities may be less interested in a criminal career, all make this a survival move. Having for so long tried to exclude Korean criminals, for example, the Japanese Yakuza is increasingly relying on them (some sources suggest they now account for 30 per cent of the membership), not least to help fight off an emerging threat from other ethnic gangs such as the Chinese Dragons, drawn especially from the *chūgoku zanryū koji* ('Chinese left-behinds'), the children and grandchildren of Japanese nationals who had been abandoned in China at the end of the Second World War, only returning later to Japan as adults.[21] Notionally 'Georgian' organised groups operating in Europe may include Russians and peoples from the North Caucasus, just as many mislabelled as 'Russian organised crime' in the USA may be anything but. The 'Shulaya Enterprise' broken in 2017 was called a Russian gang, even though its eponymous leader was Georgian, and his crew a mix of Georgians, Russians, Armenians and even Central Asians.[22]

The gentler sex?

It says something about the culture of the global underworld that in the main it took longer for the gender than race bar to fall, but it is happening. There have, of course, always been individual female gangsters who bucked the trend. The Irishwoman Anne Bonny raided Caribbean shipping aboard the infamous pirate sloop *William* alongside 'Calico Jack' Rackham in the early 1700s, for example. Kate 'Ma' Barker, who led a violent gang of her sons, topped the FBI's Public Enemy list before dying in 1935 in what was until then the longest shootout with FBI agents in its history. Phoolan Devi, born to the lowly Mallah subcaste in India's Uttar Pradesh state, became known as the 'Bandit Queen' when, having been kidnapped and raped by dacoits, bandits, she turned the tables and in due course became one of their leaders, before her arrest, election as a parliamentarian, and assassination in 2001. Hers had been a busy life.[23]

There were even female gangs. The primordially macho culture of the Russian *vorovskoi mir* ('Thieves' World') not only barred membership by women, but required its members to renounce their ties to wives, mothers and sisters. Nonetheless, gangs emerged within women prisoners of Stalin's Gulags which aped the code, slang and violent manners of their male counterparts, even while being abused by them.[24] In the 1970s, Japanese cities were even terrorised by the Sukeban, gangs of delinquent teenage girls in school uniforms and surgical masks, wielding chains and razorblades as they shoplifted, brawled and generally misbehaved like a Pacific Rim St Trinian's (a fictional anarchic British girls' private school).[25]

Nonetheless, for a variety of reasons, ranging from simple sexism to the premium put on physical strength, women's roles within organised crime have in the past largely been limited to couriers, lookouts, prostitutes, pickpockets or similar lowly roles, or as status symbols for gang leaders. At best they could often be called on to resolve intra-gang disputes, in an extension of traditional maternal stereotypes, a role sometimes taken on by the wives of Japanese Yakuza leaders, for example.[26] Since the later twentieth century, though, that has begun to change. A 2022 report by the UN Office on Drugs and Crime admitted the lack of reliable and comprehensive data but noted that women were recorded as representing 9 per cent of organised crime group members in the Netherlands, 2 per cent in Italy and 5 per cent in the UK.[27] Most noteworthy, though, is that they are – while still a small minority – increasingly assuming leadership roles.

Felia Allum has noted that even though past accounts relegating women within the Neapolitan Camorra to a minor role reflected a bias within police, journalists and academics alike, there has been a clear elevation of their status of late.[28] When godfather Gennaro Licciardi died in prison in 1994, for example, his sister Maria took over his clan, until her arrest in 2001.[29] Often this is ostensibly driven by necessity. In the case of the Camorra, it followed bloody gang wars in the 1980s and also a series of successful police operations which further decapitated the crime structures, forcing women to step in as their husband's proxies and then replacements. However, there have been gang wars and mass arrests in the past which did not lead to any kind of gender rebalancing, so one must presume that this also reflects a slow cultural change, too. Figures like Simone Jasmin did not rise to power in the violent Durban-based drug gang known as the Cartel on the coattails of a male relative, or even the three consecutive gangster boyfriends who died (earning her the nickname 'the Black Widow'), but her own drive, ambition and ruthlessness.[30] Likewise, although Xie Caiping, the violent gang boss from the Chinese city of Chongqing, sentenced to 18 years on charges from running illegal gambling dens to illegal imprisonment, was sister-in-law to a corrupt local police chief, he certainly did not set her up in business.[31]

Whether or not one quite wants to celebrate this particular assault on the glass ceiling, it reflects not just changing realities of underworld leadership (entrepreneurial ability, for example, becoming more important than simple physical strength), but also the influence of the evolving values of the upperworld, for all gangsters may like to imagine themselves a breed apart. Indeed, a new breed of 'queenpins' has even emerged within the almost caricaturishly hyper-masculine world of the Latin American *narcos*, where those women who have risen within the cartels without the support of family ties actually prove more violent, subverting the sexist assumptions of 'narco-culture' in what one study described as 'narco-feminism' (although one could question whether proving oneself more violent than the men is really 'feminism' or, as with those female Gulag gangs, merely submitting to masculine values).[32]

Of course, there are new criminal worlds, from white-collar fraud to hacking, where gender is much less directly relevant. That many female hackers still obscure their gender behind ambiguous or even explicitly masculine handles, though, suggests they at least assume there is some remaining stigma. The case of Kristina Svechinskaya, a 21-year-old Russian studying in New York who was charged with being part of a gang which stole $14 million from banks in Britain and America, suggests that it is not just the criminals who are only slowly evolving.[33] She was described in the media as 'the world's sexiest computer hacker' and *New York* magazine asked 'How Sexy Is Accused Russian Hacker Kristina Svechinskaya?'[34] Needless to say, none of her male co-defendants had their looks and clothes commented upon in the press.

Are mafias migrating?

If organised crime is crossing the gender frontier, is it also not only trading but moving across borders? There is a pervasive media myth about organised crime's capacity to 'invade' or 'colonise' new turfs, given a new lease of life of late by wider fears about migration and the dilution of national identities. To a degree, this has been based on one particular example, which has been lovingly commemorated, magnified and mythologised on screens small and large: the Sicilians' move into America. It is certainly true that a traditional Italian organised crime structure was transplanted into the United States in the late nineteenth and early twentieth centuries, entrenching itself into the marginalised and impoverished neighbourhoods where the Italian immigrants settled, such as Italian Harlem and Brooklyn in New York, Newark's First Ward, South Philadelphia and 'Little Italies' from Buffalo to San Diego. There were two reasons why Italian-American organised crime would prove so significant and long-lasting, though.

The first was scale. As of 1870, there were only some 25,000 Italian immigrants in the United States, largely more affluent and educated northern Italians. However, from the 1880s through to the 1920s, more than 4 million more would join them, predominantly escaping the miserable poverty of Sicily and southern Italy. With such a critical mass, it was inevitable not only that there were gangsters in their midst, but that they brought with them the values, assumptions and social structures of their homeland. Most had little money and less English, and arrived to find only the hardest jobs and poorest neighbourhoods open for them. There is a usual process of migrant succession at work: one generation's underdogs will seek to climb and, to this end, will often end up doing this stepping on the heads of the next. The Irish who had flocked to America earlier, fleeing poverty, persecution and then the Great Potato Famine, and who had themselves been shunned, derided and exploited, had found their place, built powerful local political machines, and looked to protect their newfound positions. The Italians would find no great allies there.

To a population which felt it had been excluded from the American Dream, to whom the legitimate state seemed distant, uncaring and alien, and legitimate economic and social opportunities denied, the social order (and economic opportunities) provided by a criminal culture was at least familiar and accessible. Organised crime was indeed *cosa nostra*, 'our thing', when the licit state and economy seemed to be 'theirs', even as the gangsters exploited and oppressed them. Under normal circumstances, this state of affairs might only have lasted a generation or two; typically, the mobster doesn't want his son following him into the business but instead wants them to be a dentist, an accountant, whatever signals safety and respectability. However, the extraordinary economic opportunities of Prohibition distorted this usual trajectory, making the Italian-American Mafia an unusual example of multi-generational criminality, even though by now it is withering, outflanked and outstripped by new ethnic crime phenomena with less to lose, from Mara Salvatrucha gangsters from El Salvador to the primarily African-American network of Bloods street gangs.

No room at the inn

The Italians were among the exceptions, though. As Federico Varese has convincingly demonstrated in *Mafias on the Move* (2011), organised crime rarely tries to 'colonise' new territories by choice, and usually fails when it does. Criminals move abroad because of pressure from rivals or the authorities, because they are weak, not ambitious. They only really succeed when they have a diaspora to hide in or stumble upon some new opportunity that local rivals have overlooked or market not yet satisfied. The Cosa Nostra in America was able first to exploit its countrymen, a community that needed protection and resources and which was neither already being predated upon by other gangs, nor adequately defended by the authorities. The sudden market expansion generated by Prohibition again created the resources that the Italian-Americans – along with many other criminals – could use to entrench themselves.

This was a relatively unusual set of circumstances, though. The Chinese Triads, themselves largely expelled from the mainland, have likewise been able to embed themselves in Chinatowns around the world, not least on the back of continued waves of migration and cultural disconnects with their host nations.[35] They too looked to build a cultural basis for their authority in the community, relying on a combination of shared values, a mythologised background and the ability to help their friends and bring terror to their enemies. Originally, they may have emerged from the seventeenth-century Tiandihui, or Heaven and Earth Society, a conspiratorial organisation dedicated to overthrowing the Qing Dynasty and restoring the Ming. (This is certainly their claim.) The Tiandihui considered themselves patriots, opposed to a dynasty dominated by the Manchus of, surprisingly enough, Manchuria, and would later support the Kuomintang or Nationalist Party in the early twentieth century, and flee to Hong Kong, Taiwan, and further parts when the Communists took power on the mainland. If the Triads were ever revolutionaries, though, they had long become little more than gangsters, dressing up their criminality in ritual and legend.

Otherwise 'mafia migration' within diasporas tends only to last a generation or so. The violent Jamaican Shower Posse, for example, spread from its origins in Kingston's violent and impoverished Tivoli Gardens neighbourhood to expatriate communities in Toronto, Miami and New York. Thanks to the activities of brokers, it has been able to develop drug- and gun-trafficking networks that have proven surprisingly resilient to law-enforcement activity, but there is an open question whether the next generation will look to the Shower Posse or some new up-and-coming rival – or be able to move away from these criminal subcultures altogether.[36] Even when criminals do migrate, their ties with home tend to attenuate. The American Mafia deals with its Sicilian forebear and namesake, but is an entirely separate organisation, just as the Russian criminals who set up shop on the Spanish Riviera, in New York's Brighton Beach or parts of Israel quickly became autonomous.

Or else they actually break their ties as they migrate. This was very much the case with the Albanians. The year 1985 saw the collapse of a brutal and bizarre neo-Stalinist regime in Albania after the death of dictator Enver Hoxha, a man who banned beards because of their association with Islam and Orthodox Christianity, and with a particular passion for books about vampires. There followed years of economic crisis and political instability, fuelled by a massive proliferation of weapons: when the government collapsed in 1997, up to a million pistols, rifles, machine guns and rocket-propelled grenade launchers disappeared from state armouries.[37] Combined with the civil war and ethnic cleansing in the neighbouring Serbian province of Kosovo, with its Albanian majority, this encouraged massive levels of emigration. By 1998, fully 20 per cent of the population was living abroad.[38] Most were, of course, hard-working and law-abiding citizens, but a minority – especially battle-hardened former guerrillas from Kosovo and backwoodsmen from the almost-medieval highlands of Albania – turned to organised crime. They did so with such vigour and violence that they shocked even their Italian counterparts and established for themselves a powerful position within Europe's heroin trade. The Albanian 'mafia' is still powerful, especially smuggling its own nationals into the EU and UK, even if it quickly lost the apparent ascendancy it had in the early 2000s, but its relations with gangsters back home is – as with the American and Sicilian mafias – essentially transactional, no more.

Otherwise, contested 'colonisations' don't tend to work. In the 1990s, Russian-based gangs crashed into Central Europe, eager to build themselves a new criminal empire that would not be dependent on the political and economic fate of the Motherland. They had money, drugs, guns and a willingness to use violence on a scale different from most of the indigenous crime gangs. They still failed.[39] There were no unclaimed markets, and as the state structures saw these thuggish newcomers as a particular security threat, they made them a priority, unexpectedly enough with the enthusiastic support of local criminals. An Estonian police officer once told me just how handy it was that almost every week some new bit of rock-solid intelligence about the Russians (and Chechens) would arrive on his desk, courtesy of native gangsters. He knew perfectly well this wasn't because they were public-spirited, but because, in his words, 'They didn't want to take the Russians on directly, and so long as we were doing the job of evicting these unwelcome newcomers for them, they were happy.'

It is telling that, having failed as conquerors in the 1990s, the Russians came back in the 2000s as merchant adventurers, not competing for turf, but offering their temptingly wide range of illicit goods and services to whoever might want them. Drugs or trafficked women? Hacking or money laundering? A market for your stolen cars or a 'torpedo' (Russian criminal slang for a hitman) to deal with some troublesome rival? Criminal concierges and wholesalers for the discerning modern godfather, the Russians could offer the lot, and for the right price, without any impolite attempts to take over your business. So much of the criminal commodities sold on the streets of Europe by local criminals (including up to a third of all the heroin) in some way, shape or form, comes through Russia or – more likely since the 2022 invasion of Ukraine closed so many direct transport routes – physically by another way, but courtesy of the Russians. Globalisation has worked a different way, not so much moving criminals around – although as individuals, of course, they do – but rather in connecting them.

Is a SPECTRE haunting Europe?

How strong are these ties, though, and do they become enough to bond disparate criminal enterprises into a single, global stricture? People have always been treated as tradeable commodities, illicit goods always trafficked, underworld empires followed upperworld ones, and ideas peddled and stolen. The question is, who (if anyone?) manages this economy? Some have warned of the emergence of transnational criminal empires and a globally integrated criminal community, the James Bond films' SPECTRE – the Special Executive for Counterintelligence, Terrorism, Revenge and Extortion – become real. The journalist Claire Sterling, for example, coyly admitted that

> there is no hard proof that the elite of the international underworld, Sicilian, American, Colombian, Turkish, Russian, Chinese, Japanese, all meet at once and vote leaders in and out of office. But they have certainly arrived at some kind of pax mafiosa.[40]

Fortunately, the reason why 'there is no hard proof' of what she goes on to call 'this planetary criminal alliance' is that it doesn't exist, and never has. Crime doesn't work that way, just as the conspiracy theories that suggest the global upperworld is controlled by the Masons, the Bilderberg Group or shape-shifting reptilians lack 'hard proof' because they are so much nonsense. There are powerful structures which, within their own territories, have considerable agency and power, but outside them must rely on deals and alliances. There are markets, which can be shaped and distorted by both human agency – cartels and monopolies, the vagaries of fashion – and the laws of supply and demand. Governance in the underworld is as much as anything else about predicting and responding to outside forces, brokering relationships and resisting rivals, and seizing new opportunities. Sound familiar? This is much like being an upper-world head of state, albeit with less pomp and more pimp (and fewer opportunities to retire with financial and physical security).

Instead, just as gangs are more likely to be networks or else operating within networks, so too the whole global criminal ecosystem is shaped not by criminal superpowers, let alone a 'planetary criminal alliance' but by economies, a series of interconnecting markets within which operate myriad smaller to larger enterprises. Some of their markets seem distinct from ours, but in practice they use the same currencies as the rest of us, funnelled largely through the same banks, to cover goods moved on the same container ships and trucking routes, by people who often went to the same schools as us and want to buy the same nice houses as us. Where and how do we draw the line between underworld and upperworld?

CHAPTER 20

CRIMINAL WORLD

Once, English families worried about the 'Resurrectionists' – body-snatchers – who would unearth recently buried cadavers to sell for medical dissection. This led to a fashion for iron coffins, or else mort-safes, heavy, padlocked iron frames placed around graves for around six weeks, after which the body was presumed too decayed to be valuable. This criminal trade has since been replaced by modern 'organleggers' as the demand for transplants outpaces supply. However, traditions continue to shape the trade in human remains. In Bhutan, the religious use of skulls and bones led to a criminal trade that has survived to the present day. In 2007, Indian police arrested a gang exhuming buried skeletons for this purpose; one courier was arrested on a bus, in possession of fully 67 human skulls and 10 other bones, the latter apparently being much prized to make ceremonial horns.[1] More recently, though, the ancient Chinese custom of the ghost marriage, originally the union of two dead people so they may be together in the afterlife, has mutated into a more gruesome version that sees living men 'married' to dead women so as to appease cultural expectations. In 2015, one village in the north-central Shanxi province saw 14 women's graves robbed in one raid to cater to this trade, which was only illegalised in 2006.[2] In an echo of European practices in the nineteenth century, families are increasingly investing in heavy, reinforced concrete coffins, and cemeteries are now being watched by CCTV.

Keeping the faith

The modern world, for all its technological marvels, is still forever in a state of transition, shaped by a mix of old and new, science and superstition, ambitious eagerness for what lies just around the corner, and conservative suspicion of the coming thing. As above, so below: the criminal world is likewise balanced between managerial innovation and diehard traditionalism.

Indeed, tradition and ritual still play a role holding organised crime groups together and allowing them to maintain their identity and 'brand' in the confusing and unmoored information age. Ghana's Sakawa Boys turn to traditional West African juju folk magic to boost their chances of conning foreigners, claiming and apparently believing that, whether by sleeping in a consecrated coffin or using appropriate charms, they can send their spirits into the internet to possess their targets.[3] In the process, they polarise opinion at home, being regarded as a terrible blight on the nation by some, but popular heroes by many. Their high-rolling lifestyles are feted in film and TV, because they spin all kinds of surreal online scams to rip off the very people who once exploited Ghana in colonial times. Yet as well as consolidating their role in the public imagination, this helps them retain a sense of common purpose and identity, an essential way of maintaining intra-group loyalty. Likewise, Nigerian people smugglers often require their clients to swear 'juju oaths' invoking illness, madness and death for them and their families should they fail to repay their debts to the criminals or inform to the police.[4]

This is not confined to Africa. Among the Latin American drug cartels are self-described priests and worshippers of Santa Muerte (Holy Death), a perverted pseudo-angelic figure, who may even offer up the severed heads of enemies to bless their operations.[5] The 'Ndrangheta still reportedly sometimes make a new member swear an oath on a Bible soaked in the blood of a sacrificed lamb. New members of the Chinese Triads similarly go through an elaborate initiation including swearing the 'Thirty-Six Oaths'. These include the invocations that 'If I rob a sworn brother, or assist an outsider to do so, I will be killed by five thunderbolts' and 'I must not disclose any address where my sworn brothers keep their wealth, nor must I conspire to make wrong use of such knowledge. If I do so I will be killed by a myriad of swords.'[6] All very dramatic, but take away the fanciful language, and this is just the usual and sensible operational code of any organised crime group, relying on threats to deter actions that might weaken or divide the gang. Criminals are essentially pragmatists, but some ritual and razzamatazz does help both internal cohesion and community legitimacy.[7]

The trickster and the optimist

After all, while it is easy to focus on the reasons why organised crime gangs rise and prosper, it is also worth noting that they are under constant pressure, too. Networked structures are harder for the police to dismantle, but also harder to hold together. The underworld has to be able to sell itself in both practical and emotional terms to current and prospective members alike. No one is truly born criminal. Sometimes, to be sure, crime is about poor impulse control, terrible upbringing, or outright rottenness. More often, though, it is, in its own terms, a rational act. We are typically ambitious for ourselves and those we hold dear, and have a keen sense of what we consider our fair share. We also often allow other factors, including peer pressure, inherited cultural values, a belief that we lack choices, sheer greed, or false hope to cloud our judgements. Nonetheless, we make our own decisions.

When legitimate society appears to offer too few opportunities to gain wealth and status, or seems to deny them to us for reasons of origin, colour, religion, accent or the like. When the intangible pressures, injunctions and role models of our society either encourage us towards a criminal life or at least fail adequately to deter us from such a step. When the opportunities available through law-breaking appear temptingly greater than those available through legitimate activities. When the dangers, whether at the hands of the state or criminal rivals, appear low proportionate to the perceived gains. When all the cool kids are doing it, or else the established role models. When all these elements of a cost-benefit analysis appear to make a life of crime more rewarding in social and monetary terms than the alternative, then it seems to make sense. Of course, we may be wrong. As Steven Levitt and Stephen Dubner noted, crack dealers in the USA take on 'the most dangerous job in America' and, according to sample data from Chicago, typically do so for less than the federal minimum wage.[8] However, they are seduced by the glamour and wealth of the handful of successful drug kingpins, sure that they will make it to that level rather than appreciating the extent to which the odds are overwhelmingly that they will soon be dead, in prison or still stuck living at home.

So long as there are unfulfilled, unaffordable or illegal needs and individuals with the greed, ambition or sociopathy to seek to fulfil them, there will be crime. But to put it another way, crime is simply another sign of our humanity, our fallible, gullible, self-interested, loophole-seeking, clannish, rules-breaking, values-questioning, risk-taking humanity. The more society is organised, the more the criminals must organise in response, but also the more ways in which criminality helps organise us. The accelerating pace of social, political, economic and technological change generates an imagination race between criminals and crime-fighters, between underworld and upperworld.

The trickster has thus not been extinguished in today's seemingly rational age.[9] In many ways, the computer hacker has become the trickster of our times, but our literature, TV and films are full of criminal as (anti)hero, whether Dexter the vigilante serial killer who only sates his blood lust on bad guys, to Han Solo, the smuggler turned revolutionary (who, of course, shot first). Many very real criminals still invoke the ambiguity of the trickster. Besides, sometimes, usually by accident, criminals do good. In the late nineteenth century, Lithuanian smugglers helped foil the tsarist Russian censors who were trying to erase the whole Lithuanian language by bringing in books and newspapers printed in neighbouring Prussia.[10] For its own reasons, the Cosa Nostra hunted Nazi spies and saboteurs in New York's docks and helped the Allies reconquer Sicily. In late Soviet times, the black-marketeers allowed people to read literature and listen to music banned by the stodgy Communist Party censors, and in the process helped keep alive a spirit of freedom that would be unleashed in the 1980s. North Korea's millennials have become known as the 'Jangmadang generation' after the Korean word for the markets which have emerged, where much of the goods for sale are contraband, whether food, or medicine in scarce supply, or smuggled foreign culture, not least films and K-pop music from the South on USB sticks. These markets provide not just a window onto the outside world, but a place to find life-saving goods for those without Party connections.[11]

The lengthening arm of the law

Either way, they face an increasingly complex challenge from the state. Pre-modern societies typically lacked police forces. Bodies like the *toxotai*, 300 publicly owned Scythian slaves of ancient Athens; the Nubian warriors known as Medjay who, by the Eighteenth Dynasty (1550–1292 BCE), were protecting Egypt's royal tombs; or the Vigiles

Urbani of Rome, were all security guards more than they were police. (Indeed, the well-to-do citizens of the Eighteenth Dynasty would keep ferocious trained guard monkeys for their own protection.) Over time, though, they would evolve if not police forces, then at least procedures that nonetheless made a life of crime riskier. Such was the threat of professional murder-for-hire in Renaissance Rome, for example, that the papal authorities banned concealable weapons like the wheel-lock carbine and required doctors treating wounds to ask the victims about the attacks, even if most preferred to give innocuous answers, as though the city was in the grip of an epidemic of slippery stairs and aggressive doors.[12] Of course, it didn't help that the *sbirri*, Rome's police, were so notoriously high-handed and unpopular that prostitutes would insult each other as '*sbirro*'s girlfriend'.

It would take time – as Allen and Barzel noted, 544 years would pass between 'the Statute of Winchester in 1285, which established private policing of criminal activity in England, and the Metropolitan Police Act in 1829, which created a public police force in London'[13] – but in due course the state in general would expand and replace the feud, the hue and cry, the mercenary thieftaker and similar measures with law-enforcement agencies of its own. Today we may grumble about how overstretched police forces respond to cases of burglary, shoplifting or stolen bicycles, but in part the very reason for that overstretch is the scale of resources thrown at serious cases such as murders and organised crime.

This is not just about their legal powers or the technology already noted – extensive though they may be – but also the scale at which states can operate, and, indeed, their own capacity to cooperate. The original London Metropolitan Police numbered around a thousand officers. In September 2014, on the other hand, Operation Archimedes became the largest ever cross-EU international law-enforcement operation to date, targeting a range of organised crime gangs involved in trafficking everything from drugs to people. Over nine days, 20,000 police and prosecutors from 34 countries made 1,150 arrests, their work supported by Interpol, as well as Europol, Eurojust and Frontex, the EU agencies responsible for police and judicial cooperation and border security, respectively.[14] It is also a matter of technique. For example, predictive policing, using the analysis of massive amounts of data to forecast likely criminal hotspots or even identify probable offenders, carries with it all kinds of risks of racial profiling and 'garbage in, garbage out' – its accuracy will depend entirely on the integrity of the data it crunches – but could be a powerful tool in combating organised rather than spontaneous crime. AI also offers the prospect of finally giving law enforcement a way of winnowing the vast and near-unmanageable amounts of information at their disposal, from financial transaction reports to text messages. (A financial crime investigation, after all, can involve millions of pages of documents.)

Criminal world

This is, of course, why organised crime itself is evolving under these Darwinian pressures, but that is not what is going to save them. Individual gangs will rise, fall, prosper or be broken, but the organised underworld is, like any shadow, indivisible from the upperworld. The modern world is defined by the interconnectivity of not just the market but the information space. A supermarket in Berlin sells oranges from South Africa and Argentinian beef; a teenager in Kent consumes Japanese manga and Korean noodles; a call centre operator in Mumbai fields customer care for a company in Houston, just as a few miles away in the Bandra Kurla Complex financial district, a banker is concluding the buy-out of some Australian real estate. Midland Bank, once one of the UK's 'big four', was bought out by the Hongkong and Shanghai Banking Corporation.

Yet this dynamic, interconnected, globalised, networked, cross-cultural world is so permeated by organised crime that we often do not see it, making it often very hard to see where upperworld ends and underworld begins. Of course, the drug barons, sex traffickers and killers for hire stand squarely outside our societies and moral economies, but even they depend on the money launderers and similar specialists who may come from, or also service, legitimate clients. Meanwhile, those processes connecting us all have become irreversibly shadowed by crime. The same network of container ships moving those oranges and noodles around the world hides drugs and guns, or terrified would-be migrants, shivering in the wave-tossed dark. That filesharing site from which copyright-busting cartoons can be downloaded, may also be being used by hackers to exchange malware. The rapid expansion of the Bandra Kurla Complex was accompanied by claims that slums were cleared fraudulently by some developers, locals cheated out of their land rights,[15] while that Australian deal may in fact be prompted by the closing of a meth lab, put out of business by the industrial laboratories in Myanmar undercutting domestic production thanks to their economies of scale.[16] The Hongkong and Shanghai Banking Corporation had its origins in a financial house set up in part to service the opium trade,[17] just as so many financial institutions around the world, which once would have bankrolled slavers, now knowingly or unknowingly launder the funds of drug traffickers and warlords, so long as they have had the good sense and better manners to prewash them thoroughly beforehand.

Without trying to pretend there is no difference between upright citizen and thuggish gangster, we have to recognise that our banks are full of dirty money, our foreign policy depends on deals with kleptocrats, our supply chains are packed with counterfeit, our glittering cities are built on foundations of stolen sand and speculative fraud, and our consumer goods and raw materials alike are produced by trafficked labour. Just as participation in organised crime is not confined to those who may seem to have no alternatives, from the ghetto kid to the impoverished Afghan opium farmer, hardly those who reap the greatest rewards, so too it is not only the slums and the banking centres which are complicit. It also extends to the complacent middle ground, where the benefits are very real, even if sufficiently concealed so that everyone can pretend not to be involved. A study of local organised crime in Scotland, for example, found that the gangs' illicit investment in the legitimate economy tended to flow into marginal, cash-in-hand sectors such as cleaning services and security, with neighbourhood residents well aware from where the money originated, but beyond that the benefits extended 'well beyond the boundaries of Scotland's most deprived neighbour-hoods, helping to fuel the consumption habits of the middle classes in the "bourgeois utopias" . . . where the most successful criminal entrepreneurs resided'.[18] Meanwhile, as discussed, the criminals – the smarter and more successful ones, at least – adopt the financial tech-nologies and business strategies of the upperworld.

Besides, none of the range of political systems evident in the twenty-first century, from mature democracies to post-truth authori-tarianisms, technocratic one-party states to ramshackle dictatorships, have managed to banish human hypocrisy, self-interest, messianism and short-sightedness. There will continue to be corruption and inefficiency and those crucial gaps between the moral economies of states and societies – or at least significant communities – within which illicit markets thrive. There will continue to be get-rich(or famous)-quick ambition and credulity. As 'BX', a former London gang member, told journalist Duncan Campbell, 'Everyone wants to be a gangster . . . Everyone's seen it on TV and that's what they want to be. They look at music videos and it looks like the people in them are making hundreds of thousands of pounds . . . So if you're broke, if you can't get a job, you're going to take the opportunity.'[19] Perversely, the real effect of the greater organisation of society and thus the growing capacity of law enforcement is to ensure that the criminals exploiting and servicing these markets will need to be all the more organised. Just like us. We are, in short, unable to sever our own shadow from ourselves.

The sixteenth-century Japanese thief, bandit and rebel Ishikawa Goemon summed it up in his funeral poem, written the night before being boiled alive for seeking to assassinate the warlord Toyotomi Hideyoshi. There are different versions, but the central message is clear:

The Ishikawa river;
the grains of pure white sand may run out,
but the seeds of thieves will never run out.

Notes

Introduction

1 For an excellent study, see Vicenzo Ruggiero, *Crime in Literature* (2003), pp. 28–37

2 Ibid., p. 39

3 All such figures need to be taken with considerable caution. A trillion dollars represents a widespread conservative assessment, while in 2017 a report from the US-based organisation Global Financial Integrity put the figure at an eye-catching upper end of $2.2 trillion; 'Transnational Crime is a $1.6 trillion to $2.2 trillion Annual "Business", Finds New GFI Report', GFI, 27 March 2017

4 Quoted in Samuel Putnam's introduction to Miguel de Cervantes, *Three Moral Tales* (1952, orig. 1613), p. xiii; we may not have a definitive date for *Miscelanea*, but Zapata died in 1593

5 Jean Riverain, *Chroniques de l'argot* (1963)

6 Jeffrey Kastner, 'Animals on trial', *Cabinet*, autumn 2001

7 Valery Chalidze, *Criminal Russia: Essays on crime in the Soviet Union* (1977)

8 Nick Fisher, 'Workshops of villains', in Keith Hopwood (ed.), *Organised Crime in Antiquity* (1999), p. 81

9 Pascal Vernus, *Affairs and Scandals in Ancient Egypt* (2003)

10 Michel Foucault, *Discipline and Punish: The Birth of the Prison* (1977), p. 281

11 Frances Berdan, 'Crime and control in Aztec society', in Keith Hopwood (ed.), *Organised Crime in Antiquity* (1999), p. 265

12 'Organized crime is a nonideological enterprise involving a number of persons in close social interaction, organized on a hierarchical basis . . . for the purpose of securing profit and power by engaging in illegal and legal activities. Positions in the hierarchy and positions involving functional specialization may be assigned on the basis of kinship or friendship, or rationally assigned according to skill . . . Permanency is assumed by the members who strive to keep the enterprise integral and active in pursuit of its goals. It eschews competition and strives for monopoly on an industry or territorial basis. There is a willingness to use violence and/or bribery to achieve ends or to maintain discipline. Membership is restricted . . . There are explicit rules, oral or written, which are enforced by sanctions that include murder.' Howard Abadinsky, *Organized Crime* (1990), p. 6

13 The *Independent*, 18 July 2024; 'The world's most liveable cities', *The Economist*, 26 June 2024

PART ONE: THE AGE OF STATE-BUILDING

Chapter 1: 'Robbers of the Better Sort' and Makers of States

1 Marcelo Duhalde, 'How an army of eunuchs ran the Forbidden City', *South China Morning Post*, 23 July 2018

2 David Robinson, *Bandits, Eunuchs and the Son of Heaven: Rebellion and the Economy of Violence in Mid-Ming China* (2001)

3 Brent Shaw, 'Bandits in the Roman Empire', *Past & Present* 105 (1984), pp. 24–5

4 Quoted in Philip Hitti & Walid Khalidi, *History of the Arabs, revised, 10th ed.* (2002), p. 25

5 Josephus, *Antiquities of the Jews*, 18.274, quoted in Lincoln Blumell, 'Beware of bandits! Banditry and land travel in the Roman Empire', *Journeys* 8:1–2 (2007)

6 Anton Blok, *De Bokkerijders* (1991)

7 Maurice Keen, *The Outlaws of Medieval Legend, revised edition* (2000), pp. 11–22

8 Frances Berdan, 'Living on the edge in an ancient imperial world: Aztec crime and deviance', *Global Crime* 9:1–2 (2008)

9 Charles Tilly, 'War making and state making as organised crime', in Peter Evans, Dietrich Rueschemeyer & Theda Skocpol (eds), *Bringing the State Back In* (1985), pp. 170, 172

10 Mancur Olson, 'Dictatorship, democracy, and development', *American Political Science Review* 87 (1993)

11 Quoted in Ludwig Friedländer, *Roman Life and Manners under the Early Empire, vol. I* (1970), p. 297

12 Andrew Young, 'What does it take for a roving bandit settle down? Theory and an illustrative history of the Visigoths', *Public Choice* 168 (2016)

13 Matthew Baker & Erwin Bulte, 'Kings and Vikings: on the dynamics of competitive agglomeration', *Economics of Governance* 11:3 (2010)

14 Peter Kurrild-Klitgaard & Gert Tinggard Svendsen, 'Rational bandits: plunder, public good and the Vikings', *Public Choice* 117:3–4 (2003)

15 Frances Stonor Saunders, *The Devil's Broker* (2004), p. 19

16 Eric Hobsbawm, *Bandits* (1969), p. 95

17 Barbara Hanawalt, 'Fur-collar crime: the pattern of crime among the fourteenth-century English nobility', *Journal of Social History* 8:4 (1975), p. 4

18 Trevor Dean, *Crime in Medieval Europe* (2001), p. 30

19 For an excellent summary of his career, see Roy Hunnisett & J.B. Post (eds), *Medieval Legal Records edited in memory of C.A.F. Meekings* (1978), pp. 198–207

20 John Keepe, 'Bandits and the law in Muscovy', *Slavonic & East European Review* 35: 1 (1956), p. 220

21 Vadim Volkov, *Violent Entrepreneurs* (2002)

22 Jonathan Sumption, *Trial by Fire, vol. II* (2001), p. 156

23 Augustine, *City of God* (Penguin Classics edition, 2003), p. 139

24 Frances Stonor Saunders, *The Devil's Broker* (2004), p. 95

25 David Robinson, 'Banditry and the subversion of state authority in China: the Capital region during the Middle Ming period (1450–1525)', *Journal of Social History* 33:3 (2000), p. 535

26 Donald Crummey, 'Banditry and resistance: noble and peasant in nineteenth-century Ethiopia', in Crummey (ed.), *Banditry, Rebellion & Social Protest in Africa* (1986), pp. 138–40

Chapter 2: Between Extortion and Protection

1 Allan MacInnes, 'Crown, clans and fine: the "civilizing" of Scottish Gaeldom', *Northern Scotland* 14:1 (1993)

2 Diego Gambetta, *The Sicilian Mafia. The Business of Private Protection* (1996), Appendix A

3 Anton Blok, *The Mafia of a Sicilian Village, 1860–1960: A Study of Violent Peasant Entrepreneurs* (1974), p. 11

4 Federico Varese, *The Russian Mafia: private protection in a new market economy* (2001); Peter Hill, *The Japanese Mafia: Yakuza, law and the state* (2003)

5 Eric Hobsbawm, *Bandits*, 4th ed. (2000), p. 20

6 For example, Anton Blok, 'The peasant and the brigand: social banditry reconsidered', *Comparative Studies in Society and History* 14:4 (1972); Pat O'Malley, 'Social bandits, modern capitalism and the traditional peasantry. A critique of Hobsbawm', *Journal of Peasant Studies* 6:4 (1979); and Richard Slatta, 'Eric J. Hobsbawm's Social Bandit: A critique and revision', *Contracorriente*, 1:2 (2004)

7 Minsoo Kang, *Invincible and Righteous Outlaw: The Korean Hero Hong Gildong in Literature, History, and Culture* (2018)

8 Ruth Pike, 'The Reality and Legend of the Spanish Bandit Diego Corrientes', *Folklore* 99:2 (1988)

9 Tomas Balkelis, 'Social banditry and nation-making: The myth of a Lithuanian robber', *Past & Present* 198:1 (2008)

10 He himself denied he ever said this, crediting it to 'some enterprising reporter who apparently felt the need to fill out his copy'; Willie Sutton & Edward Linn, *Where the Money Was: the memoirs of a bank robber* (2004), p. 161

11 Charles Tilly, 'War making and state making as organised crime', in Peter Evans, Dietrich Rueschemeyer & Theda Skocpol (eds), *Bringing the State Back In* (1985), p. 169

12 Ibid.

13 Ibid., p. 173

14 Julius Ruff, *Violence in Early Modern Europe 1500–1800* (2001), pp. 231–2; Florike Egmond, *Underworlds: organized crime in Netherlands, 1650–1800* (1993), p. 104

15 Kellow Chesney, *The Victorian Underworld* (1970), p. 39
16 Greg Bankoff, 'Bandits, banditry and landscapes of crime in the nineteenth-century Philippines', *Journal of Southeast Asian Studies* 29:2 (1998)
17 The *Independent*, 26 February 2012
18 Nene Mburu, 'Contemporary banditry in the Horn of Africa: causes, history and political implications', *Nordic Journal of African Studies* 8:2 (1999), p. 98
19 Vanda Felbab-Brown, 'Puntland's problems', *Foreign Affairs*, 15 June 2017
20 Mark Galeotti, *The Vory: Russia's super mafia* (2018)
21 Reuters, 25 March 2011

Chapter 3: Cocoa Beans and Currency Counterfeiters

1   Frances Berdan, 'Crime and control in Aztec society', in Keith Hopwood (ed.), *Organised Crime in Antiquity* (1999)
2   Glyn Davies, *A History of Money* (2002)
3   Edoardo Grendi, 'Counterfeit coins and monetary exchange structures in the Republic of Genoa during the sixteenth and seventeenth centuries', in Edward Muir & Guido Ruggiero (eds), *History from Crime* (1994), pp. 172–3
4   Richard Pankhurst, 'The perpetuation of the Maria Teresa dollar and currency problems in Italian-occupied Ethiopia (1936–41)', *Journal of Ethiopian Studies* 8:2 (1970)
5   Richard Finlay & Anny Francis, 'A brief history of currency counterfeiting', *Bulletin of the Reserve Bank of Australia*, 19 September 2019
6   The *Guardian*, 22 December 1999; Stephen Jory, *Funny Money* (2012)
7   Niv Horesh, 'From Chengdu to Stockholm: a comparative study of the emergence of paper money in east and west', *Provincial China* 4:1 (2012)
8   *Time*, 18 January 1926
9   Adolf Burger, *The Devil's Workshop: A Memoir of the Nazi Counterfeiting Operation* (2022); Lawrence Malkin, *Krueger's Men: The Secret Nazi Counterfeit Plot and the Prisoners of Block 19* (2006)
10 Stephen Mercado, 'The Japanese Army's Noborito Research Institute', *International Journal of Intelligence & Counterintelligence* 17:2 (2004)
11 *New York Times*, 23 July 2006
12 US Senate, 'Why Congress Needs To ACT: Lessons Learned from the FTX Collapse', 1 December 2022

Chapter 4: Gamblers, Crafty Criminals, and the Early Organised Underworld

1   Geoffrey Chaucer, *The Canterbury Tales: Selected Tales in Modern English* (trans. Percy MacKaye) (2022), p. 90
2   Serina Patterson (ed.), *Games and Gaming in Medieval Literature* (2015)
3   Mary McIntosh, 'Changes in the organization of thieving', in Stanley Cohen (ed.), *Images of Deviance* (1971), p. 102

4   Ibid., p. 104
5   Alexander Lyon Macfie, 'Thuggee: an orientalist construction?', *Rethinking History* 12:3 (2008)
6   Kim Wagner, 'The deconstructed stranglers: A reassessment of thuggee', *Modern Asian Studies* 38:4 (2004)
7   Mike Dash, *Thug* (2005), pp. 66–78
8   Gamini Salgado, *The Elizabethan Underworld* (1992), p. 147
9   W. Bruce Lincoln, *In War's Dark Shadow* (1983), p. 127
10   Uwe Danker, 'Bandits and the state', in Richard Evans (ed.), *The German Underworld* (1988), p. 98
11   Mary Perry, *Crime and Society in Early Modern Seville* (1980), p. 32
12   Karl Friday, 'Teeth and Claws. Provincial Warriors and the Heian Court', *Monumenta Nipponica* 43:2 (1988)
13   Guy Geltner, 'Rural policing in the long trecento', *English Historical Review* 137:584 (2022); John Keep, 'Bandits and the law in Muscovy', *Slavic & East European Review* 35:84 (1956)
14   Franco Franceschi, 'The economy: work and wealth', in John Najemy (ed.), *Italy in the Age of the Renaissance* (2004), pp. 135–6
15   Fernand Braudel, *The Wheels of Commerce, vol. II* (1983), p. 303
16   Uwe Danker, 'Bandits and the state', in Richard Evans (ed.), *The German Underworld* (1988), p. 85

Chapter 5: Beggar Kings and Rookeries

1   Jonathon Green, *The Vulgar Tongue: Green's history of slang* (2015), p. 15
2   Victor Hugo, *The Hunchback of Notre Dame* (1831; Signet Classics translation 2001), p. 82
3   Franco Franceschi, 'The economy: work and wealth', in John Najemy (ed.), *Italy in the Age of the Renaissance* (2004), p. 131
4   Farah Karim-Cooper, 'Strangers in the city: the cosmopolitan nature of 16th-century Venice', British Library, 15 March 2016
5   Samuel Berner, 'Florentine society in the late sixteenth and early seventeenth centuries', *Studies in the Renaissance* 18 (1971), p. 241
6   Edward Muir, 'The idea of community in Renaissance Italy', *Renaissance Quarterly* 55:1 (2002), p. 1
7   Juvenal, cited in Jérome Carcopino, *Daily Life in Ancient Rome* (1956), p. 60
8   James Short, 'Criminology, the Chicago School, and sociological theory', *Crime, Law and Social Change* 37:2 (2002)
9   First espoused in Edwin Sutherland, *Principles of Criminology, 3rd ed.* (1939)
10   Mark Galeotti, *Paths of Wickedness and Crime: the underworlds of the Renaissance Italian city* (2012)
11   Lauro Martines, *Power and Imagination* (2002), p. 74
12   John Brackett, *Criminal Justice and Crime in Late Renaissance Florence, 1537–1609* (1992), pp. 137–8

13 Fergus Linnane, *London's Underworld* (2004), p. 62

14 Thomas Shadwell, *The Squire of Alsatia* (1688), quoted in the *New York Times*, 14 February 2012

15 Hugh Bellot, *The Inner and Middle Temple* (1902), p. 202

16 Mary Perry, *Crime and Society in Early Modern Seville* (1980), pp. 21, 45–6

17 Thomas Holloway, *Policing Rio de Janeiro* (1993), pp. 223–5

18 Douglas Hay, 'Crime and justice in eighteenth- and nineteenth-century England', *Crime & Justice* 2:1 (1980), p. 47

19 *News24* (South Africa), 14 March 2020

20 *France24*, 23 January 2022

21 Amnesty International, *'They come in shooting': Policing socially excluded communities* (2005), p. 14

22 Brendan O'Flaherty & Rajiv Sethi, 'Peaceable Kingdoms and War Zones. Preemption, Ballistics, and Murder in Newark', in Rafael Di Tella, Sebastian Edwards & Ernesto Schargrodsky (eds), *The Economics of Crime: Lessons for and from Latin America* (2010), p. 305

23 Aditi Kumar & Eric Rosenbach, 'The Truth about the Dark Web', *IMF Finance & Development*, September 2019

24 Europol, 8 June 2021; *New York Times*, 9 June 2021

PART TWO: THE AGE OF CAPITALISM

Chapter 6: Hurrah for the Pirate Kings

1 Polybius, *Histories*, XVIII.54, and Diodoros, *Historical Library*, XXVII.1, cited in Henry Ormerod, *Piracy in the Ancient World* (1924), p. 148, and Gary Reger, *Regionalism and Change in the Economy of Independent Delos* (1994), p. 19

2 Diodoros, *Historical Library*, XX.110, cited in Henry Ormerod, *Piracy in the Ancient World* (1924), p. 122

3 David Bjork, 'Piracy in the Baltic, 1375–1398', *Speculum* 18:1 (1943)

4 Domingo Non, 'Moro piracy during the Spanish period and its impact', *Japanese Journal of Southeast Asian Studies* 30:4 (1993), p. 408

5 Thomas Heywood & William Rowley, *Fortune by Land and Sea* (1607–9), Act V, scene 1, quoted in Claire Jowitt, 'Piracy and politics in Heywood and Rowley's Fortune by Land and Sea (1607–9)', *Renaissance Studies* 16:2 (2002), p. 223

6 David Bjork, 'Piracy in the Baltic, 1375–1398', *Speculum* 18:1 (1943)

7 Irene Katele, 'Piracy and the Venetian state: the dilemma of maritime defence in the fourteenth century', *Speculum* 63:4 (1988)

8 Janice Thomson, *Mercenaries, Pirates & Sovereigns* (1994), pp. 22–3

9 Claire Jowitt, 'Piracy and politics in Heywood and Rowley's Fortune by Land and Sea (1607–9)', *Renaissance Studies* 16:2 (2002), p. 218

10 Quoted in Kenneth Andrews, 'Sir Robert Cecil and Mediterranean plunder', *English Historical Review* 344 (1972), p. 514

11 John Appleby & Paul Dalton (eds), *Outlaws in Medieval and Early Modern England* (2009), pp. 155 & 157

12 Ibid., pp. 162–3

13 Kenneth Andrews, 'Sir Robert Cecil and Mediterranean plunder', *English Historical Review* 344 (1972), p. 521

14 Ibid., p. 530

15 Claire Jowitt, 'Piracy and politics in Heywood and Rowley's Fortune by Land and Sea (1607–9)', *Renaissance Studies* 16:2 (2002), p. 219

16 Janice Thomson, *Mercenaries, Pirates & Sovereigns* (1994), p. 47

17 Fernand Braudel, *The Mediterranean and the Mediterranean World in the Age of Philip II, vol. II* (1973), p. 867

18 Janice Thomson, *Mercenaries, Pirates & Sovereigns* (1994), pp. 25–6, 70–1

19 Margaret Small, 'From jellied seas to open waterways: redefining the northern limit of the knowable world', *Renaissance Studies* 21:3 (2007), pp. 335–6

20 Barbara Fuchs, 'Faithless empires: pirates, renegades and the English nation', *English Literary History* 67 (2000), p. 51

21 Kenneth Andrews, *Elizabethan Privateering* (1964), p. 228

22 Angus Konstam, *Blackbeard* (2007), p. 23

23 Nuala Zahedieh, 'Trade, plunder and economic development in Early English Jamaica, 1655–1689', *Economic History Review* 39 (1986)

24 Janice Thomson, *Mercenaries, Pirates & Sovereigns* (1994), p. 44

25 Ruby Maloni, 'The Angres and the English – Contenders for Power on the West Coast of India', *Proceedings of the Indian History Congress* 66 (2005)

26 Marcus Rediker, '"Under the banner of King Death": the social world of Anglo-American pirates, 1716 to 1726', *William & Mary Quarterly* 38:2 (1981), p. 214

27 *Seattle Times*, 14 May 2010

Chapter 7: Corruption, Bureaucracy, Forgery and Fraud

1 Niccolò Machiavelli, *Discourses on Livy* (1517; University of Chicago edition, 1996), p. 148

2 Following a corruption case brought by the US Department of Justice, he reached a settlement in 2014 to surrender some $34 million in assets held in the States. He was also found guilty in a separate case in France, receiving a suspended sentence and fine of €30 million and having his property there seized, including 17 luxury cars. In 2012, the UK also placed him under sanctions on the grounds of his corruption.

3 Christopher Eyre, 'Patronage, power, and corruption in pharaonic Egypt', *International Journal of Public Administration* 34:11 (2011)

4 William Chester Jordan, 'Anti-corruption campaigns in thirteenth-century Europe', *Journal of Medieval History* 35 (2009)

5   Brian Davies, 'The Politics of Give and Take: Kormlenie as Service Remuneration and Generalized Exchange, 1488–1726', in A. Kleimola & G. Lenhoff (eds), *Culture and Identity in Muscovy, 1359–1584* (1997)

6   Samuel Huntington, *Political Order in Changing Societies* (1968), p. 69

7   Andy Barnett, Bruce Yandle & George Naufal, 'Regulation, trust, and cronyism in Middle Eastern societies: The simple economics of "wasta"', *Journal of Socio-Economics* 44 (2013); Alena Ledeneva, *Russia's Economy of Favours: Blat, Networking and Informal Exchange* (1998); Yanjie Bian, 'The Prevalence and the Increasing Significance of Guanxi', *China Quarterly* 235 (2018)

8   Mary Perry, *Crime and Society in Early Modern Seville* (1980), pp. 64–5

9   Nick Fisher, '"Workshops of villains": was there much organised crime in classical Athens?', in Keith Hopwood (ed.), *Organised Crime in Antiquity* (1999), pp. 56–7

10 Alexandr Osipian, 'Forgeries and Their Social Circulation in the Context of Historical Culture: The Usable Past as a Resource for Social Advance in Early Modern Lemberg/Lviv', *Kyiv-Mohyla Humanities Journal* 1:1 (2014)

11 Jacqueline Hylkema, *Books, Crooks and Readers. The Seduction of Forgery, 1600–1800* (2014), p. 7

12 Mary Perry, *Crime and Society in Early Modern Seville* (1980), p. 34

13 Paul Gillingham, 'The strange business of memory: relic forgery in Latin America', *Past & Present* 205:5 (2010), p. 213

14 Randall McGowen, 'Making the "bloody code": forgery legislation in eighteenth-century England', in Norma Landau (ed.), *Law, Crime and English Society 1630–1830* (2002), p. 119

15 'Why businesses don't report cybercrimes to law enforcement', CSO, 30 May 2019

16 David Robinson, 'Banditry and the subversion of state authority in China: the Capital region during the Middle Ming period (1450–1525)', *Journal of Social History* 33:3 (2000), p. 547

17 TASS, 8 January 2024

18 BBC, 22 July 2016

19 *Kyiv Post*, 11 March 2021; Reuters, 25 April 2022

20 The *Spectator*, 21 May 2022

21 As well as Oliver Bullough's *Moneyland: Why Thieves And Crooks Now Rule The World And How To Take It Back* (2018) and *Butler to the World* (2022), I'd especially note Sarah Chayes, *Thieves of State* (2015), Tom Burgis, *Kleptopia* (2020) and Robert Barrington, Elizabeth David-Barrett, Sam Power & Dan Hough (eds), *Understanding Corruption: How Corruption Works in Practice* (2022)

22 'Danske Bank Pleads Guilty to Fraud on U.S. Banks in Multi-Billion Dollar Scheme to Access the U.S. Financial System', *US Department of Justice*, 13 December 2022

23 Lisa Marriott, 'NZ's white-collar crime gap: just 1% of serious fraud complaints result in prosecution', *Conversation*, 19 August 2024

24 'Glencore to pay £289 million for "highly corrosive" and "endemic" corruption', UK Serious Fraud Office, 3 November 2022
25 *Los Angeles Times*, 17 October 2024

Chapter 8: A Nice Cuppa and Some Smuggling

1   David Christian, 'Vodka and Corruption in Russia on the Eve of Emancipation', *Slavic Review* 46:3–4 (2017)
2   Richard Platt, *Smuggling in the British Isles: A History* (2011)
3   Evan Jones, 'Illicit business: accounting for smuggling in mid-sixteenth-century Bristol', *Economic History Review* 54:1 (2001), p. 17
4   Ibid., pp. 30–1
5   Julius Ruff, *Violence in Early Modern Europe 1500–1800* (2001), p. 242
6   Tao-Chang Chiang, 'The salt industry of Ming China', *Geographical Review* 65:1 (1975), p. 93
7   Mark Kurlansky, *Salt* (2002), p. 154
8   John Wesley, 'A word to the smuggler' (1783), quoted in Allan Karras, *Smuggling: Contraband and Corruption in World History* (2011), p. 20
9   E.P. Thompson, 'The Moral Economy of the English Crowd in the Eighteenth Century', *Past and Present* 50:1 (1971), pp. 78–9
10 Matt Raven, 'Wool Smuggling and the Royal Government in England, c. 1337–63: Law Enforcement and the Moral Economy in the Late Middle Ages', *Law and History Review* 40:4 (2022)
11 Hind Abdul-Jabbar, 'Smuggled in the bustle', *Fashion Studies Journal* 8 (2017); Peter Andreas, *Smuggler Nation: How Illicit Trade Made America* (2013), p. 186
12 'Gentleman of Chichester', *A Full and Genuine History of the Inhuman and Unparallel'd Murders of Mr. William Galley, A Custom-House Officer at the Port of Southampton and Mr. Daniel Chater, a Shoemaker, at Fordingbridge in Hampshire, by Fourteen Notorious Smugglers* (1749)
13 Quoted in Hannes Ziegler, 'Rebel, Traitor, Sailor, Spy: The Social Figure of the Smuggler in Mid-Eighteenth-Century Britain', *Trahir* 29 (2024)
14 Christian Koot, 'Smuggling in Early America', *Oxford Research Encyclopedia of American History* (2016)
15 George Smith, *The American Revolution and the Declaration of Independence: The Essays of George H. Smith* (2017), p. 8
16 Pauline Croft, 'Trading with the enemy, 1585–1604', *Historical Journal* 32:2 (1989)
17 *Novaya Gazeta*, 12 June 2000
18 Gavin Daly, 'Napoleon and the "City of Smugglers", 1810–1814', *Historical Journal* 50:2 (2007)
19 Stephen Wise, *Lifeline of the Confederacy: Blockade running during the Civil War* (1998), p. 226
20 Vanda Felbab-Brown & Diana Paz García, 'Russia, Ukraine, and organized crime and illicit economies in 2024', *Brookings Commentary*, 6 February

2024; Mark Galeotti, *Time of Troubles: the Russian underworld since the Ukraine invasion* (Global Initiative Against Transnational Organized Crime, 2023)

21 'Illegal tobacco factory producing 2,000 cigarettes a minute dismantled', Europol, 11 July 2019

Chapter 9: Rustling and Fencing Everything from Cattle to Cars

1 Christine Worobec, 'Horse Thieves and Peasant Justice in Post-Emancipation Imperial Russia', *Journal of Social History* 21:2 (1987)

2 Christian Seignobos, 'The phenomenon of the Zaraguina in Northern Cameroon – A crisis of Mbororo society', *Afrique Contemporaine* 239:3 (2011)

3 *Irish Independent*, 26 August 2020

4 Mary McIntosh, 'Changes in the organization of thieving', in Stanley Cohen (ed.), *Images of Deviance* (1971), p. 118

5 Uwe Danker, 'Bandits and the state', in Richard Evans (ed.), *The German Underworld* (1988), pp. 82–3, 88

6 Mary McIntosh, 'Changes in the organization of thieving', in Stanley Cohen (ed.), *Images of Deviance* (1971), pp. 116–22

7 *Washington Post*, 27 July 1997

8 Martin Gill, 'The craft of robbers of cash-in-transit vans: crime facilitators and the entrepreneurial approach', *International Journal of the Sociology of Law* 29:3 (2001)

9 Nick Fisher, ' "Workshops of villains": was there much organised crime in classical Athens?', in Keith Hopwood (ed.), *Organised Crime in Antiquity* (1999), pp. 56–7

10 L. Shaw, *The Code of Hammurabi* (2004), pp. 3–4

11 Brent Shaw, 'Bandits in the Roman Empire', *Past & Present* 105 (1984), p. 38

12 Ausonius, *Ep.* 14.22–7, quoted in Andrew Wallace-Hadrill (ed.), *Patronage in Ancient Society* (1989), p. 182

13 Esther Cohen, for example, notes that while those trying to sell stolen silverware or the like in Paris often turned to Jewish moneylenders, they frequently informed the authorities: Esther Cohen, 'Patterns of crime in fourteenth-century Paris', *French Historical Studies* 11:3 (1980), p. 325

14 See, for example, Shaul Stampfer, 'Jews as fences in early modern Poland and beyond: function, ideology, almost philanthropy and almost diplomacy in a complex society', *Jewish Culture and History* 19:1 (2018)

15 Evelyn Welch, *Shopping in the Renaissance* (2005), p. 200

16 Frank Bennett, 'Secondhand Japan: Used Goods Regulation 1645–Present (Part 1)', *Zeitschrift für Japanisches Recht* 11:21 (2006), pp. 37–8

17 '[A]lmost all those mentioned as receivers of stolen goods [in seventeenth and early eighteenth century Germany] were Jewish . . .' Uwe Danker, 'Bandits and the state', in Richard Evans (ed.), *The German Underworld* (1988), p. 91; see also accounts of fencing in Jenna Weissman Joselit, *Our Gang: Jewish crime and the New York Jewish community, 1900–1940* (1983)

18 Robert Antony, *Unruly People: Crime, Community, and State in Late Imperial South China* (2016), p. 156

19 Meena Radhakrishna, 'Colonial construction of a "criminal" tribe: Yerukulas of Madras Presidency', *Economic and Political Weekly*, 15 July 2000

20 Nand Hart Nibbrig, 'Rascals in paradise: urban gangs in Papua New Guinea', *Pacific Studies* 15 (1992)

21 For a useful typology, see Robert Blakey, & Michael Goldsmith, 'Criminal redistribution of stolen property: the need for law reform', *Michigan Law Review* 74:8 (1976)

22 Jonathan Lipman, '"A Fierce and Brutal People". On Islam and Muslims in Qing Law', in Pamela Kyle Crossley, Helen Siu & Donald Sutton (eds), *Empire at the margins: Culture, ethnicity, and frontier in early modern China* (2006), p. 90

23 *The Economist*, 21 May 1998

Chapter 10: What's the Problem with Bootleggers, Pornographers and Drug Pushers?

1 For an engaging *tour d'horizon* about the politics of alcohol in Russia and the role of vodka taxation predating the Bolsheviks, see Mark Schrad, *Vodka Politics: Alcohol, Autocracy, and the Secret History of the Russian State* (2014)

2 Vladimir Treml, 'Alcohol abuse and quality of life in the USSR', in Helmut Sonnenfeldt (ed.), *Soviet Politics in the 1980s* (2019)

3 Mark Galeotti, *The Vory: Russia's super mafia* (2018), pp. 99–101

4 'Chinese Authorities Double Down on Tibetan Reincarnations', Human Rights Watch, 15 December 2021

5 'Rock 'n' Roll and Military Dictatorships Almost Destroyed Argentine Tango', *Atlas Obscura*, 7 December 2016; BBC, 16 June 2014

6 Anna Knutsson & Hanna Hodacs, 'When coffee was banned: strategies of labour and leisure among Stockholm's poor women, 1794–1796 and 1799–1802', *Scandinavian Economic History Review* 71:2 (2023)

7 Gāmini Salgādo, *The Elizabethan Underworld* (1977), pp. 37–9

8 Robert Haney, *Comstockery in America: Patterns of Censorship and Control* (1960), p. 16

9 Ibid., p. 20

10 Y. Yvon Wang, *Reinventing Licentiousness: Pornography and Modern China* (2021), p. 154

11 *NBC News*, 20 January 2015

12 Quoted in Marc-Antoine Crocq, 'Historical and cultural aspects of man's relationship with addictive drugs', *Dialogues in Clinical Neuroscience* 94:4 (2007), p. 357

13 In his *A Counterblaste to Tobacco* (1604), quoted in Matthew Romaniello, 'Through the filter of tobacco: the limits of global trade in the early modern world', *Comparative Studies in Society and History* 49:4 (2007), p. 916

14 Sheldon Zhang & Ko-lin Chin, *A People's War: China's Struggle to Contain its Illicit Drug Problem* (Brookings, 2016)

15 UNODC, *World Drug Report 2023, vol. 1* (2021), p. 12
16 Ibid., p. 22
17 WHO, 'Tobacco', 24 May 2022, https://www.who.int/news-room/fact-sheets/detail/tobacco
18 Decriminalisation is a step below legalisation – not making the drugs wholly legal, but not policing personal use
19 Reuters, 16 January 2012
20 *Financial Times*, 12 January 2022

PART THREE: THE AGE OF GLOBALISATION

Chapter 11: Drug Traffickers, Apostles of the Market

1 Ilaria Sacchettoni, 'Operazione Odessa. Alla sbarra Garrido, il boss dei narcos', *Corriere della Sera*, 19 January 2022
2 'Cae alias Cachano o El Viejo, el denominado "Rey de los Semisumergibles" del narcotráfico', Fiscalia (Colombian Attorney General's Office) Boletín 41728, 8 January 2022; as of writing, Óscar Moreno Ricardo is still awaiting trial
3 The *Guardian*, 4 February 2022; all three men were convicted on drug trafficking charges
4 'Drug Sub-Culture', *New York Times* magazine, 26 April 2009
5 Afghanistan figures from conversation with UN Office on Drugs & Crime (UNODC) analyst in 2020; Irish figure from the *Irish Times*, 27 June 2019
6 The *Telegraph*, 25 May 2017
7 Richard Nixon, 'Special Message to the Congress on Drug Abuse Prevention and Control', 17 June 1971
8 Justin Rowlatt, 'How the US military's opium war in Afghanistan was lost', BBC, 25 April 2019
9 U. Zerell, B. Ahrens & P. Gerz, 'Documentation of a heroin manufacturing process in Afghanistan', *Bulletin on Narcotics* 57:1–2 (2005)
10 'Prepared statement of Ralf Mutschke, assistant director, Sub-Directorate for Crimes Against Person and Property, Interpol General Secretariat, Lyon, France', to the Subcommittee on Crime of the Committee on the Judiciary, US House of Representatives, 13 December 2000
11 *South China Morning Post*, 21 February 2024
12 *New Front Lines. Organized criminal economies in Ukraine in 2022* (Global Initiative against Transnational Organized Crime, 2023)
13 The outline of this particular heroin trafficking route was explained to me by Russian police officers in 2018, and key elements of this were subsequently corroborated in conversations with an analyst at Europol and a European law-enforcement liaison officer serving in Moscow
14 Robert Bunker & Byron Ramirez (eds), *Narco Armor* (2013)

15 INCB, *Report of the International Narcotics Control Board for 2002* (2002), p. 7

16 *Le Monde*, 4 November 2024; *Times of India*, 15 November 2024

17 *NBC News*, 2 September 2009

18 'What Percentage of Shipping Containers Are Inspected? The Surprising Truth', *Shipping Container Lab*, 13 April 2023

Chapter 12: People as Customers and Commodities

1 *Arizona Republic*, 19 June 2024

2 UN Tourism, Tourism Statistics Database @ https://www.unwto.org/tourism-statistics/tourism-statistics-database

3 ILO/IOM, *Global Estimates of Modern Slavery: Forced Labour and Forced Marriage* (2022), p. 19

4 Hassan al-Thawadi, secretary general of Qatar's World Cup organising committee, originally said that 'around 400, between 400 and 500' migrant labourers died; he later walked that figure back, but many human and labour rights organisations put the real toll in the thousands; *Time*, 2 December 2022

5 Thomas Grunewald, *Bandits in the Roman Empire: myth and reality* (2004), pp. 110–36

6 George La Rue, 'Slave Trades and Diaspora in the Middle East, 700 to 1900 CE', *Oxford Research Encyclopedia of African History* (2021)

7 John Cotton Richmond, 'Less than half of 1 percent of human trafficking victims are identified. That needs to change', *New Atlanticist*, 16 June 2023

8 For an interesting rumination on the numbers, then and now, see Brandon Gerrard, 'Are There Really More Slaves Now Than Anytime In History?', *Medium*, 31 October 2020

9 ILO, *Profits and Poverty: The Economics of Forced Labour* (2014)

10 ILO/IOM, *Global Estimates of Modern Slavery: Forced Labour and Forced Marriage* (2022), pp. 2–3

11 'Together Against Trafficking in Human Beings', European Commission, 23 April 2024

12 The *Guardian*, 3 January 2021

13 Laura T. Murphy, Jim Vallette & Nyrola Elimä, *Built on Repression. PVC Building Materials' Reliance on Labor and Environmental Abuses in the Uyghur Region*, Sheffield Hallam University Helena Kennedy Centre for International Justice (2022)

14 Joseph Whittle, 'Snakehead: the extent to which Chinese organised crime groups are involved in human smuggling from China to the UK', *Trends in Organised Crime* 25:3 (2022)

15 European Commission, *A Study on Smuggling of Migrants. Characteristics, responses and cooperation with third countries* (2015), p. 37

16 'The Facebook smugglers selling the dream of Europe', BBC, 13 May 2015

17 Sheldon Zhang & Ko-Lin Chin, 'Enter the Dragon: Inside Chinese Human Smuggling Organizations', *Criminology* 40:4 (2006)
18 The *Guardian*, 5 February 2023
19 Patrick Radden Keefe, *The Snakehead: an Epic Tale of the Chinatown Underworld and the American Dream* (2023)
20 Rong Xiaoqing, 'The Fading American Dreams of China's Most Notorious Snakehead', *Foreign Policy*, 4 January 2017
21 Abdulaziz Almulhim et al., 'Climate-induced migration in the Global South: an in-depth analysis', *npj Climate Action* 3:47 (2024)
22 Ines Kohl, 'Afrod, le business Touareg avec la frontière: nouvelles conditions et nouveaux défis', *Politique africaine* 132 (2013)

Chapter 13: Knock-Off Magnates and Counterfeit Consumerism

1 'Counterfeit drugs raise Africa's temperature', *Africa Renewal*, May 2013
2 *BusinessWire*, 10 January 2023
3 Thomas Hoving, *False Impressions: The Hunt for Big-time Art Fakes* (1996), p. 31
4 Marco Beretta, *The Alchemy of Glass: Counterfeit, Imitation, and Transmutation in Ancient Glassmaking* (2009)
5 Jane MacLaren Walsh, 'What is Real? A New Look at Pre-Columbian Mesoamerican Collections', *AnthroNotes* 26:1 (2005)
6 OECD, *Global Trade in Fakes. A Worrying Threat* (2021)
7 Europol, *Intellectual Property Crime Threat Assessment 2022* (2022), p. 5
8 *Hürriyet Daily News*, 21 February 2017
9 'The Truth Behind Counterfeits', US Customs & Border Protection, https://www.cbp.gov/trade/fakegoodsrealdangers
10 *USA Today*, 21 January 2020
11 The *Independent*, 23 December 2021
12 Andrew Chubb, 'China's *Shanzhai* Culture: "Grabism" and the politics of hybridity', *Journal of Contemporary China* 24:92 (2015)
13 'China's Black Market Boom', *Forbes*, 6 February 2009
14 *Variety*, 6 June 2018
15 YouGov, 'Why we pirate', 10 September 2024
16 BSA, *Global Software Survey: Software Management: Security Imperative, Business Opportunity* (2018)
17 *The Drinks Business*, 3 August 2022
18 The *Guardian*, 21 December 2016

Chapter 14: Selling the Earth

1 Mark Harris, 'Ghost ships, crop circles, and soft gold: A GPS mystery in Shanghai', *MIT Technology Review*, 15 November 2019

2   Vince Beiser, 'The Deadly Global War for Sand', *Wired*, 26 March 2015

3   Robert Marks, *China: Its Environment and History* (2011), p. 334

4   'IUCN SSC statement on World Wildlife Day', International Union for Conservation, 3 March 2023

5   World Bank, *Illegal Logging, Fishing, and Wildlife Trade: the Costs and How to Combat it* (2019), p. 8

6   Khadija Sharife, 'Made in China: The Secret of Mugabe's Election Success', *100 Reporters*, 28 October 2013

7   Rep. Christopher H. Smith, remarks to 'Child Labor and Human Rights Violations in the Mining Industry of the Democratic Republic of Congo', Tom Lantos Human Rights Commission Hearing, 14 July 2022

8   World Bank, *Illegal Logging, Fishing, and Wildlife Trade: the Costs and How to Combat it* (2019), p. 15

9   *Quartz*, 2 November 2021

10 UK Centre for Ecology & Hydrology, 'Deforestation increases risk of flash flooding in fast-growing West African coastal cities', 4 January 2022

11 UNIDO, *Some Like it Cool: UNIDO and the Montreal Protocol* (2017), p. 9

12 Juli Berwald, 'One overlooked way to fight climate change? Dispose of old CFCs', *National Geographic*, 29 April 2019

13 *Environmental Health Perspectives* 112:2 (2004), p. A98

14 Mustapha Tolba, 'The Global Agenda and the Hazardous Wastes Challenge', *Marine Policy* 14:3 (1990), p. 206

15 Greenpeace, *The Waste Invasion of Asia* (1994)

16 Daan van Uhm & Dina Siegel, 'The illegal trade in black caviar', *Trends in Organised Crime* 19:1 (2016)

17 Dina Fine Maron, 'Siberian tigers are being hunted at night for their body parts', *National Geographic*, 19 January 2022

18 *World Bank Voices*, 29 October 2019

19 Shelley Clarke, E.J. Milner-Gulland & Trond Bjørndal Cemar, 'Social, Economic, and Regulatory Drivers of the Shark Fin Trade', *Marine Resource Economics* 22 (2007)

20 Rosaleen Duffy, *Security and Conservation: The Politics of the Illegal Wildlife Trade* (2022)

Chapter 15: Old Masters for Sale and Security

1   Noah Charney, 'The myth of the art thief: It's not a gentleman's crime', *Salon*, 24 September 2017

2   'The art of money-laundering', *IMF Finance & Development*, September 2019

3   Lidija McKnight, 'The crocodile with eight heads', the *Guardian*, 30 September 2015

4   John Calvin, *A Treatise on Relics* (1543), translated from the French by Count Valerian Krasinski (1870), p. 173

5   Ibid., p. 166
6   Paul Gillingham, 'The strange business of memory: relic forgery in Latin America', *Past & Present* 205:5 (2010)
7   Erin Thompson, 'The True Cost of Museum Fakes', *Hyperallergic*, 26 March 2020
8   Jane MacLaren Walsh & Brett Topping, *The Man Who Invented Aztec Crystal Skulls* (2018)
9   *Time*, 24 February 1961
10 *Newsweek*, 22 July 2014
11 *Artfix Daily*, 28 September 2011
12 *New York Times*, 19 July 2012
13 The *Independent*, 22 July 2015
14 *Claims Journal*, 15 June 2015
15 'The Strange Story of Marie Antoinette's Watch', *Wired*, 17 May 2013
16 Simon Mackenzie & Tess Davis, 'Temple looting in Cambodia: Anatomy of a statue trafficking network', *British Journal of Criminology* 54:5 (2016)
17 'United States Files Civil Action To Forfeit Thousands Of Ancient Iraqi Artifacts Imported By Hobby Lobby', Department of Justice US Attorney's Office, Eastern District of New York, 5 July 2017
18 Judith Harris, 'Financing terror', *Journal of Art Crime* 2:1 (2009)
19 'Following the trail of Syria's looted history', *CBS News*, 9 September 2015
20 The *Guardian*, 15 June 2014
21 *La Stampa*, 16 October 2016
22 Cited in UNESCO, 'Intergovernmental Committee For Promoting The Return Of Cultural Property To Its Countries Of Origin Or Its Restitution In Case Of Illicit Appropriation Twentieth Session, 29–30 September 2016' (2016), p. 2

Chapter 16: White-Collar Mobsters and the Global Economy

1   Russian Organized Crime in the United States: hearing before the Permanent Subcommittee on Investigations of the Committee on Governmental Affairs, US Senate, 15 May 1996
2   Robert Friedman, *Red Mafiya: How the Russian Mob Has Invaded America* (2000), pp. 69–96
3   This was later recounted to me by an NYPD officer who had been monitoring the conversation
4   Angus Konstam, *Pirates 1660–1730* (1998), p. 51
5   Sterling Seagrave, *Lords of the Rim: The Invisible Empire of the Overseas Chinese* (1995)
6   Wim Decock et al., *Law and Religion: The Legal Teachings of the Protestant and Catholic Reformations* (2014), pp. 22–3
7   *Boston Globe*, 18 July 1995; the authorities successfully petitioned a court to seize Bulger's share of the winnings

8   Maryam Razavy, 'Hawala: An underground haven for terrorists or social phe-
     nomenon?', *Crime, Law & Social Change* 44:3 (2005); Ido Levy & Abdi Yusuf,
     'How do terrorist organizations make money? Terrorist funding and innova-
     tion in the case of Al-Shabaab', *Studies in Conflict & Terrorism* 44:12 (2021)
9   'The growing threat of organized crime groups in the Tri-Border Area of
     South America', PMI, 13 December 2019
10   Loretta Napoleoni, *Rogue Economics* (2008), p. 65
11   *New York Times*, 9 November 2005
12   In 2022, Danske Bank pleaded guilty and paid a $2 billion forfeit: 'Danske
     Bank Pleads Guilty to Fraud on U.S. Banks in Multi-Billion Dollar Scheme
     to Access the U.S. Financial System', US Department of Justice, 13
     December 2022
13   Refinitiv, *Revealing the True Cost of Financial Crime. 2018 survey report* (2018), p. 5
14   CNN, 23 February 2014
15   Jørgen Juel Andersen, Niels Johannesen & Bob Rijkers, 'Elite capture of
     foreign aid: Evidence from offshore bank accounts', *Journal of Political Econ-
     omy* 130:2 (2022)
16   The *Guardian*, 12 December 2009

PART FOUR: BRAVE NEW WORLD

Chapter 17: Wankers, Vishers, Cybercrime and Semantics

1   Paul Marks, 'Dot-dash-diss: The gentleman hacker's 1903 lulz', *New Scien-
     tist*, 20 December 2011
2   Dan Stuckey, 'The mystery of the creepiest television hack', *Motherboard*, 25
     November 2013
3   Emil Hozan, 'My Journey into the Dark Web: At Your Service', *Secplicity*, 9
     January 2019
4   AFP, 10 May 2022
5   *Cybercrime Magazine*, 13 November 2020
6   Reuters, 25 January 2008
7   ' "Fortune 50" Company Made Record-Breaking $75M Ransomware Pay-
     ment', *PC Mag*, 30 July 2024
8   FBI, *Internet Crime Report 2023* (2024), p. 13
9   Alexander Martin, 'Ransomware incidents now make up majority of
     British government's crisis management "Cobra" meetings', *Record*, 18
     November 2022
10   BBC, 19 December 2017
11   Chris Kanich et al., 'Spamalytics: An Empirical Analysis of Spam Mar-
     keting Conversion', *Proceedings of the 15th ACM Conference on Computer and
     Communications Security* (2008)
12   David Wall, *Cybercrime: The Transformation of Crime in the Information Age*
     (2007), pp. 147–56

13 David Wall, 'Cybercrime and the Culture of Fear: Social Science Fiction(s) and the Production of Knowledge about Cybercrime', *Information, Communication & Society* 11:6 (2008)

14 'New Report Looks at the Rising Influence of Online Communities', *Social Media Today*, 24 February 2021

15 The *Guardian*, 16 May 2013; in fairness, LulzSec as a group was involved in hacks to have fun and inconvenience those they disliked, but a number of their members did also have money-making online side-hustles

16 The *Telegraph*, 24 December 2016

17 Lora Hadzhidimova & Brian Payne, 'The profile of the international cyber offender in the US', *International Journal of Cybersecurity Intelligence & Cybercrime* 2:1 (2019)

18 *The Economist*, 30 August 2007

19 The *Guardian*, 15 November 2007

20 Kevin Poulsen, 'One Hacker's Audacious Plan to Rule the Black Market in Stolen Credit Cards', *Wired*, 22 December 2008

21 Roberto Musotto & David Wall, 'More Amazon than Mafia: analysing a DDoS stresser service as organised cybercrime', *Trends in Organized Crime* 25:2 (2022)

22 'Two Arrested for Alleged Conspiracy to Launder $4.5 Billion in Stolen Cryptocurrency', US Department of Justice, 8 February 2022

23 Parma Bains et al., 'Regulating the Crypto Ecosystem: the Case of Unbacked Crypto Assets', *IMF Fintech Note*, September 2022

24 BBC News, 26 January 2022

25 *Kommersant*, 12 December 2022

26 'Common Social Media Posts That Help Out Burglars', SafeZone, 28 January 2022

27 John Bohannon, 'Why criminals can't hide behind Bitcoin', *Science*, 9 March 2016

28 *Wall Street Journal*, 30 August 2019

Chapter 18: Imagination Races and the Crimes of the Future

1 William Helmer, *The Gun That Made the Twenties Roar* (1969)

2 *Belfast Telegraph*, 8 August 2016

3 The *Guardian*, 5 December 2014

4 *New York Times*, 22 November 1994

5 NATO, *The Alliance's Strategic Concept* (1999), paragraph 24

6 Peter Andreas & Richard Price, 'From war fighting to crime fighting: Transforming the American national security state', *International Studies Review* 3:3 (2001)

7 Matthew La Lime, 'Black Axe – Nigeria's Most Notorious Transnational Criminal Organization', *Africa Centre for Strategic Studies Spotlight*, 29 October 2024

8 Ibrahim has been designated as a terrorist by the US government
9 Bill Park, 'Turkey's Deep State: Ergenekon and the Threat to Democrati-sation in the Republic', *RUSI Journal* 153:5 (2008)
10 Ryan Gingeras, 'In the hunt for the "sultans of smack": dope, gang-sters and the construction of the Turkish deep state', *Middle East Journal* 65:3 (2011)
11 Jane Schneider, 'Fifty years of mafia corruption and anti-mafia reform', *Current Anthropology* 59:18 (2018)
12 Eiko Maruko Siniawer, *Ruffians, Yakuza, Nationalists: The Violent Politics of Modern Japan, 1860–1960* (2008)
13 T. Wing Lo, 'Beyond social capital: Triad organized crime in Hong Kong and China', *British Journal of Criminology* 50:5 (2010)
14 James Cockayne, *Hidden Power* (2016), pp. 160–5
15 Thomas Maier, 'Inside the CIA's Plot to Kill Fidel Castro – With Mafia Help', *Politico*, 24 February 2018
16 Peter Scott, 'Washington and the politics of drugs', *New York Review of Books*, 25 June 1992
17 Max Smeets, 'Hack Global, Buy Local: The Inefficiencies of the Zero-Day Exploit Market', *Lawfare*, 6 June 2022
18 Mark Galeotti, *The Weaponisation of Everything* (2022), p. 14
19 'Treasury Designates Iranian Qods Force General Overseeing Afghan Heroin Trafficking Through Iran', US Treasury, 7 March 2012
20 Mark Galeotti, *The Weaponisation of Everything* (2022), chapter 6
21 Mark Galeotti, *The Vory: Russia's super mafia* (2018), chapters 4 and 15
22 'Try This One Weird Trick Russian Hackers Hate', *KrebsOnSecurity*, 17 May 2021
23 The assassin, going under the fake identity of Vadim Sokolov, was con-victed of murder, and the court also determined that the murder was ordered by the Russian government: *Deutsche Welle*, 15 December 2021
24 BBC, 26 April 2024
25 'Estonian Spy Hunters', *Warsaw Institute Review*, 12 March 2018
26 CNN, 14 December 2022
27 *The Times*, 7 November 2022
28 *New York Times*, 21 October 2022
29 Mark Galeotti, *Gangsters at War: Russia's Use of Organized Crime as an Instrument of Statecraft* (Global Initiative Against Transnational Organized Crime, 2024)
30 For my personal favourites, read Charles Stross's *Halting State* (2008) and *Rule 34* (2011)
31 Reuters, 3 April 2014
32 M. Caldwell et al., 'AI-enabled future crime', *Crime Science* 9:14 (2020)
33 Andy Greenberg, 'Hackers Remotely Kill a Jeep on the Highway – With Me in It', *Wired*, 21 July 2015
34 'The Modern Manhunt Began With An Arrest by Wireless Telegraph', *Atlas Obscura*, 2 March 2016

35 Danielle Cave et al., *Mapping China's Tech Giants*, Australian Strategic Policy Institute (2019)

36 Susan Canney, 'The Mali Elephant Project: protecting elephants amidst conflict and poverty', *International Zoo Yearbook* 53 (2019), pp. 174–88; Jeff Muntifering et al., 'Lessons from a conservation and tourism cooperative: the Namibian black rhinoceros case', *Annals of Tourism Research* 82:6 (2020); Achyut Aryal et al., 'Global lessons from successful rhinoceros conservation in Nepal', *Conservation Biology* 31:6 (2017)

Chapter 19: Gangsters with Five-Star Reviews: The Power of the Network

1   I have changed and withheld some details as this is still a live investigation, as recounted to me by a Dutch police officer, who nonetheless was not at the time (2024) holding out much hope that a case would or could be brought to court

2   Diego Gambetta, *Codes of the Underworld* (2009), p. 7

3   Andreas Baranowski et al., 'The CSI-education effect: Do potential criminals benefit from forensic TV series?', *International Journal of Law, Crime and Justice* 52 (2018)

4   Eduardo Guerrero, 'Towards a Transformation of Mexico's Security Strategy: Priorities and Challenges', *RUSI Journal* 158:3 (2013)

5   Carlo Morselli, *Inside Criminal Networks* (2009)

6   Paul Duijn, Victor Kashirin & Peter Sloot, 'The Relative Ineffectiveness of Criminal Network Disruption', *Scientific Reports* 4238 (2014)

7   Joseph Hanlon, 'The Uberization of Mozambique's heroin trade', *LSE Department of International Development Working Paper* 18-190 (2018), p. 17

8   'Two baggage handlers have been convicted of being part of a plot to smuggle cocaine through Heathrow Airport', National Crime Agency, 19 October 2017

9   Anthea McCarthy-Jones & Mark Turner, 'Dark Networks, Transnational Crime and Security: The Critical Role of Brokers', *Journal of Illicit Economies & Development* 5:1 (2023)

10 *Insight Crime*, 30 April 2021; *Sydney Morning Herald*, 30 August 2010

11 Pat Akey et al., 'Price revelation from insider trading: Evidence from hacked earnings news', *Journal of Financial Economics* 143:3 (2022)

12 *New Front Lines. Organized criminal economies in Ukraine in 2022* (Global Initiative against Transnational Organized Crime, 2023)

13 'The ice pipeline', ABC, 22 April 2024

14 The Russian news agency *Sputnik* presents a series of photos at https://sputnikmediabank.com/story/list_43646/

15 James Quinn & D. Shane Koch, 'The nature of criminality within one-percent motorcycle clubs', *Deviant Behavior* 24:3 (2003)

16 'Show them the money: Profit, contacts trump biker lifestyle as Hells Angels evolve', *London Free Press*, 6 June 2024

17 Alexander Stille, *Excellent Cadavers* (1995), pp. 21–2; Vincenzo Scalia, 'The production of the Mafioso space. A spatial analysis of the Sack of Palermo', *Trends in Organized Crime* 24:2 (2020)

18 Ernesto Savona, 'The Businesses of Italian Mafias', *European Journal on Criminal Policy and Research* 21:2 (2015)

19 Misha Glenny, *McMafia* (2008), p. 77

20 Tom Wainwright, *Narconomics* (2017), pp. 153–6

21 Martina Baradel, 'Yakuza battle Chinese gangs for control of Japan's criminal underworld', *Conversation*, 30 January 2023

22 US Attorney's Office – Southern District of New York, 'Members And Associates Of Russian Crime Syndicate Arrested For Racketeering, Extortion, Robbery, Murder-For-Hire Conspiracy, Fraud, Narcotics, And Firearms Offenses', 7 June 2017

23 Mary Anne Weaver, 'India's Bandit Queen', *Atlantic*, November 1996

24 Mark Galeotti, *The Vory: Russia's super mafia* (2018), p. 77

25 Beth Webb, 'How Vicious Schoolgirl Gangs Sparked a Media Frenzy in Japan', *Vice*, 16 February 2016

26 Ryu Otomo, 'Women in Organised Crime in Japan', in Giovanni Fiandaca (ed.), *Women and the Mafia: female roles in organised crime structures* (2007)

27 UNODC, *Organized Crime and Gender: issues relating to the United Nations Convention Against Transnational Organized Crime* (2022), p. 9

28 Felia Allum, *Women of the Mafia: Power and Influence in the Neapolitan Camorra* (2024)

29 She was convicted of membership of a mafia-style criminal association

30 Jasmin was gunned down in 2020; *Times Live* (South Africa), 3 November 2020

31 The *Guardian*, 3 November 2009

32 Lauren Gillespie et al., 'Queenpins: an exploratory study of female participation in high-level drug distribution networks', *Trends in Organized Crime*, forthcoming

33 She pleaded guilty to her crimes in 2010

34 'How Sexy Is Accused Russian Hacker Kristina Svechinskaya?', *New York* magazine, 1 October 2010

35 Jeffrey Scott McIllwain, *Organizing Crime in Chinatown* (2004); Peng Wang, 'The increasing threat of Chinese organised crime', *RUSI Journal* 158:4 (2013)

36 Christian Leuprecht, Andrew Aulthouse & Olivier Walther, 'The puzzling resilience of transnational organized criminal networks', *Police Practice & Research* 17:4 (2016)

37 Rachel Stohl & Dan Smith, 'Small arms in failed states: a deadly combination', memorandum written for the Failed States and International Security Conference, April 1999

38 Dhori Kule et al., *The Causes and Consequences of Albanian Emigration During Transition*, University of Kent Discussion Paper (2000), p. 1

39 Mark Galeotti, *The Vory: Russia's super mafia* (2018), pp. 181–205

40 Claire Sterling, *Crime Without Frontiers: The Worldwide Expansion of Organised Crime and the Pax Mafiosa* (1994), p. 22

Chapter 20: Criminal World

1   *National News* (UAE), 12 February 2009

2   BBC, 24 August 2016

3   Alice Armstrong, 'Sakawa Rumours: Occult Internet Fraud and Ghanaian Identity', *UCL Working Paper in Anthropology* 8/2011

4   'Trafficking, ritual oaths and criminal investigations', *Forced Migration Review* 64 (2020)

5   Robert Bunker, 'Santa Muerte: Inspired and Ritualistic Killings', *FBI Law Enforcement Bulletin*, 5 February 2013

6   Barend Ter Haar, *The Ritual and Mythology of the Chinese Triads: Creating an Identity* (2021)

7   David Skarbek & Peng Wang, 'Criminal rituals', *Global Crime* 16:4 (2015)

8   Steven Levitt & Stephen Dubner, *Freakonomics* (2005), p. 104

9   Chema Salinas, 'Ambiguous Trickster liminality: two anti-mythological ideas', *Review of Communication* 13:2 (2013)

10 'The 19th-Century Lithuanians Who Smuggled Books to Save Their Language', *Atlas Obscura*, 19 July 2017

11 *Washington Post*, 15 December 2017

12 Peter Blastenbrei, 'Violence, arms and criminal justice in papal Rome, 1560–1600', *Renaissance Studies* 20:1 (2006), pp. 73–6

13 Douglas Allen & Yoram Barzel, 'The Evolution of Criminal Law and Police during the Pre-modern Era', *Journal of Law, Economics & Organization* 27:3 (2011), p. 541

14 'Operation Archimedes', Europol, 15 February 2023

15 *Hindustan Times*, 5 January 2024

16 'The ice pipeline', ABC, 22 April 2024

17 There is no reason to believe that HSBC is either any better or worse than other major banks in preventing its use for money laundering and similar operations, but it is worth noting that, for example, in 2021, British regulators fined it £64 million for failings in its anti-money-laundering processes over a period of eight years, and in 2019, it agreed to pay $336 million to settle a case with the Belgian authorities relating to accusations of tax fraud and money laundering. This is not to single out HSBC: pretty much all major banks have similar incidents on their record

18 Andy Clark, Alistair Fraser & Niall Hamilton-Smith, 'Networked territorialism: the routes and roots of organised crime', *Trends in Organised Crime* 24:2 (2021), p. 257

19 Duncan Campbell, 'Inside the 21st-century British criminal underworld', the *Guardian*, 4 July 2019

Acknowledgements

At times it can be hard to distinguish serious research from my continued fascination with the shadow worlds in which a nerdy scholar is not meant to intrude, but nonetheless I must thank those cops and robbers who, in different ways and different times, were willing to share their worlds with me. Those police officers who nonetheless took me with them on ridealongs in Moscow and London and on a New Jersey State Trooper raid in Newark, as well as letting me sit in on or give briefings from Vegas to Vilnius, and all the other, often even more enlightening, conversations over beers or cuppas. And for that matter, those criminals also willing to talk about 'their thing', even if usually in rather less direct terms!

I must recognise that I am an interdisciplinary scholar in the sense that I have self-indulgently followed my interests where they will, from history and politics to criminology and anthropology. As such, I owe a particular debt to those more focused and serious scholars who have, knowingly or unknowingly, especially guided my thinking on matters criminal, although they share no guilt for my errors and flights of fancy, including Pino Arlacchi, Sarah Chayes, James Finckenauer, Diego Gambetta, Carolyn Nordstrom, Nancy Ries, Roberto Saviano, Federico Varese, Katherine Wilkins and Phil Williams. My thanks are also due to Robyn Drury at Ebury for her detailed and thoughtful suggested revisions, which made this a much more focused book.

Index